the oracles of
Apollω

About the Author

John Opsopaus, PhD, (Tennessee) has practiced magic and divination since the 1960s, and his fiction and nonfiction have been published in various magical and Neopagan magazines (more than thirty publications). He designed the Pythagorean Tarot and wrote the comprehensive *Guide to the Pythagorean Tarot* (Llewellyn, 2001). He frequently presents workshops on Hellenic magic and Neopaganism, Pythagorean theurgy and spiritual practices, divination, and related topics. Opsopaus was a Third Circle member of the Church of All Worlds, past coordinator of the Scholars Guild for CAW, and past Arkhon of the Hellenic Kin of ADF (A Druid Fellowship). He is also a university professor with more than forty years of experience reading Ancient Greek and Latin.

THE ORACLES of
Apollꭥ

Practical Ancient Greek
Divination for Today

JOHN OPSOPAUS, PhD

Llewellyn Publications
Woodbury, Minnesota

FIRST EDITION
First Printing, 2017

Cover design by Kevin R. Brown
Interior art and photos provided by the author

Llewellyn Publications is a registered trademark of Llewellyn Worldwide Ltd.

Library of Congress Cataloging-in-Publication Data
Names: Opsopaus, John, author.
  Title: The oracles of Apollo : practical ancient Greek divination for today /
    John Opsopaus, PhD.
  Description: First edition. | Woodbury : Llewellyn Worldwide, Ltd, 2017. |
    Includes bibliographical references and index.
  Identifiers: LCCN 2017009345 (print) | LCCN 2017021001 (ebook) | ISBN
    9780738752259 (ebook) | ISBN 9780738751979 (alk. paper)
  Subjects: LCSH: Divination--Greece--History--To 1500.
  Classification: LCC BF1765 (ebook) | LCC BF1765 .O87 2017 (print) | DDC
    133.30938--dc23
  LC record available at https://lccn.loc.gov/2017009345

Llewellyn Publications
A Division of Llewellyn Worldwide Ltd.
2143 Wooddale Drive
Woodbury, MN 55125-2989
www.llewellyn.com

Printed in the United States of America

Other Books by John Opsopaus

The Pythagorean Tarot

Contents

Part III. The Oracle of the Seven Sages

Acknowledgments

It is a pleasure to be able to thank those who have facilitated the production of this book. First, I'm grateful to the many people who, over the past twenty years since I first put my translations of the Alphabet Oracle and the Counsels of the Seven Sages online, have urged me to provide more information and have told me how valuable these texts have been to them. Second, I'm grateful to Llewellyn Worldwide and their support for this project. In particular, Elysia Gallo, Senior Acquisitions Editor, made many suggestions that have improved immeasurably the content and readability of this book, and the production editor, Stephanie Finne, edited the manuscript closely, catching errors and improving consistency and organization. It is always a pleasure to work with the dedicated and professional Llewellyn staff.

Part i
ancient greek divination

ΙΔΡΩΤΕΣΕΙΣΙΝΙΠΛΗΝΑΠΑΝ

ΟΛΩΣΕΤΡΟΝΩΝ

Chapter 1

What You Will Learn

"Only sacred divination united with the gods truly gives a share in the divine life, participating in foreknowledge and divine thoughts, and truly makes us divine." This was written by Iamblichus (ca. 250–ca. 330 CE), a Pagan philosopher and teacher of theurgy (the art of communicating with gods). He also tells us that the Pythagoreans—the ancient Pagan masters of magic and the Mysteries—considered divination (along with medicine and music) the highest among the sciences, for divination "alone is the means of interpreting the intentions of the gods."

Since ancient times, divination has been an important tool for seeking guidance from the gods, and most modern Pagans, Wiccans, and others who practice the old faiths are familiar with divination and many practice some divinatory art, such as tarot, runes, I Ching, or scrying. In restoring the faiths of our ancient ancestors, we would like to understand the arts by which they sought divine guidance. Unfortunately, there is little documentation to guide us. Although there are legends of the tarot's origin in ancient Egypt, history traces it back to a fifteenth-century Italian card game, and its documented use for divination is no older than the late eighteenth century. The runes indeed date from our Pagan past, but we do not have documentation of how they were used for divination in ancient times. Of course older is not necessarily better, and new divinatory arts can be developed. Esoteric, Neopagan, and Wiccan tarots have been developed (including my own *Pythagorean Tarot*), which work well for us. Nevertheless, we would like to understand divination as it was practiced by our Pagan predecessors.[1]

This was my motivation more than twenty years ago when I made the first English translation of the ancient Greek Alphabet Oracle and made it available on the Internet. Although I had practiced magic since the 1960s and studied Ancient Greek in college so that I could read ancient mythology, literature, and philosophy, it was in the 1980s that I realized it was the Greek gods who spoke most clearly to me. At that time there were few groups practicing Hellenic Neopaganism, and so it was difficult to organize group rituals. Therefore, in 1995 I founded the Omphalos, a networking group for Greek and Roman Neopagans, which was listed in the *Circle Guide to Pagan Groups* from 1997 onward. This was in the early days of the Internet, and so contact information was distributed on paper through the post office! As more people got online in the 1990s, I moved operations to the Internet and established the *Stêlê*, the homepage for the Omphalos (still online, but not actively maintained).

At that time, many devotees of the Greek gods were practicing "Wicca with Greek god names," but I was interested in practicing in the ancient way established by our Pagan forebearers (with, of course, some adaptations for the world today). There was little available of a practical nature, so I began doing research into ancient practices and adapting them for contemporary use. I made these rituals, developed by myself and other Pagans, available with other information on the *Stêlê*.

Although I had used the tarot, runes, the I Ching, and other divination systems for many years, they didn't fit well with the Greek pantheon. One outcome of my discomfort was the *Pythagorean Tarot*, which I developed in the late 1990s. However, it was a conscious adaptation of a post-Pagan divination system to ancient Paganism, and I wanted to understand how my Hellenic predecessors had practiced divination. Until very recently, Halliday's *Greek Divination* (1913) was about the only book on the subject, and it did not give enough information for practical use. Therefore, I started on a long quest, aided by a good research library and much use of interlibrary loan—again before the modern Internet

---

1. Iamblichus's quotations from *Iamblichus on the Mysteries*, X.4 (2003), ¶289; p. 346, and *On the Pythagorean Way of Life* (1991), ¶¶138, 163; pp. 156–7, 179, respectively. I use ¶ for the Parthey page numbers. On tarot history, see Decker, Depaulis, and Dummett, *A Wicked Pack of Cards* (New York: St. Martins, 1996, ch. 2). See also https://marygreer.wordpress.com/2008/04/01/origins-of-divination-with-playing-cards/ (accessed Nov. 6, 2015).

era—to get access to rare books and epigraphic reference material.[2] From these I made the first English translation of the Greek Alphabet Oracle—imperfect in many respects—and published it on the *Stêlê* in 1995. In part 2 of this book, you will see an improved translation based on corrected readings of the original inscriptions along with much previously unpublished supplementary material to help you put the Oracle to good use.

Indeed, this book will teach you two divination systems. The first is the Alphabet Oracle, which uses the ancient Greek alphabet much like the runes are used. The difference is that we have actual ancient stone tablets (dating from the early third century CE[3]) that give the divinatory meanings of the letters. About a dozen of these tablets are known and survive in whole or in part. Although there are differences, they are amazingly consistent, and those are the meanings you will learn. In part 2, I will explain several techniques for consulting this Oracle, including the use of alphabet stones (analogous to rune stones), dice, staves, beads, and coins. The Alphabet Oracle has proved to be valuable to many modern people, as it was to the Ancients, in the twenty years since I first made it available on the Internet.

The second oracle is based on the Counsels of the Seven Sages, which were inscribed on tablets at the Temple of Apollo at Delphi. Although the original tablets do not survive (so far as we know), there are both written and inscribed copies, so we can be confident of the text. The Counsels are short, somewhat enigmatic, oracular statements from the Seven Sages of ancient Greece. I don't know of any evidence that they were used for divination in ancient times, but they were inscribed at the Temple of Apollo at Delphi, the most important oracular site of the ancient world, dedicated to the god whose gift is divination. They beg to be used for divination, and I provide a means for doing so in the Oracle of the Seven Sages in part 3.

Both oracles are especially suited to giving advice about practical matters. Stone tablets and pillars with the Alphabet Oracle were set up in town squares and similar places where wayfarers could get practical advice on their enterprises. The Oracle of the Seven Sages gives advice on how to live well, but it is also practical, for the Seven Sages were practical men. (Yes, I'm afraid they were all men, but I have no doubt that much of their wisdom was learned at their mothers' knees.)

---

2. E.g., Sterrett, *The Wolfe Expedition to Asia Minor* (Boston, MA: Damrell & Upham, 1888) and *Leaflets from the Notebook of an Archaeological Traveler in Asia Minor* (Austin, TX: University of Texas, 1889) and Heinevetter, *Würfel- und Buchstabenorakel in Griechenland und Kleinasien* (Breslau, Germany: Universität Breslau, 1912).

3. Nollé, *Kleinasiatische Losorakel* (München, Germany: C.H. Beck, 2007), 226.

In the remainder of part 1, I will also tell you a little of the history and mythology of ancient divination, which I think you will find interesting. And I will explain a little of the ancient theory of divination and how it facilitates communication with the gods. This will help you to improve your practice of these authentic ancient arts of divination. Finally, in part 1 you will learn rituals, based in ancient practice, for consecrating your divinatory tools and for conducting divinations, which are, of course, communications with the gods. These rituals are based in the Hellenic tradition, but you will have no trouble adapting them to your own tradition. Of course you can do impromptu divinations and get good results, but an effective ritual can tune your soul more closely to the divine energies and ensure clearer communication. All this will lay a solid foundation for using effectively the divinatory arts taught in parts 2 and 3.

Chapter 2

Divination in the Ancient World

In this chapter, you will learn some of the background information that will help you to practice ancient divination more successfully. First, I will tell some of the important Greek myths about the origins of divination, which will acquaint you with the gods who oversee the ancient art. Next, I will survey briefly the many arts of divination practiced in the ancient Greek and Roman worlds, some of which are quite familiar, others quite strange. Finally, I will explain the theory of divination taught in ancient Neoplatonism, the deepest and richest Pagan philosophy and theology. You can always use a tool more effectively if you know a little about how it works.

Mythical Origins of Divination

Neopaganism adapts the religions of our ancient Pagan ancestors to the world we live in today, and so the lore that lies behind ancient practices can help us to use them today. Therefore, I will begin with the sacred myths that tell how the gods gave divination to mortals.[4] Treating these myths as mere stories or as psychological metaphors dilutes the illumination and power they offer. Accept their gifts!

The Bee Nymphs of Mount Parnassus

As you might expect, I will have something to say about the Delphic Oracle, but not yet, for our story begins long before Delphi was established. Delphi is perched on the side of Mount Parnassus, which (like all mountains) is haunted by nymphs, who are daughters of Zeus. They often appear as attractive young women, who may seduce shepherds and take them as husbands. They frequent the oracular springs from which prophets draw their inspiration, for Earth is the font of wisdom.

In the earliest times, before the Greeks came and before Apollo arrived at Delphi, priestesses delivered oracles received from Earth goddesses. There were oracles of Gaia, the Earth herself (more commonly named Gê in Ancient Greek).[5] There were also oracles of Demeter, the grain goddess whose name *Dê-mêtêr* is a variant of *Gê-mêtêr*, which means "Earth Mother." Ancient lore also tells us that the goddess Themis delivered oracles at various sites, including Delphi, and she might have inherited this site from her mother, Gaia. (She is a daughter of Ouranos and Gaia: Heaven and Earth.) You might not be familiar with Themis. Her name is the word for something that has been established, and is often translated as custom, order, law, and what is right; in the plural it refers to decrees

---

4. There are many different versions of these myths, and scholars differ on some matters, such as the Thriai. The following stories are drawn primarily from Homeric Hymn III, *To Pythian Apollo,* and Homeric Hymn IV, *To Hermes* both in Evelyn-White translation of Hesiod, *Hesiod, the Homeric Hymns, and Homerica* (Cambridge, MA: Harvard University Press, 1936), Apollodorus's *The Library* translated by James G. Frazer (Cambridge, MA: Harvard University Press, 1921, III.10), and Kerényi, *The Gods of the Greeks* (London: Thames & Hudson, 1979, X.1). Kerényi's *Apollo* (Dallas, TX: Spring, 1983) and *Hermes* (Dallas, TX: Spring, 1995) contain deep insights into the nature of Apollo and Hermes, respectively; Karl Kerényi (1897–1973) was a student of the Neopagan scholar Walter Otto (1874–1958). Additional information is from Fowler, *Early Greek Mythography II* (Oxford: Oxford University Press, 2013), 81–83; Gantz, *Early Greek Myth* (Baltimore, MD: Johns Hopkins University Press, 1993), 37–38, 87–88; Keightley, *The Mythology of Ancient Greece and Italy* (London: George Bell & Sons, 1896), 100–124; and Otto, *The Homeric Gods* (New York: Pantheon, 1954), 104–124. On bees and nymphs, see also Cook, "The Bee in Greek Mythology," *Journal of Hellenic Studies* 15 (1895): 1–24; Larson, *Greek Nymphs* (Oxford: Oxford University Press, 2001); and Scheinberg, "The Bee Maidens of the Homeric Hymn to Hermes," *Harvard Studies in Classical Philology* 83 (1979): 1–28. On the Delphic tripod, see Cook, *Zeus,* Vol. 2 (New York: Biblo and Tannen, 1965), 193–221.

5. In general, I will use familiar English names when they exist (e.g., Apollo, Gaia, Circe), as opposed to transcribed ancient Greek names (e.g., Apollôn, Gê, Kirkê), but I do use the Greek names in invocations and to show etymological connections.

and oracles of the gods. Some say the Moirai (Three Fates), who spin and measure out the destiny of every mortal, are her daughters. Thus it is not surprising that the priestesses of Themis would deliver oracles by which mortals might guide their actions.

The Corycian Cave, on Mount Parnassus above Delphi, was such an oracular site, where people sought oracles from the nymphs inhabiting the springs in the cave. Occupied since Neolithic times, there is evidence that the Mycenaean Greeks were visiting the cave for oracles from at least 1400 BCE. More than 23,000 *astragaloi* (ankle bones used for divination) and a large number of dice have been found along with many goddess statues dedicated in gratitude. Delphi had a long history of divination before Apollo arrived around 800 BCE.

Homeric Hymn IV, *To Hermes,* tells of three nymphs who dwell on Mount Parnassus and use small stones for divination. They are described like bees—winged, buzzing, swarming, eating honey, etc.—but this is not as unusual as it sounds, for bees are associated with many oracles, including Delphi. In fact, the Pythia (the prophetess of Delphi) is called "the Delphic Bee." The priestesses of Demeter were called Bees (Grk., *Melissai*), as were those of some other goddesses. What is the connection with bees?

Both nymphs and bees haunt caves and trees and live near water, but there are deeper connections. Not only do bees have souls, but Virgil (*Georgics* IV) says they are pure souls and have a portion of the divine mind. They subsist on honey, "the sweet food of the gods," which inspires them with divine enthusiasm. Some ancient authors noted that bees reproduce parthenogenetically (by "virgin birth") and that some priestesses were chaste, and thus like bees. Moreover, bees are clean, orderly, and civilized, and nymphs taught these virtues to our earliest ancestors. They taught morals and many practical skills to shepherds, who often encountered nymphs in the grottos and groves. For example, bee nymphs (Grk., *melissai*) first taught humans to eat the fruit of trees instead of human flesh. And a nymph named Melissa was the first to taste honey and to mix it with water to make *hydromel*. The bee (Grk., *melissa*) was named in her honor, and ever since, bees are sacred to her.

Another connection between oracles and bee nymphs is that prophecy is aided by taking in the divine spirit (Grk., *pneuma*; Lat., *spiritus*) in the form of a substance inhaled, drunk, or eaten. In early times, honey was the principal inspirational drink, often in the form of hydromel (which can be slightly alcoholic) or mead. Moreover, honey can be hallucinogenic if the bees frequent certain plants. (Wine as an inspirational drink arrived later with Dionysos.) Honey was the traditional food of the gods, often identified with nectar and ambrosia, which confer divine immortality. As you will see, Apollo governs both poetry and prophecy, which are identical in origin, and both are compared to honey when they are divinely inspired and, as a consequence, are both true and beautiful. Bees serve the Muses, the divine patrons of the arts and sciences, who were described as bees and sent bees to inspire their devotees with honey.

Bees attended many of the greatest poets in their infancy and fed them honey. This was told of Plato himself, and also of Hesiod, Pindar, and Virgil, among others. For example, Euadnê, a daughter of Poseidon and the nymph Pitanê, bore a son to Apollo. Because she was ashamed of her illicit pregnancy, she gave birth in secret in a field of violets, and abandoned the child there. Bees came and fed the infant honey, or some say that Mother Earth sent serpents to bring him the honey, which is called their blameless venom (Grk., *ios*). Either way, he acquired the gift of prophecy. Euadnê dwelled in the palace of King Aigyptos of Arcadia, and when he realized she had given birth, he asked the Delphic Oracle about the father. The Pythia replied that it was Apollo and that the boy would be a famous prophet. Therefore, the king ordered Euadnê to rescue the child, and since he was lying in a field of violets (Grk., *ia*), she named him "Iamos." When he was a young man, he descended by night into the Alpheos River and invoked his father Apollo and his grandfather Zeus, seeking his destiny. Apollo led him then to Olympia and taught him prophecy. After Heracles established the Olympic Games, Iamos established the oracle there, and founded the lineage of Iamidai prophets, who were still active in the third century CE.

To return to the nymphs, the three bee nymphs of the Corycian Cave are named Melaina (Black One), Kleodôra (Famed for Her Gifts), and Daphnis (Laurel) or Corycia (Grk., *Kôrukia*, named for the cave). Daphnis was said to be the first prophetess of the oracle of Gaia at Delphi. Apollo says that when they are offered honey, the bee nymphs rave and give true prophecies.

These prophetic nymphs are perhaps the same as the "Thriai," daughters of Zeus, whom Hesychius calls the first prophets. They invented divination using small stones or pebbles, which was the earliest form of divination in ancient Greece, for *thriai* is the word for pebble divination, and *thriasthai* means "to divine." You might wonder, is this method of divination named for the nymphs, or are the nymphs the spirits of the pebbles and named for them? Another possibility is that the nymphs originally taught divination by leaves or petals (Grk., *thria*), and that the name of this form of divination came to be applied to other kinds of lots, including pebbles, and that the Thriai nymphs are the patrons of all these kinds of divination. No one knows.

There is an old story that Athena, the goddess of wisdom, learned pebble divination from the Thriai nymphs, or perhaps it is the other way around. Regardless, when Apollo was granted the exclusive right to know Zeus's plans, he demanded that other forms of divination be made unreliable. Therefore, Athena discarded the thriai pebbles in a place since known as the Thriasian Plain (the region around Eleusis, where the Mysteries were celebrated). This is why the Pythia said, "Many are the pebble-casters (*thrioboloi*), but prophets are few." No doubt she saw them as competition! Apollo learned prophecy from the bee nymphs when he was a shepherd on Mount Parnassus, which is the next story.

Pythian Apollo

Apollo is the archer god, ruler of the solar energies (which purify and reveal), lord of Delphi, patron of music and leader of the chorus of Muses (patrons of the arts and sciences), and a god of purification, clear thought, and wisdom. He is also the principal deity of oracles and divination. His twin sister, Artemis, is also an archer god, ruler of lunar energies (which nourish growth), virgin goddess of the chase, and the leader of a troupe of nymphs. The arrows of Apollo and Artemis symbolize the rays of the sun and moon, respectively. They are distant deities; they stand apart and shoot from afar. He has the epithet *Hekatos* and she has *Hekatê*, which come from *hekas*, meaning "far off." Their mother is the gentle Titan goddess Leto, whose name refers to the heavenly darkness from which the twin lights are born. Together they are called the Delian Triad, as I shall explain.

When Leto was pregnant with Artemis and Apollo, she was driven out of every land, for Hera had declared that she could give birth nowhere on Mother Earth. (Hera was angry, naturally, because the father was Zeus, her husband.) When Leto came to Delphi, she was chased away by the monstrous serpent Pythôn, who was born from Gaia. He dwelled there with his wife, the dragoness Delphunê, where they guarded the Omphalos, the sacred stone marking the Earth's navel. (The name "Delphi" is related to *delphus*, which refers to the womb.) They delivered oracles, as do oracular serpents in many sanctuaries of Earth goddesses.

After seven months, Leto came to Delos where she was able to give birth because it was a floating island unconnected to Earth; at Zeus's command, four columns grew up through the sea from the roots of earth to anchor the island. Others say that the island appeared from beneath the sea, which is why it is called *Dêlos*, which means visible, manifest, clear to the mind (Apollonian attributes!). Leto was in labor for nine days, until Eileithuia, the birth goddess, was brought secretly to the island. Artemis was born first, on the sixth day after the new moon, which has been sacred to her ever since. It is said that she was born before her brother so she could midwife at his birth, which is why women in labor call on her. Leto grasped the holy palm tree, and a choir of snow white swans, sacred to the god, flew seven times around the island to herald Apollo's birth, as is described in the *Hymn to Apollo*:

> *What force, what sudden impulse thus can make*
> *The laurel-branch, and all the temple shake!*
> *Depart ye souls profane; hence, hence! O fly*
> *Far from this holy place! Apollo's nigh;*
> *He knocks with gentle foot; The Delian palm*
> *Submissive bends, and breathes a sweeter balm:*
> *Soft swans, high hov'ring catch the auspicious sign,*
> *Wave their white wings, and pour their notes divine.*
> *Ye bolts fly back; ye brazen doors expand,*
> *Leap from your hinges, Phoibos is at hand!*
>
> —Callimachus (ca. 310/305–240 BCE), *Hymn to Apollo*,
> adapted from a translation by H. W. Tytler (1793)

Apollo, then, was born at dawn on the seventh day, which is sacred to him. This was during the seventh month, Delphinios, which began with the new moon after the constellation Delphinus (the Dolphin) became visible in the morning. This month, which was the first after the winter solstice, contained festivals for Apollo Delphinios and Apollo Lukaios (Light Bringer). Pilgrims would plan their journeys to Delphi after Apollo returned in the following month, Bysios, when Delphinus became visible over the sheer cliffs east of Delphi.[6]

Leto fed the newborns on nectar and ambrosia so they became big and strong. Four days after his birth (gods grow quickly!), Apollo asked for a bow and arrows, and the Delian Triad went to Delphi to punish Pythôn. Cradled in his mother's arms, he shot a golden arrow into the all-devouring creature of darkness, and then another, and a hundred gleaming

---

6. The Delphic month, Bysios, corresponds approximately to February but could occur as early as late-January, or as late as mid-March. See Salt and Boutsikas, "Knowing When to Consult the Oracle at Delphi," *Antiquity* 79 (2005): 564–572.

arrows, flashing forth like the rays of the rising sun, and soon the dark dragon was dead. Some say Leto urged on her child (*Ie, pai!*), but others say it was the mountain nymphs who hailed him (*Iê Ie Paian!* using his name among the Mycenaean Greeks, "Paian"). In any case, he is thus invoked to this day, and their battle was reenacted in Delphic rituals. We find this myth in the *Hymn to Apollo*:

> *Now Iê! Ie Paian! rings around*
> *As first from Delphi rose the sacred sound,*
> *When Phoibos swift descending deigned to show*
> *His heav'nly skill to draw the golden bow.*
> *For when no mortal weapons could repel*
> *Enormous Python horrible and fell,*
> *From his bright bow incessant arrows flew,*
> *And, as he rose, the hissing serpent flew.*
> *Whilst Iê! Ie Paian! numbers cry,*
> *Haste launch thy darts, for surely from the sky,*
> *Thou came the great preserver of mankind,*
> *As thy fair mother at thy birth designed.*
>
> —Callimachus (ca. 310/305–240 BCE), *Hymn to Apollo*,
> adapted from a translation by H. W. Tytler (1793)

Apollo buried the corpse at the foot of Mount Parnassus and commanded it "Rot!" (Grk., *Putheu!*), and so it putrefied in the gentle heat of Helios the sun and was reduced to its essence, which returned to Mother Earth. (Alchemists will understand the significance of putrefaction.) Whenever the serpent stirs, Delphi feels the quaking earth. Some say the serpent is now called Pythôn (Grk., *Puthôn*) because of this putrefaction (Grk., *puthein*, to putrefy), and his original name might have been Delphunês (a masculine form of Delphunê). Delphi is also called Pythô after the serpent, and the Delphic prophetess is called the Pythia. She delivers her oracles while sitting astride a metal tripod over a cleft in the earth from which arise the prophecy-inspiring vapors (the *pneuma Puthônos*), which are also called Pythôn, for they are the spirit of the serpent. Apollo himself is called "the Pythian." His gleaming arrows bring illumination and dispel darkness, but they are penetrating and can destroy.

Gaia complained to Zeus, and Apollo had to atone for killing her son Pythôn in the sacred precinct of Delphi. He was sent to the Vale of Tempe to serve King Admetos. When his purification was accomplished, he returned to Delphi wearing a laurel wreath and bearing a laurel wand, both from the sacred laurel tree in the Vale of Tempe. Thereafter he was known as *Phoibos*, the Pure. He taught mortals the healing songs called *paeans* (Grk., *paian*). He also inaugurated the Pythian Games in the serpent's honor, enshrining its teeth and bones as relics in the cauldron on the Delphic tripod. The story shows that even a god must atone for shedding blood.

To learn the prophetic arts, Apollo sought out the Corycian nymphs and learned pebble divination from them. Since Apollo had killed Pythôn, he acquired the oracular site at Delphi from Themis and kept the Pythia as its prophetess. Lot divination continued to be used at Delphi until at least the time of Plutarch (ca. 46–120 CE), who was a lifetime priest there from 95 CE. He tells us that there was a bowl of thriai, and that before the Pythia sat astride her tripod and was ready to prophesy, the thriai would rattle. Others say it was the Pythôn's teeth and bones that rattled in their cauldron; it amounts to the same thing.

The cauldron is an instrument of apotheosis, of rebirth into a divine state. The initiate is symbolically dismembered and boiled in order to be reborn as a prophet or seer (as in the Black Sea shamanic practices, which the Greeks learned in the seventh century BCE).[7] In this way the prophetic Python was reborn in the Delphic tripod. By its means the Pythia is divinized and becomes the bride of Apollo, who impregnates her with his divine Ideas. The tripod is a celestial seat, which raises the priestess above the earthly realm, so she can survey both land and sea. Sometimes the Delphic tripod is depicted with wings, for it conveys the seeress through all the realms of heaven and earth. Some tripod cauldrons were fitted with hemispherical lids, some of which were decorated with stars and astronomical zones. Thus the tripod becomes a microcosm through which the seer surveys the macrocosm.

According to Homeric Hymn III, *To Pythian Apollo*, the god appeared as a dolphin (Grk., *delphin*) to some Cretan sailors and recruited them to build his first temple at Delphi and to become his priests. Pausanias informs us that the second temple was built by bees (Grk., *melissai*) out of beeswax and feathers. Apollo later sent this temple to Hyperborea, the land beyond the North Wind (Boreas), where he has his winter residence, for Apollo

---

7. For example, Dionysos was dismembered, boiled, and eaten by the Titans. Apollo brought his essence to Delphi for divine rebirth. Other examples include the myths of Pelias, Iason, Pelops, Melikertes, and the Rites of Leukothea.

and Dionysos share Delphi, and Dionysos holds it in the three winter months, when the constellation Dolphin is not visible. Then Apollo ascends his swan-drawn chariot, given to him by Zeus, and journeys north to the Hyperboreans, who are holy people who suffer neither death nor disease. There the god delights in sacred festivals, with laurel-wreathed celebrants, maiden choirs, and music of flutes and lyres. Apollo's garden is in Hyperborea, which can be reached by neither land nor sea unless Apollo shows the way. Three months later, when the Dolphin rises above the eastern mountains at dawn, choirs of Delphic youths chant a *paean* around the tripod, and the god ascends his chariot to return to Delphi, bringing song and prophecy. His golden lyre sings summer songs, while nightingales, swallows, and even cicadas sing their hymns to the god. The Castalian Spring flows with silver streams to purify the Pythia and her attendant priests.[8]

The Birth of Hermes

The other god who plays a major role in divination is Hermes, master of ingenuity, lord of barter, preeminent guide, boundary crosser, and interpreter (Grk., *hermêneus*). (The name of the corresponding Roman god, Mercurius, was explained as *mentium currus*, "mental activity."[9]) Therefore, Hermes is a god of clever speech, including eloquence, but also trickery and deceit: whatever works. He is a messenger for Zeus, communicating between Olympus and our world, and, as soul leader (Grk., *psychopompos*), he conducts souls into the underworld and back out, so we call on him when journeying to these realms. In addition to his winged shoes, by which he travels swiftly, he possesses the Cap of Hades, by which he becomes invisible, and a wand, the threefold caduceus, which represents the Cosmic Tree by which he can journey into the heavens or the underworld.[10] Often he is accompanied by three nymphs or goddesses (and so he makes four, which is his number).

Whereas Apollo acts from afar, Hermes is suddenly present, giving uncanny guidance, arranging chance encounters and surprises, for better or worse. A *hermaion* is a windfall or god-sent bit of luck. Whenever a conversation is suddenly silent, we say Hermes has

---

8. The description of Apollo's return is from a lost hymn by Alcaeus, which was described by Himerius (Keightley, *The Mythology of Ancient Greece and Italy*, 112; Otto, *The Homeric Gods*, 63–64).

9. Bernardus Silvestris (fl. 1136 CE), *Commentary on the First Six Books of Virgil's* Aeneid, Bk. 4 (Lincoln, NE: University of Nebraska, 1979), 26.

10. Butterworth, *Some Traces of the Pre-Olympian World in Greek Literature and Myth* (Berlin, Germany: Walter de Gruyter, 1966), 147–150 and 158–161. I use "shamanic" in a generic sense, but there are historical connections to ancient Greece, as I will mention later.

passed by. Apollo brings the bright clarity of day, but Hermes is at home in the night, when appearances are obscure, indistinct, confused, and changeable; when it is easy to become lost unless he appears and shows the way. For the night demands that we be more vigilant and perceptive, to peer into the darkness and be wary, to seek illumination, to be open to his aid. Out of the darkness the truth is revealed.

Hermes puts people to sleep and wakes them up with his golden wand; thus he is called "ruler of dreams" (Grk., *hêgêtôr oneirôn*). Hermes also brings these nocturnal surprises and transformations during the light of day, and so he became a god of mystery and magic. Therefore, in later times, Greeks and Romans understood Hermes and the Egyptian god Thoth to be related aspects of the same god of magic and theurgy. As such, he is known as Hermes Trismegistus ("Thrice Greatest") and credited with revealing or inspiring the Hermetic books.

Hermes's mother is the nymph Maia, one of the Seven Sisters, the Pleiades, daughters of the Titans Atlas and Pleionê, daughter of Oceanus. She lived apart from the other Immortals in a cave on Mount Cyllene (Grk., Kullênê) in Arcadia. There, in the depths of night, she had her trysts with Zeus and soon was pregnant. After ten months, she gave birth to Hermes on the fourth day after the new moon, which has been sacred to him ever since. This was in the fourth month (called *Hermaios* in Argos), the first month after the fall equinox.[11]

Maia caressed the child, kissing and stroking him. He grew quickly and became strong. Soon he was able to stand up on his own and was looking for adventure. As Helios the sun, who sees all things, was setting on the day he was born, Hermes poked his way out of his swaddling clothes and went thieving.

Hermes found Apollo's cattle in Pieria, where they were pastured. Since he desired the savor of meat, he cut fifty head from the herd and devised a clever plan to steal them. He drove the cattle backward and walked backward himself to confuse pursuers. He crafted sandals from bark so that he would make large, unrecognizable footprints. He drove the cattle hard through the night, fording the River Alpheos just as Helios arose in the east, and he hid the stolen herd in a spacious grotto near Pylos.

Baby Hermes selected the two best cattle for the first sacrifice. He slaughtered and skinned them, placing the skins on the rocks to dry. Using laurel for tinder, he made the first fire, divided the meat into twelve portions, and burned them for the gods. He enjoyed

---

11. Kerényi, *Hermes*, 56–57.

the savor of the burning fat, wafting toward heaven, but didn't taste the meat, for gods don't eat meat.

Then Hermes spied a tortoise crawling out of the cave and conceived a clever invention. He killed the tortoise and made the first lyre from its shell, stringing it with cow gut. As the evening of his second day approached, Hermes entertained himself on the lyre, celebrating his accomplishments. The next morning, he sneaked silently back to Mount Cyllene—as only Hermes can do—slipped through the keyhole like a mist or autumn breeze, wrapped himself in his swaddling clothes, and climbed into his cradle.

But Maia knew what he had been up to and scolded him. Hermes pleaded innocence, but he also promised his mother that he had a plan by which they could live as immortals among the Immortals on Olympus, rather than in a dismal cave.

As soon as Apollo discovered the theft of his cattle, he set out in pursuit. He was confused by the strange tracks, but he used his power of divination—specifically, reading the flight of birds—to find his way to the thief. Thus he came to Maia's cave, where he accused the infant of theft. Hermes pretended to be an innocent baby and to know nothing of cattle, and so Apollo brought him before Zeus. He continued to protest his innocence, but Zeus, who knows everything, ordered him to lead Apollo to the cattle. All the gods, including Apollo, laughed at Hermes's precocious cleverness and praised him for it.

The two sons of Zeus went to Pylos, where Apollo saw the ox hides drying in the sun. Hermes explained that he had sacrificed two cattle to the Twelve Olympian Gods.

"Twelve?" asked Apollo. "There are only eleven."

"I am to be the twelfth," Hermes modestly announced.

Apollo wondered that a tiny baby could do such a deed. "You do not need to grow any longer!" he said. He tried to restrain Hermes with strong bands, but they could not keep Hermes down, for they fell magically from the young god.

To soothe his older brother, Hermes pulled out his lyre and began to sing a hymn to the Immortals. Apollo was so enchanted by the lyre that he offered to trade the stolen cattle for it, to give Hermes the golden shepherd's crook, and to make him keeper of herds. Hermes happily agreed and explained that one must have the proper knowledge and preparation for the lyre to answer pleasingly. (So also with divination!) Some say that Apollo increased the number of strings to seven from the four that Hermes had (seven and four being their special numbers). These seven strings represent the harmony of the seven planetary spheres, symbolized in the seven Greek vowels. Apollo's gold plectrum symbolizes the rays of the sun, which evoke the music of the spheres. Hermes agreed never to steal anything else of Apollo's, and in return Apollo gave him a golden three-branched magic wand capable of any task.

To amuse himself while he tended the herds, Hermes made a reed pipe (Grk., *syrinx*), which Apollo heard and desired very much. He offered Hermes whatever he might want, and the shepherd asked for the art of prophecy, for which Apollo was famous. Apollo said he could not grant this, for only Zeus knew his thoughts and plans, and Apollo had been granted the exclusive right to reveal them to mortals. He had sworn an inviolable oath to reveal the art to no one of gods or mortals. Instead, Apollo offered the divinatory art that he had practiced as a shepherd, but in the form of a riddle or enigma (Grk., *ainigma*).

"There are certain holy ones," he said, "virgin sisters with wings, their hair dusted with pollen, who hum and swarm about. If Hermes seeks them out, he can learn this ancient art." Were they the bee nymphs of the Corycian Cave under the ridge of Parnassus? Were they the same as the Thriai? We don't know, but Apollodorus [12] says Apollo gave Hermes the art of pebble divination. Apollo further informed Hermes that the sisters must be offered honey in order to speak the truth, otherwise their prophecies would be unreliable.

Apollo granted Hermes permission to teach this art to mortals. If these holy sisters are approached with appropriate respect and wisdom, they will tell the truth, otherwise their responses will be unreliable. It is the same, Apollo explains, with the Delphic Oracle: if through preliminary divination Apollo reveals that a consultation is permitted, then it will be truthful. If an inquirer persists in consulting the oracle in spite of inauspicious omens, then the response will be unreliable. An important warning to keep in mind!

Hermes and Apollo are both riddlers. Apollo was called "Loxias," which probably refers to his pronouncements being ambiguous and oblique (Grk., *loxos*). Delphic oracular verses are notoriously obscure. Greeks understood them to be a challenge to mortals to use their wits and wisdom to understand them correctly. Like Zen koans, they are enigmas (Grk., *ainigmata*) that act as spells—blessing or cursing their recipients according to how they are understood (more on this important topic later). Through their exchange of gifts, Apollo and Hermes became similar in bringing mortals both inspired divination and inspired poetry and song.

Now you know the story of how the bee nymphs first taught divination by pebbles, of how Pythian Apollo came to Delphi and became lord of prophecy, and of how Hermes learned divination by lots. Let's move on to the divining, which this book will teach to you.

---

12. For convenience, I use this traditional name for the unknown author of *The Library* (Grk., *Biblioteca*), which dates to the first or second century CE.

Methods of Divination

"Divination is at the heart of Greek religion."[13] This is because, as the Stoic philosopher Chrysippus (ca. 279–ca. 206 BCE) explains, divination is the power to see, to understand, and to interpret the signs that the gods give to people.[14] This is evident in the Latin word *divinatio* (divination), which comes from the same root as *divinus* (divine). Divination is not limited to predicting the future; thus, Homer sings of the famous seer:

> *Calchas, an augur foremost in his art,*
> *Who all things, present, past, and future knew (Iliad I.70)*

Often indeed, divination is intended to discover something about the past in order to illuminate the present. In this section, I will describe the various methods of divination used in the ancient Greek and Roman worlds.[15]

In his *Phaedrus*, Plato (ca. 428–348 BCE) might have been the first to distinguish two kinds of divination: natural and artificial. According to Plato, natural divination (also called intuitive or inspired) is superior, for through it the gods communicate directly to mortals. This is experienced as a kind of madness (Grk., *mania*, from the Indo-European root *men*, referring to mental power), which is why *mantikê* is the Ancient Greek word for divination, and *mantis* is the word for a diviner or seer. This is the sort of divination practiced by the Pythia, but also that in which we interpret those dreams that are sent by the gods. It is closely related to another kind of madness that comes from Apollo: the divine inspiration of poets and musicians. Oracles too are often expressed in verse, which indicates their divine origin, as does their obscurity.

Dream interpretation was commonly classified as natural divination, but there definitely was art involved in its practice. Artemidorus's book of dream symbols still survives from the second century CE, but there were many others. The Neoplatonist Synesius (ca. 370–ca. 413 CE) wrote a treatise defending dream divination, but he thought that such

---

13. Hornblower and Spawforth, *The Oxford Classical Dictionary* (Oxford: Oxford University Press, 1996), s.v. Divination.

14. Cicero, *On Divination* (Oxford: Clarendon, 2006), 2.130.

15. Homeric quotation from William Cowper translation, 1791. Information in this section is primarily from Halliday, *Greek Divination* (London: Macmillan, 1913); Luck, *Arcana Mundi* (Baltimore, MD: Johns Hopkins University Press, 1985), ch. IV; and Johnston, *Ancient Greek Divination* (Chichester, England: Blackwell, 2008), which is the best contemporary treatment of ancient Greek divination.

dream books were useless, since dreams are so individual. In fact, as psychologist Carl Jung showed, there are common, archetypal symbols, but they take some analysis to interpret.

The other sort of divination, artificial (also, technical, inductive) depends on some learned technique or art (Grk., *technê*; Lat., *ars*). It depends on human skill and reason rather than on divine illumination, and therefore it is more fallible. We have seen this distinction already in the myth of Hermes's birth, when he receives the divinatory art from Apollo, who reserved inspired prophecy for himself. In the divinatory arts, it is necessary to learn to read and interpret the signs, an error-prone process.

In practice, the distinction between natural and artificial divination is not so clear. On the one hand, natural divination usually requires some technique and skill. For example, a dream might be sent by the gods, but some skill is required to distinguish such dreams (which, Homer says, come through the Gate of Horn) from ordinary, mundane, insignificant dreams (which come through the Gate of Ivory).[16] Second, skill is required to interpret the dreams, which is why the ancients had dream interpretation handbooks, as we still do today. Finally, while dreams might come unbidden, ritual and magical techniques can be used to seek an oracular dream, and there is definitely skill involved in these arts. There were certainly sophisticated ritual techniques deployed at the Asclepieia—the healing shrines of the god Asclepius—for seeking and interpreting the healing dreams. The Pythia also used specific techniques to enter her trance state, and there were elaborate rituals at other oracular shrines, such as the Oracle of Trophonius. Certainly, theurgy (rituals and practices for communing with gods and ascending to the divine) is a complex art.

On the other hand, the artificial divination techniques are not entirely a human enterprise. Typically, they involve a ritual to invoke Apollo or another god to bring a true oracle; the god's presence is necessary for a successful divination. Moreover, wise diviners seek the god's aid in finding the best interpretation of the signs. That is, they seek divinely inspired interpretations and do not depend on their own human wits alone.

In Aeschylus's *Prometheus Bound*, the Titan god Prometheus—whose name means "Forethought"—informs us that he taught mortals to interpret dreams and to find omens in chance utterances, the flight of birds, the organs of sacrificed animals, and sacrificial fires. This might seem to contradict the myths about Apollo and Hermes, but I think it refers to the earlier history of divination, for Prometheus belongs to the older generation of Titans, who preceded the Olympian gods, such as Apollo, Hermes, Athena, and Zeus.

---

16. *Odyssey,* 19.560–9. The Greek word for horn, *keras,* is similar to the word for "fulfill," *krainô,* and the word for "ivory," *elephas,* is similar to the word for "deceive," *elephairomai.*

According to some myths, Prometheus created humankind and was also the great human benefactor, bringing us fire and teaching many things, including the alphabet, numbers, agriculture, astronomy, medicine, and other arts and sciences. In particular, he taught mortals how to sacrifice to the gods, tricking Zeus into accepting the inedible parts so that people could keep the meat for themselves. Therefore, it is natural that he also taught us how to interpret the omens accompanying sacrifice, such as the condition of the victim's internal organs and the behavior of the flames and smoke from the altar fire. These religious practices were well established before Apollo came to Delphi and Hermes acquired the divinatory arts from him.

Indeed, many divinatory arts may have their origin in omens accompanying sacrifice. When you make an offering to a god, it is natural to watch for signs that the god has accepted it. When you pour a wine libation on the altar fire and it flares up, the omen is auspicious. When you burn an incense offering, you look for signs the god has accepted it. And in ancient times, when an animal was sacrificed, specialists inspected its internal organs to divine the god's reception of the offering. The liver was especially significant, because the ancients believed it was the source of blood, the seat of life, and the mirror in animals of the divine life force. The specialists in these kinds of divination—the *haruspices* (sing., *haruspex*)—also interpreted lightning and other ominous occurrences. No general would begin a battle without concurrence of the haruspices.

It is an easy path from observing the omens that accompany a sacrifice and indicate its success to performing a sacrifice for the sake of the omens that accompany it. For example, in ancient times it was customary to make offerings to the nymphs at their sacred springs. As people prayed, they tossed coins, medals, gemstones, cakes, and other small objects into the springs and watched for signs that they were accepted: if it sank, the offering was welcome. They also paid attention to the sound and ripples when it hit the water, and watched as it sank. These omens hinted at whether the prayer would be answered. From this, it is a small step to cast an object into the spring while praying for advice or for the answer to a query, and then to observe its behavior as a sign from the nymphs. The sign could be the side on which a coin landed, giving a positive or negative response. Casting dice or astragaloi could answer more complicated queries. As you have learned, such divination was performed at the Corycian Cave on Mount Parnassus.

Divination at sacred springs may have developed into bowl divination (*lecanomancy*, from Grk. *lekanê*, "dish," and *manteia*, "divination"), a common method in the ancient world.[17] Rather than conducting the rite at the sacred spring, a jug of its water could be poured in a dish. We know that the ancients sometimes divined by casting dice, astragaloi, or stones into dishes of water. Lots were also drawn, without looking, from such bowls. What happens if you are fresh out of water from a sacred spring? In this case you can invoke a deity into any dish of water before casting the lots into it. We have invocations to do this from the *Greek Magical Papyri*.[18]

Scrying might have a similar origin. At a sacred spring you can observe the ripples in the water to discern the nymphs' response, or peer more deeply into the depths to observe images and other signs. The same can be done in a consecrated dish of water, but other liquids are also used, such as ink. Or you can dribble a little oil in the water and scry in the resulting patterns. Orpheus, who attached cosmic significance to the egg, wrote a lost book *Ooscopy*, which we know from descriptions of the book to be divination by scrying the forms assumed by egg white when dropped into hot water; it is practiced to this day. The ancient Greeks also scried in other reflective objects, such as mirrors and the polished blades of swords and daggers. Crystal gazing commonly used beryls of various colors. Ancient scriers often placed a candle or oil lamp so its light reflected in a bowl or mirror. They might also scry directly in the candle or lamp flame, which is akin to divining from the sacrificial altar fire.

Pausanias (second century CE) tells us that at a certain Oracle of Demeter a sick person could find out their fate. The querent lowered a mirror into a sacred spring until it just touched the surface. After burning incense and praying, the mirror was withdrawn and on its surface would be an image of the sufferer, either dead or alive.

As you can see, the ancients used many different media for divination. In another lost work, the scholar Marcus Varro (116–27 BCE) classified divination systems according to the four elements, earth, water, air, and fire. Hydromancy (water divination) includes, of course, divination in sacred pools and bowls. Empyromancy (fire divination) includes scrying in a candle, lamp, or other flame, but also observing how objects behave when they

---

17. There are technical terms for all of these methods of divination, such as "lecanomancy" for bowl divination. You can find lists of them online, but in most cases I don't think it's important to know them. I mention only a few, which are relevant.

18. *The Greek Magical Papyri*—cited as *PGM* for *Papyri Graecae Magicae*—is a modern collection of magical papyri from Graeco-Roman Egypt, which date from the first century BCE to the fifth century CE; see Betz, *The Greek Magical Papyri in Translation, Including the Demotic Spells* (Chicago, IL: University of Chicago, 1992) for a translation.

are burned, such as how they sizzle or crack in an altar fire. Earth divination (geomancy) depends on the power of the earth and includes the observation of oracular snakes; this might have been the practice when Pythôn still lived at Delphi. Finally, air divination (aeromancy) includes taking the auspices—observing the flight, calls, and other behavior of birds—but also observing lightning, clouds, smoke from incense or altar fires, and how barley, flour, or other materials behave when thrown in the air.

Roman *auspicium* refers primarily to the observation of birds (from Lat. *avis*, "bird," and *specio*, "to look at"), but also to lightning and other aerial phenomena. Such omens might be sought (technically termed *impetrative*) or come unbidden (*oblative*). The diviner (called an *auspex*) might also seek auspices by observing how eagerly the sacred chickens ate their feed! They also noted unsought omens from the way quadrupeds fed and from unusual, ominous occurrences. In ancient times, the auspices were taken only to ascertain the gods' concurrence with the timing of an action, and pertained to one day. If the outcome was inauspicious, you could try again the next day. To ascertain both the timing and the advisability of the action, the Romans resorted to augury, which was closely related, but the province of specialist augurs. They assisted in establishing temples and installing priests, which is where we get our word "inaugurate."

Birds were also important in ancient Greek divination. The same word (*oiônos*) was used for any large bird of prey, for divination by means of them, and by extension for all kinds of divination. Due to their ability to fly and speak, birds are important messengers between mortals and gods. Birds are supposed to know all languages, and many legendary seers could understand the language of birds. Moreover, shamans use feathers and bird costumes for their ritual ascents, and Greek "healer-seers" (*iatromanteis*; sing. *iatromantis*) learned shamanic techniques after the Greeks established trade with the Black Sea in the seventh century BCE. Many myths, including Hermes's birthday escapade, can be interpreted as shamanic journeys.[19] For example, the legendary Latin king Picus (Lat. for "Woodpecker") was turned into a woodpecker by the witch Circe (Grk., Kirkê, a feminine form of *kirkos*, a wheeling hawk or falcon), after which he delivered oracles. He is described wearing the ritual garb of an augur, so perhaps the woodpecker was his familiar. (There is an interesting parallel in the bee nymphs, who may have divined by the flight and buzzing of bees; the Pythia was called "the Delphic Bee.")

---

19. Butterworth, *Some Traces of the Pre-Olympian World*, 155–160.

The Sanctuary of Zeus at Dodona is perhaps the oldest Greek oracle (ca. 2000 BCE). Three priestesses called "Doves" prophesied and interpreted the splashing of the sacred spring, the rustling leaves of the Sacred Oak, and the behavior of oracular doves. Staff at the oracle would give a thin lead tablet to a querent, who would scratch their question into the tablet. Then they rolled it up and scratched their initials on the outside. In trance, a Dove would pull each rolled tablet out of a jug, read aloud the initials, and pronounce the answer to the question without unrolling it. Hundreds of these tablets have been found.

A common method of divination made use of chance utterances (Grk., *klêdones*), which could be understood as omens or oracles from the gods. These might come unbidden, but there are techniques for obtaining them. For example, Pausanias tells us that in the middle of the marketplace at Pharai (in Achaia, Greece) there was an oracle in the form of a *herm*, a four-sided pillar surmounted by a bust of Hermes.[20] There was a stone hearth in front of it and bronze oil lamps on both sides. Querents would come at nighttime, pray for an oracle, burn some incense on the altar, fill and light the lamps, and place a copper coin to the right of the image. After whispering their question in Hermes's ear, they covered their own ears, left the marketplace, uncovered their ears, and took the first words they heard as an oracle. Hermes is the appropriate god as the patron of merchants and wayfarers, but also a god of chance and the lucky accident. This simple method (called cledonomancy, but don't bother remembering it) was practiced in many places.

Diogenes Laertius (third century CE) tells us that Pittacus, one of the Seven Sages, was consulted by a man who couldn't decide which of two women to marry. Pittacus pointed his staff at children spinning tops some distance away and said, "They will give you a message; follow their track." When the man approached, he heard them saying, as they whipped their tops, "Drive your own!" The man interpreted this to mean that he should marry the woman of his own class and not the one of higher station. The Greek words, however, are ambiguous and enigmatic, like most oracles. We don't even know what the phrase meant in the context of the children's game, for it could be telling the other children to keep to their own tops, or it could be encouraging the top to follow its own path (the usual meaning of the Greek phrase, which is proverbial) as it spins and wanders about. It might be a sort of ritual or magical command to keep it spinning. Nor is it coincidental that Pittacus directed the querent toward children whipping tops, for spinning tops and disks are traditional instruments of love magic, as is whipping. Moreover, after

---

20. Pausanias, *Pausanias Guide to Greece,* translated by Peter Levi (London: Penguin, 1979), VII.22.2–3; p. 285.

the top is whipped fiercely, it wanders indecisively, first one way, then another, like the querent in this case. More generally, spinning tops are symbols of the celestial spheres and the Spindle of Destiny, so it is unsurprising they are used for divination and invoking gods.[21]

These synchronistic utterances can be understood as a divine pronouncement (*klêdôn, phêmê, omphê*) granted in answer to prior prayer. Indeed, as the bringers of oracles, Klêdôn was sometimes worshipped as a god and Phêmê as a goddess, with their own sanctuaries, altars, priests, and sacrifices. They are also aspects of oracular gods, including Hermes, Apollo, Athena, and Zeus.

The mystic, mage, and healer-seer Pythagoras (sixth century BCE), who stands at the origin of the Western spiritual and philosophical tradition, practiced cledonomancy, hydromancy, augury, and numerology. Once he was visited by Abaris, a priest-magician of Apollo from Hyperborea, "the land beyond the North Wind," who used his golden dart to travel around the world, including Greece. Some scholars believe that he came from Central Asia, perhaps Tibet, and that his "dart" was a *phurba* (Sanskrit, *kîla*), the Indo-Tibetan ritual dagger.[22] On the other hand, Hecataeus of Abdera (ca. 360–290 BCE) identified Hyperborea with Britain, and said the Hyperboreans had a circular temple (Stonehenge?) where they worshipped Apollo, so perhaps he was a Druid. In any case, Pythagoras and Abaris instructed each other in their Mysteries. Abaris gave his dart to Pythagoras, and Pythagoras taught Abaris divination by numbers, for the inner circle of Pythagoreans were vegetarians and rejected animal sacrifice. Moreover, divination by numbers is more spiritual and less materialistic than divination from entrails, and so it is more suited to spiritual adepts. Unfortunately, we do not know what method Pythagoras used, but it's highly unlikely to be the sort of "Pythagorean numerology" taught nowadays. The divination systems you will learn from this book can be consulted by means of numbers.

The ancients also practiced pendulum divination, in the simplest case to answer yes-or-no questions. Usually they used a finger ring hanging from a cord for their pendulums. (Rings symbolize the manifestation of eternity in the material world; they are receptive of divine power.) For a more complex question, they might hold the pendulum in a bowl with the alphabet inscribed around the rim. The pendulum would move from letter to letter (like the planchette on a Ouija® board) spelling out, for example, the name of the next

---

21. Diogenes Laertius, *Lives of the Eminent Philosophers* (Cambridge, MA: Harvard University Press, 1925), I.80; Livrea, "From Pittacus to Byzantium," *The Classical Quarterly* 45, 2 (1995): 474–480.

22. On the Tibetan connection see Kingsley, *A Story Waiting to Pierce You* (Point Reyers, CA: Golden Sufi, 2010) and Opsopaus, "Apollo's Dagger," *Circle Magazine* 108 (Spring 2011): 10–12.

emperor (which didn't make you popular with the current emperor). A related method, which was popular in ancient Greece but is still used today, is sieve divination, in which a wooden sieve is held between the blades of a pair of scissors. The answer is read from the way the sieve turns.

Divination by icons is similar. After praying for an answer, the querent lifts a small statue of the god or a sacred stone near it; if it is easy to lift, the answer is favorable, but if it pulls the arm down, unfavorable. A sacred icon can give the sensitive mantis an answer in other ways, such as appearing to nod, smile, speak, shine, sweat, or exhibit other changes.

Astrology was, of course, practiced in ancient Greece and Rome, and astrological timing was used in magical operations, but it does not seem to have been especially popular as a method of divination. Palmistry was practiced on similar principles, discerning trines, squares, and other aspects in the lines of the palm. Necromancy (divination by communication with the dead) does not seem to have been important in ancient Greece or Rome outside of literary depictions.

Cleromancy

Let's turn now to cleromancy, the kind of divination you will learn in this book. (You will be a cleromancer!) The term comes from the Greek word *klêros*, which means "lot," and cleromancy is thus divination by casting or drawing lots. The Latin word for "lot" is *sors* (plural, *sortes*), and so the Latin word for one who draws (*legere*) lots is *sortilegus*. From it we have the English word "sortilege" for drawing or casting lots and "sortileger" for one who practices this art.

Many varieties of cleromancy were used in ancient Greece and Rome. Pebbles, stones, dice, and astragaloi might be cast into sacred springs, bowls of liquids, or dice trays. Stones, clay balls, beans, or inscribed objects (stones, wooden staves, thin metal leaves) were drawn from bowls, jars, or other containers (sometimes filled with water), or shaken out of them.

Sortilege was practiced at many of the shrines that are known primarily for inspired divination. There is no archaeological evidence that it was practiced at Delphi, but astragaloi and dice are found in the Corycian Cave, just seven miles away. We are also told that at Delphi the pebbles in a bowl above the tripod rattled before the Pythia was brought in to prophesy. It was perhaps a preliminary divination to determine the god's willingness to speak through her. We also read that the "two-bean method of divination" (some kind of lot drawing) was conducted at Delphi. Plutarch tells of a situation in which several men wanted to be king of Thessaly, so each marked his name on a bean and put it in a jug, which was sent to Delphi. The Pythia drew a bean from the jug and thus decided the king. Cleromancy might have provided a less expensive or more accessible means of divination than consulting the Pythia, for she prophesied only on the seventh day of the nine non-winter months, when Apollo resided at Delphi, and consultants had to offer a sheep (expensive!). Astragaloi and dice are found among the ruins of many temples, and so we assume cleromancy was practiced at them.

Inspired or venerated texts, such as Homer's *Iliad* and *Odyssey* and Virgil's *Aeneid*, are used for book divination (bibliomancy). With your eyes closed, open one of those books to a random page and put your finger on a random line. That is your oracle. A related technique is the *Homer Oracle,* which lists the 216 throws of three dice, with a line from Homer for each one. You throw the dice and the corresponding Homeric verse is your oracle. Other collections of oracles, such as the Sibylline Oracles, were consulted by casting lots. In chapter 5, you will learn a similar art, the Oracle of the Seven Sages.

The *Sortes Astrampsychi* (Lots of Astrampsychus) dates to the second century CE and is known from several papyri from the third to sixth centuries and from later manuscripts. It is a system of divination, supposedly from Astrampsychus, an ancient Egyptian sage or Persian magus, who credits the work to Pythagoras. It took the form of two books and a table. From a book of ninety-two questions, querents selected the one that best expressed their query. Next, the gods led them to pick a number from one to ten. An arithmetical procedure combined the two and used the table to find an appropriate answer in the second book. (An English translation is now available.[23])

Cicero recounts a story told in the annals of the city Praeneste (modern Palestrina, Italy). A certain Numerius Suffustius was plagued by dreams urging him to go to a certain place and split open a flint rock. Eventually the dreams became threatening, and so, in spite of the laughter of others, he went to the place, found the rock, and broke it open. Out fell a number of oak tablets inscribed in ancient characters (presumably the archaic Roman alphabet). These were the *Sortes Numerii* (Lots of Numerius), also known as the *Sortes Praenestinae* (Praenestine Lots). The place was declared sacred, and a statue of the infants Jupiter and Juno in the lap of Fortuna was erected by it. When the lots were found, a nearby olive tree began to exude honey, and the soothsayers declared that an arc or chest for the tablets should be made of the olive wood. A temple of Fortuna was built where

---

23. Hansen, *Anthology of Ancient Greek Popular Literature* (Bloomington, IN: Indiana University Press, 1998), ch. 10.

the olive tree had been; it eventually became one of the largest sanctuaries in Italy (it's still there). Consultation of the oracle was permitted only if the Fortuna statue agreed by nodding her head. Then, the lots would be taken out, shuffled, and a child would draw them. It is unknown whether the lots contained whole sentences, single words, or perhaps just letters, which would have to be arranged. Many thankful inscriptions from consultants of the oracle survive to this day.

The details in the story are not coincidental. The lots came out of a stone, which connects them with Gaia, but they were made of oak, which connects them with divination (recall the Sacred Oak of Zeus at Dodona, which gave oracles). The olive tree exuded honey, which is connected with divination, as you have seen. Finally, when ancient Greeks drew lots, they sometimes put an olive leaf in the jug, because the olive is good luck.

According to Suetonius, the Emperor Tiberius (42 BCE–37 CE) was afraid of divination (explained in the next section) and ordered all the oracles destroyed. He commanded that the *Sortes Praenestinae* be sealed in their arc and brought to him, but when the arc was opened, it was found to be empty. When it was returned to the temple, the lots miraculously reappeared in the arc. The oracle was closed by the Christian Emperors Constantine (272–337 CE) and Theodosius I (347–395 CE), never to reopen.

Pausanias described a shrine of Heracles in a grotto by the Boura River in Achaea, Greece.[24] Inside was a statue of Heracles with a large number of astragaloi nearby. After praying, you picked up four and cast them on a table. There was an engraved tablet that gave the meaning for each combination of astragaloi. The method of consulting these oracles was probably similar to the Hermes of Pharai described earlier. Perhaps too there were local oracle interpreters hanging around to explain the oracle's meaning—for a price! This grotto still existed as late as 1817, but it was obliterated by an earthquake in 1898. Fortunately, similar oracular tablets survive from other shrines; Nollé lists twenty-one in various states of completeness, most dating from the second century CE.[25] The most common form uses five astragaloi, for which there are fifty-six possible throws (interestingly, the number of minor arcana in the tarot). These were commonly inscribed on the four sides of a stone pillar, six feet high and two feet wide. Sometimes they took the form of a

---

24. Pausanias, *Pausanias Guide to Greece, Vol. I: Central Greece*, Translated by Peter Levi (London: Penguin Books, 1979), VII.25.6[10]; pp. 298–299.

25. Nollé, *Kleinasiatische Losorakel.*

herm, the characteristic bust of Hermes atop a four-sided pillar, because four is the sacred number of Hermes, who was born on the fourth day of the fourth month. The oracles are in the first person, and it seems that Apollo is the speaker. Hermes is involved for several reasons. He is the patron of travelers and merchants, but, as you know, he is also involved in cleromancy, as appropriate for the god of chance and good luck. Here he seems to function as Apollo's prophet and messenger (another of Hermes's offices). A prayer accompanying one astragalos oracle confirms his role:

> *Thou, Muses' servant, Hermes, god, Apollo's seer,*
> *Hail, well-spoken Zeus' and Maia's son, my guide,*
> *Reveal to me divine decrees in oracles.*[26]

Closely related are the alphabet oracles, which are stone tablets (typically from three to five feet high) inscribed with twenty-four verse oracles, each of which begins with one of the twenty-four letters of the Greek alphabet in order. By some (unknown) process of drawing or casting lots (perhaps like rune casting), a letter was chosen, and the corresponding oracle was the answer to the query. I won't say more about the Alphabet Oracle here, since it is the subject of part 2, where you will learn how to use it.

Theory of Divination

In this section, I will say a little about how our Pagan ancestors understood divination. Although you don't need to know this to use the systems in this book, the information you will learn will help you to improve your practice. As with any tools, you will be able to use them more effectively if you understand a little about how they work.

I will begin with the simplest explanation of divination, which is probably the way most of our Pagan ancestors understood it. The gods care for humankind and often answer our prayers (when it accords with their plans). For example, Prometheus, who created humans, has been our benefactor—bringing us fire, for example. In Aeschylus's *Prometheus*

---

26. My translation of Greek text in Nollé, *Kleinasiatische Losorakel*, 213, from a seven-astragalos oracle from Termessos.

Bound, he recalls how ignorant people were at first, how "beholding, they beheld in vain, / And hearing, heard not." [27] Therefore,

> *I made them wise and true in aim of soul!—*
> *And I will tell you—not as taunting them,*
> *But teaching you the intention of my gift.*

Among many other arts, he taught us divination: "I fixed the various rules of mantic art," he says, and proceeds to describe a few of them.

Clearly, divination will be most successful if accompanied by a sincere petition to the gods. This may be accompanied by a vow to be fulfilled if the god helps you out. Of course, you should fulfill your vow, or you're asking for trouble! Think about that before you make your vow!

The ancient Stoic philosophers worked hard to understand divination, for they said that the efficacy of divination proves the existence of the gods, and the existence of the gods implies that they will aid us through divination. The Stoic Chrysippus (ca. 279–ca. 206 BCE) defined divination as "the power to see, to understand, and to interpret the signs that are given to humans by the gods." [28] This power is a consequence of the universe being a harmonious whole. As Marcus Aurelius (IV.130) says,

> *Always think of the cosmos as one living being,*
> *having one substance and one soul, …*
> *and how intertwined is the fabric*
> *and how closely woven the web.*[29]

This fabric or web is a spirit (Grk., *pneuma*) that pervades the cosmos, just as a spirit pervades each of us, which integrates all the parts into one. This is manifested by a cosmic *sympatheia*, a sympathy, concord, or mutual affinity by which everything affects everything

---

27. This and the following two quotations are from Aeschylus's *Prometheus Bound*, lines 447–8, 443–6, and 484 found in Browning, *Prometheus Bound and Other Poems* (New York: C. S. Francis, 1851), 27–28.

28. Cicero, *On Divination*, 2.130. This work presents the Stoic theory of divination, which Cicero subjects to a rationalistic critique.

29. See MacLennan, *The Wisdom of Hypatia* (Woodbury, MN: Llewellyn, 2013), ch. 6, for an introduction to the Stoic view of Nature.

else. Therefore, the intentions and actions of the gods are mirrored throughout the universe and can affect, in particular, the casting or drawing of lots. Through divination, Stoics seek to discern the Providence of the gods, so that by living in conscious accord with it, they fulfill their individual destinies in the divine plan.

The Stoic Posidonius (135–51 BCE) explained that there are three ways by which dreams can reveal hidden truths.[30] First, since the human soul is divine, being made of the same incorporeal substance as the gods, it has the same visionary powers as they do, but these powers are obscured and confounded by the soul's entanglement with the body. When the soul is loosened from the body in sleep, however, it recovers some of its divine powers and can see more clearly. (The same happens when people are near death or in trance.) Second, the air is pervaded by *daimons*, which are spirits who mediate between gods and mortals, in particular, facilitating communication. When the sleeper's soul is free of the body, it is better able to communicate with the daimons who are the messengers (Grk., *angeloi*, "angels") of the gods. Third, the gods may speak to us directly, for that is their power. Although this is Posidonius's explanation of prophetic dreams, it is applicable to other kinds of divination as well. It suggests that our divinations will be more successful if we do them in a meditative state, focusing inward and away from our bodies and the visible world. Invite the gods or their assistant daimons to bring the knowledge you seek.

The Neoplatonic philosophers developed the most complete and sophisticated theory of divination.[31] "Neoplatonism" is the name that modern philosophers give to the new direction in Platonic philosophy first taught by Plotinus (204–270 CE). Neoplatonic spiritual practices center around theurgy, a kind of spiritual magic directed toward direct communion with the gods, and so divination is an essential practice for Neoplatonists.

To understand the role of divination in Neoplatonism and to use it to improve your skill in the art, I will have to explain a little about Neoplatonic philosophy. In addition to the ordinary, mundane world, in which everything is changing, both coming to be but also passing away, Neoplatonists are aware of another realm or plane of reality: the realm of the Platonic Forms, which are eternal, unchanging Ideas that exist independently of individual minds. Think of mathematical objects such as the perfect Circle or numbers such as

---

30. Cicero, *On Divination*, 1.64.

31. The primary source for Neoplatonic theurgy and divination is Iamblichus's book commonly known as *De Mysteriis* (*On the Mysteries*). Of secondary sources, Addey, *Divination and Theurgy in Neoplatonism* (Surrey, England: Ashgate, 2014), esp. ch. 7, is especially valuable for understanding the Neoplatonic theory and practice of divination.

One and Two. They are unchanging and eternal, unlike objects in this world. Our physical circles are inevitably imperfect images of Circle, and of course physical circles must be created and will eventually decay. Since a mind is composed of ideas, the sum total of Platonic Ideas makes up a sort of eternal Cosmic Mind. The material universe, in contrast, is the Cosmic Body.

More important for our purposes is the fact that the gods also reside in the Platonic realm. They may be considered the eternal Forms or Ideas of certain powers, energies, or patterns of action. The traditional myths about the gods hint at their nature, but cannot fully comprehend it. Neoplatonists treat these myths as enigmas, which must be solved by allegorical interpretation in order to understand the nature of the gods.

Like the Stoics, Neoplatonists perceive an all-pervading harmony in the Cosmos; Pythagoras coined the Greek word *kosmos* to refer to order and harmonious beauty. All of the Platonic Ideas—and thus all the gods—collectively create a divine Providence governing our world. This is in spite of the fact the gods may disagree with each other and even strive against each other. In fact, this contrast of their natures and intentions is necessary for our world to exist. (The ancient philosopher Empedocles [ca. 490–ca. 430 BCE]—who first explained the four elements—said all things come to be through Love and Strife, the powers of union and division, the yin and yang of ancient Greek philosophy.)

This principle of unity, this principle by which any thing is *one thing*, Neoplatonists call *The Inexpressible One (To Arrhêton Hen)*. It is inexpressible because it cannot be described in words. This in turn is because, as the ultimate principle of unity, it is beyond duality, and therefore beyond *is* and *is not*. The only way to know it is by a process of mystical union, which is one of the goals of Neoplatonic theurgy. The Greek word *arrhêton* can also be translated "ineffable" and "unspeakable," and can refer to the ancient Mysteries, about which it is unlawful to speak. The Inexpressible One is not a personal god, such as monotheists believe in; all the personal gods reside at the level of the Platonic Ideas.

We live in a world of time and space, but the Platonic realm is immaterial and eternal; it is outside of time and space. (The geometric Circle is not merely perpetual; it is literally *timeless*.) Now it is a principle of Neoplatonic philosophy that whenever opposites are joined, there must be some mediating element to make them a unity, a mediator that shares something with each of the opposites. Therefore, joining the Cosmic Mind and the Cosmic Body is a mediating spirit, the Cosmic Soul or *Anima Mundi*. It brings the timeless, spaceless Ideas into manifestation in space and time. The Cosmic Soul is often understood as a goddess—usually Hekatê or Isis—who is impregnated by the Ideas in the

Cosmic Mind and gives birth to physical forms and embodied ideas in the material world (the Cosmic Body). She gives the Ideas substance and material existence. She turns being into becoming.

Because they reside in the Platonic realm, the gods are universal forces, and not so concerned with us as individuals (although their energies certainly affect our attitudes and actions). We are very much enmeshed in space and time, materially embodied, but the gods are not. Therefore, there are mediating spirits between them and us. They are eternal and immaterial like the gods, but nevertheless embedded in space and time like us. The ancient Greeks called them *daimons*. Because of their existence in space and time they are able to interact with us, to hear us and to communicate to us. Thus they are effective mediators between the gods and us; as the wise woman Diotima in Plato's *Symposium* says, a daimon is:

> A power that interprets and conveys to the gods the prayers and sacrifices of mortals, and to mortals the commands and rewards of the gods; and this power spans the chasm that divides them, and in this all is bound together, and through this the arts of the prophet and the priest, their sacrifices and mysteries and charms, and all prophecy and incantation, find their way.[32]

When we think we are communicating with a god, usually we are communicating with one of their daimons, which is okay, since that is their job in the Cosmic Bureaucracy. In particular, it is daimons who assist in our divinations. (It should be apparent that there is nothing demonic about daimons—that is a Christian slander!—they are the rightful assistants of the gods.) Our individual souls are also daimonic and are part of the Cosmic Soul.

In summary, these are the planes of reality, from top down: (1) The Inexpressible One; (2) the Cosmic Mind, where the gods reside, Heaven or Olympus; (3) the Cosmic Soul, which we can think of as the air where the daimons reside; and (4) the Cosmic Body, earth, where we mortals spend most of our time. Of course, these planes are metaphorical, for all these realms exist everywhere simultaneously.

Neoplatonists understand that there are chains, lines, or lineages (Grk., *seirai*), originating in The One, that bind the planes of reality together. They are like rays of emanation by which The One imparts identity on the Ideas, which through the mediation of the Cosmic Soul give form, being, and life to material things, including us. Therefore, everything in

---

32. *Symposium* (202e–203a) in Plato, *The Dialogues of Plato*, Vol. 1, translated by Jowett (New York: Scribners, 1909), 495.

the material world is in the lineage of some god; it is a manifestation of that god's energy, and therefore a symbol (Grk., *symbolon*; Lat., *signum*) by which that god can be invoked, if we learn the correspondences. Through theurgy, we can use these chains to ascend toward the gods. Therefore, Neoplatonists understand that there are vertical lines of sympathy in addition to the horizontal lines recognized by Stoics.

Neoplatonists distinguish inspired (or natural) divination from artificial methods of divination. Inspired divination uses symbolic correspondences and vertical sympathies to attune the seer's soul to the god's energy. The *mantis* communes with the god by means of supra-rational, intuitive part of the soul, which ancient Greeks called the *nous* (pronounced "noose"). The individual's nous is the image in the individual microcosm of the Cosmic Mind (*Nous*) in the macrocosm. Inspired divination is thus direct illumination from the gods (or their daimons), but it may be difficult to express or interpret in words, for these are rational processes that are lower than the nous. This is why at Delphi there were "prophets" to interpret the Pythia's oracles. In Greek, a *prophêtês* is one who speaks (*phêmi*) on behalf of (*pro*) another. Inspired divination is the most direct kind of divination and the most beneficial. Iamblichus tells us that only divine divination (*theia mantikê*) allows us to participate in the divine life, experiencing the gods' foreknowledge and noetic understanding of the Ideas.[33] In this way, we experience divine benevolence.

Artificial divination, in contrast, depends on some teachable and learnable art. It makes use of skilled observation, language, discursive reason, conjecture, and interpretation. These are faculties of the nonintuitive, rational mind, which thinks sequentially in time. It is more horizontally focused than vertically. It depends on fallible human thinking rather than on direct insight from the gods. In these respects, it is inferior to inspired divination.

Nevertheless, as Iamblichus explains, the objects observed or manipulated in artificial divination are in the lineages of gods and are symbols of them.[34] Moreover, artificial divination is often conducted in a ritual context, which invokes the gods, and uses consecrated tools for divination. Therefore, the gods are present, both to guide the fall of the lots and to guide our interpretation of them. Further, divining in a contemplative and mindful manner puts the diviner in a meditative state, opening them to inspiration from the gods. Therefore, while artificial divination relies more on art than does inspired divination, they are both directed to the same end: communion with gods and daimons.

---

33. Iamblichus, *On the Mysteries*, X.4 (¶289; pp. 346–7).

34. Iamblichus, *On the Mysteries*, III.16–17 (¶138–43), V.10 (¶209–10); pp. 160–1, 238–41.

In divinization by lots, the element of chance invites the gods to intervene in our world. The outcome is undetermined and can go in different ways; which way it goes is left in the laps of the gods. Therefore, it is a communication from the gods, in their symbolic language, and the subsequent interpretation completes the transmission of the message from the divine to the human world. Chance creates the bridge between the worlds, and divination is thus a dialogue between gods and mortals. In Cicero's book *On Divination*, his brother Quintus explains that when a meaningful discourse arises from lots drawn by chance, it is by the will of the gods, and "among all people the interpreters of such lots are nearest to divinity." [35]

The objective of divination is happiness or well-being, in Greek: *eudaimonia*, which is literally to have a flourishing inner *daimôn* (soul). Iamblichus claims that the only way to achieve this is through knowledge (*gnôsis*) of the gods, by which we can align our wills with theirs. Our souls are in tune with the greater cosmic harmony. In this way, we free ourselves from the bonds of blind fate and manifest the goodness of the gods. Through self-knowledge we become more godlike, which is the ultimate goal of theurgy.

> With *gnôsis* of the gods, there follows a turning toward ourselves and *gnôsis* of ourselves. [36]

Paradoxically, the gods' concern for our spiritual development explains the enigmatic character of their oracles. Certainly, it was common opinion in the ancient world that oracles were obscure and ambiguous. Heraclitus (ca. 540–ca. 480 BCE) said that the god in Delphi neither speaks plainly nor hides, but "signifies." Like Apollo and Nature herself, Pythagoras conveyed his wisdom in short enigmatic sayings, called "symbols" (*symbola*), which are like tiny seeds, which must be cultivated to bring forth fruit, or like embers of truth, which must be tended until they burn bright and illuminate the soul. [37] The Emperor Julian (who temporarily restored Paganism in the Roman Empire, 361–363 CE) said that the gods make the oracles obscure so that we learn to use our own wits, to inquire into philosophy, and not to trust blindly the opinions of others. The gods reveal the truth,

---

35. Cicero's *On Divination* (I.34); see Cicero, M. *Tulli Ciceronis De Divinatione Liber Primus* (1920), 151–3, and *On Divination*, 57. Scholars dispute the precise significance of the word here translated "divinity."

36. Iamblichus, *On the Mysteries*, X.1 (¶286.9–10).

37. Iamblichus, *On the Pythagorean Way of Life* (¶¶161–2; pp. 176–7). Several examples of these *symbola* are discussed in the Oracle of the Seven Sages.

says Iamblichus, when it will benefit us, but withhold it when the uncertainty will lead to our greater moral development. The Neoplatonist Porphyry (ca. 234–ca. 305 CE), who wrote *Philosophy from Oracles,* said that oracles are enigmas (*ainigmata*) to hide their meaning from the profane and uninitiated, for whom they would be worse than useless. They must be read properly—allegorically and symbolically—to reveal their true meaning. Plato said that oracles must be solved, like riddles. They encourage the particular dialectical process that is, according to Plato, the means by which we ascend to The One. Like koans, paradoxical oracles defeat our rational minds. To solve them we must work with them symbolically, contemplating their allegorical meaning, exercising their symbols, until we grasp them noetically (in one's *nous*). This is how you are initiated into the Mysteries, which cannot be expressed in words but must be transmitted in symbols. Therefore, we should not despair at the ambiguity and obscurity of the oracles. Rather, we should welcome them as challenges through which we win the benevolence of the gods. They are spells that transform our souls.

Divination is akin to magic. Or, to put it in Neoplatonic terms, divination is a part of theurgy, the arts by which we come into contact with the gods and consciously realize the destiny of the world and ourselves. Through divination the gods reveal potencies and potentialities (Grk., *dynamis*; Lat., *potentia*) in which we may participate. The process of actualizing these powers, this destiny, of manifesting their energies as actuality (Grk., *energeia*; Lat., *actus*), begins with interpretation of the oracle or omen. Prior to interpretation, the meaning of the oracle is open, though constrained by the signs.

This is why in ancient times prophets and lay people might compete to find the best interpretation of an oracle, and why emperors didn't like someone divining about their death or successor! The most famous example is the story of Oedipus and the Sphinx, in which the price of failure is, as is often the case, death. Other examples are the divination contest of Mopsus and Calchas, and the ancient *Contest of Homer and Hesiod*, in which Hesiod challenged Homer with a series of riddles (a legend, for they did not live at the same time). Finally, there is the competition among the Seven Sages to interpret the Delphic oracle concerning the Tripod of Helen, about which you will learn in chapter 8.

Once an oracle's meaning is expressed in words and accepted, the potentials begin to collapse into one possibility. Therefore, it is important to formally reject the worst interpretations and to consciously and explicitly accept the best, thus manifesting the benevolence of the gods. Thus the wise mantis does not so much predict the future as guide it.

Once the oracle's meaning has been accepted, the oracle (Grk., *chrêsmos*; Lat., *oraculum*) and its meaning become talismans—magical instruments to facilitate and reinforce its actualization. Thus divination blends seamlessly into magic. The oracle can be embodied in a concrete talisman (as explained in chapter 6) in order to strengthen the manifestation of the oracle's interpretation. Indeed, the ancients called omens and oracles "symbols" (*symbola*) because they are manifestations in our world of the power of the gods. As symbols, they can be used as vehicles of contemplation, theurgy, and magic to connect us with the gods.

Therefore, ancient philosophers collected oracles and used them in philosophy and theurgy. In fact, some scholars think one of the first uses of the alphabet was to record oracles.[38] Someone who collects oracles is called a *chrêsmologos*, and the corresponding (art of) divination from them is *chrêsmologikê (technê)*.[39] The most famous oracle collection is the *Chaldean Oracles* (second century CE), which resulted from the divination of Julian the Theurgist and his father, Julian the Chaldean. These oracles were central to the theurgy of Iamblichus, Proclus, and other Neoplatonists. Other collections of oracles circulated, or were kept under wraps to prevent their misuse. According to Suetonius, Emperor Augustus (63 BCE–14 CE) had two thousand books of oracles burned in one day! Books of *Orphic Oracles* circulated, said to have come from the legendary mystic and religious reformer, Orpheus. The *Bakic Oracles* (eighth–sixth centuries BCE) were attributed to several different prophets named Bakis, one of whom was supposed to have learned divination from the Corycian nymphs. The oracles of Musaeus were collected during the reign of Peisistratus at Athens (561–527 BCE). The Roman senate and emperors kept tight control of their *Sibylline Books* (*Libri Sibyllini*), Greek oracles collected from the ten Sibyls, inspired prophetesses from around the Mediterranean. None of these books survive complete. On the other hand, we do have the ancient text of the Alphabet Oracle and the Oracle of the Seven Sages, both of which you will learn in this book (and therefore become a *chrêsmologos*!).

---

38. Burkert, *Greek Religion*, translated by John Raffan (Cambridge, MA: Harvard University Press, 1985), II.8.5; 117.

39. Johnston and Struck, eds., *Mantikê: Studies in Ancient Divination* (Leiden, Germany: Brill, 2005), 18–19, 167–231.

Chapter 3

Rituals

Divination brings you into contact with the gods so that you can learn the truth from them and benefit from their advice. Rituals provide techniques for contacting the gods more effectively, and using appropriate rituals will improve the effectiveness of your divination. In this chapter, you will learn rituals for consecrating your divination tools and for doing a divination. If you have practiced other kinds of divination, then you may already know rituals for consecration and divination. If so, you certainly can use them with the oracles in this book; you do not have to use the rituals I will present. They are, however, drawn from the ancient Graeco-Egyptian tradition, and I think you will find them useful.

Consecration Ritual

In later chapters, you will discover that you can consult these oracles with many different kinds of divinatory instruments: dice, marked stones (like rune stones), coins, staves, etc. If you learn to use several of these techniques, you will be able to improvise divinations with available materials even if you do not have your instruments available. Nevertheless, you also will want to have one or more sets of lots that you have consecrated specifically for divination. Consecration purifies these objects of extraneous influences, dedicates them to a sacred purpose, and divinely empowers them to perform it well. Moreover, through repeated use, you will become psychically attuned to your instruments and they will work better for you.

If you already have a consecration ritual that you use for your magical and ritual tools, by all means use it to consecrate your divinatory lots. In case you don't, or in case you want to learn a new one, I will explain a consecration drawn from the Graeco-Egyptian magical tradition.[40]

Preparation:

You should have an altar facing east and a clean white linen altar cloth. If you have a statue or image of Apollo (or the patron god of divination in your tradition), you can do the consecration in its presence. Seasonal flowers on the altar will please the god. You should also have a censer and such incenses as frankincense, myrrh, and Egyptian *kyphi*. For a libation you can use honey (especially), wine, olive oil, milk, or rainwater. If you are working indoors, you will need a vessel in which to pour the libations. Have seven offerings of, for example, seasonal fruit, fresh bread, cakes, or cookies. You can use a laurel branch as a wand (ideally, with seven leaves).

Abstain from sex for seven days and take a ritual bath before the operation to purify yourself. Dress in a clean white linen robe unbound by a belt. Crown yourself with a laurel wreath, which is sacred to Pythian Apollo, Lord of Oracles.

The seventh day after the new moon (that is, the first quarter) is celebrated as Apollo's birthday and is especially auspicious for this consecration.

The Operation:

1. If you are not working in consecrated space, then cast a circle or create sacred space in your accustomed way.

2. Light the incense.

3. *Invocation:* Pour libations and make offerings, saying *Spondê!* (pron., *spon-DAY*) whenever you pour a libation. Invoke Apollo as follows:

> *Blest Paian, come in answer to my prayer,*
> *O god of Delphi, whom we all revere,*
> *O Delian king, whose light-producing eye*
> *views all within and all beneath the sky,*
> *whose locks are gold, whose oracles are sure,*
> *who, omens good reveals and precepts pure.*

---

40. The ritual is adapted from consecrations in the *Great Magical Papyrus* of Paris (PGM IV. 1596–1715, 2179–2205, 3210–3214) and other *Greek Magical Papyri* (PGM III. 291–310; V. 213–248; XII. 211–269, 285–334). See Betz, *The Greek Magical Papyri in Translation* for English translations.

Hear me entreating for the human kind,

hear, and be present with a gracious mind! [41]

4. If you are using the laurel branch, hold it in your right hand during the following invocation. The vowel chants should be intoned long and sonorously.

I invoke Thee, O Paian, O Phoibos of Parnassus,

Apollôn of Claros EÊU (eh ay ü),

Castalian One AÊA (ah ay ah),

Pythian ÔAE (oh ah eh),

Apollôn of the Muses IEÔÔEI (ih eh oh oh eh ih). [42]

5. *Purification:* Hold your lots to be consecrated in the incense smoke and pray:

I have called on thee, the greatest god,

and through thee on all other gods

to purify these lots of every taint.

Protect these lots today and for all time,

and give them strength supreme, divine.

Give power, truth, and fortune to these lots.

For this consecration I beseech you,

gods of the heavens,

gods under the earth,

gods residing in the middle,

masters of the living and the dead,

you who hear the needs of gods and mortals,

you who reveal what's been concealed!

Immortal gods! Attend my prayers and grant

that I may fill with spirit these, my lots. [43]

6. *Potentiation:* For additional strength, the remainder of the consecration up to the release can be repeated seven times with increasing force and power:

I conjure Earth and Heaven!

I conjure Light and Darkness!

I call the god who hath created all,

---

41. Adapted from the "Orphic Hymn to Apollo" (Thomas Taylor translation).

42. Adapted from the PGM II. 124–40; III. 258–9.

43. Adapted from PGM IV.1615–1620; XII.216–224, 301–304.

> *Complete this sacred consecration now!*
> *The Gates of Earth are opened!*
> *The Gates of Sea are opened!*
> *The Gates of Sky are opened!*
> *The Gates of Sun and Moon*
> *and all the Stars are opened!*
> *My spirit has been heard by all the gods,*
> *So give now spirit to this mystery*
> *that I have made, O gods whom I have named,*
> *O gracious gods on whom I've called.*
> *Give breath to this, the mystery I've made!*
> *Esto!*[44]

7. *Release:* It is important to bring the ritual to a definite end. Make final offerings and libations of thanks while reciting a dismissal such as this:

> *Depart, O Master, to thy realm,*
> *to thine own palace, to thy throne.*
> *Restore the order of the world.*
> *Be gracious and protect me, Lord.*
> *I thank thee for thy presence here.*
> *Depart in peace and joy. Farewell!*[45]

For a more comprehensive procedure, see the *Greater Tool Consecration*, which I have made available online (see the bibliography).

For a more potent consecration of the Alphabet Oracle, you can invoke the daimons or spirits of each letter.[46] Between steps five and six, chant these names sonorously and visualize the glowing letters descending into your lots from progressively higher spheres. The names are given in Greek letters with the individual oracles in chapter 7. Here I write them phonetically so you can use them in the ritual. Each is preceded by the Greek letter for visualization:

---

44. Adapted from PGM XII.325–334. "Esto!" means "So be it!"

45. Based on releases such as PGM I.94–95; II.180–183; IV.1061–1065, 3120–3124; V.41–50.

46. From PGM CI. 23–29. These are called *voces magicae* (Lat., "magic words") or *onomata barbara* (Grk., "barbarian names").

A	*Ah-blah-nah-thah-nahl-bah!*
B	*Boo-law-men-taw-reb!*
Γ	*Geh-nih-awe-moo-thig!*
Δ	*Day-maw-geh-nayd!*
E	*En-kü-klih-eh!*
Z	*Zay-naw-bih-oh-thiz!*
H	*Ay-skoh-thoh-ray!*
Θ	*Thoh-thoo-thoth!*
I	*Ih-ah-eh-awe-ü-oh-ih!*
K	*Kor-kaw-oo-naw-oak!*
Λ	*Loo-law-eh-nay-el!*
M	*Maw-raw-thaw-ape-nam!*
N	*Nehr-xih-are-xin!*
Ξ	*Xaw-naw-faw-ay-nax!*
O	*Or-neh-awe-fah-oh!*
Π	*Pü-raw-bah-rüp!*
P	*Reh-roo-taw-ayr!*
Σ	*Seh-sen-meh-noo-ress!*
T	*Tau-raw-paw-lit!*
Y	*Ü-peh-feh-noo-rü!*
Φ	*Fih-meh-mah-mef!*
X	*Khen-neh-awe-feh-awkh!*
Ψ	*Psü-khom-poi-aps!*
Ω	*Oh-rih-own!*

Divination Rituals

I'm giving you two rituals for divination, a more formal one for important divinations, and a simpler one for impromptu readings. I'll also address the issue of miscasts (e.g., dice rolling off the table) and what to do about them, the all-important act of accepting an oracle response, and when you can repeat a question.

Formal Divination

In general, divination will be more effective if you go to some effort to attune your soul to the energy of the god with whom you wish to communicate. Therefore, for an important divination, I suggest that you prepare yourself ritually, for example, taking a ritual bath, donning robes, and burning incense. Here is a suggestion for a formal divination ritual: [47]

1. Light the incense.

2. While sitting or standing comfortably, ground and center yourself.

3. For an especially important divination, anoint your lips with honey or drink a honeyed drink (e.g., mead, honeyed wine, or milk and honey). Make an offering as well.

4. Pray with a sonorous voice:

O Lord Apollôn, come with Paian now.

Give answers to my questions, all-wise one.

Leave Mount Parnassus and from Delphi fly

whenever I have said thy secret name:

AKRAKANARBA

KRAKANARBA

RAKANARBA

AKANARBA

KANARBA

ANARBA

NARBA

ARBA

RBA

BA

A

O Pythian Apollôn, answer me! [48]

As you chant the "wing" above, visualize Apollo appearing in all his glory and standing in front of and above you. Picture a young man with piercing eyes and longish blond hair

---

47. This divination spell is adapted from one in the text of a dice oracle.

48. Adapted from PGM I. 296–9; II. 1, 65.

crowned with a laurel wreath. He is nude or draped in a yellow *himation* (toga) and holds a seven-string lyre in his left hand and a golden arrow in his right.

1. Silently, in your mind, ask the question.

2. Mix up or shuffle the lots as you hold the question in your mind.

3. If you are casting, then you can blow into the hand holding the lots to inspire them before you cast. If you are drawing, then rub your hands together, generating heat, before you draw.

4. When the time seems right (the *kairos*[49]) or the god moves you, cast or draw your lots. (Specific instructions are given in chapters 5 and 9.)

5. Interpret the oracle, praying to Apollo that he guides you to the truth:

> *Explain thy prophecy in lucid words,*
> *reveal all things: both when they will occur*
> *and how they will be done. Reveal the truth!*[50]

6. When you are done, thank the god for his assistance. You can use the release I gave for the consecration ritual.

Informal Divination

Sometimes you don't have the time or equipment at hand for a formal divination, and a more informal procedure is appropriate. In these cases, first center yourself, and then think or speak a spell such as this (which you can memorize):

> *Come hither to thy prophet, haste to sing*
> *divine precepts to me, and to proclaim*
> *pure words, and through these lots to bring*
> *me oracles. Thus I invoke thy name:*
> *Akti Kara Abaiôth (Ahk-tih Kah-rah Ah-buy-oath).*[51]

---

49. See under B (Beta) in the Alphabet Oracle (chapter 7) for a discussion of *kairos*.

50. Adapted from PGM VI. 16–19.

51. Adapted from PGM VI. 41–5; II. 79.

Instead of the *Akti* formula, you can recite the *AKRAKANARBA* wing. Or improvise your own prayer. Before casting your lots, visualize Apollo standing above and before you as you contemplate the question. Pray as follows when you cast:

> *O Pythian Apollôn, answer me!*

To invoke Hermes for your divination, you can use the prayer to him in chapter 2 (page 29). If you would prefer to invoke a goddess for your divinations, a good choice is Daphne, who is Apollo's assistant and messenger, or Athena, goddess of wisdom.

Dealing with Miscasts

Occasionally something will go wrong in a divination: a die will roll off the table, you'll miscount the beads, you'll fumble the alphabet stones, etc. You should not ignore such unforeseen happenings in a divination ritual. Often, it means that the god is reluctant to answer the query, either because it is better if you do not know the answer or because there is something more important for you to inquire about. Nevertheless, it is reasonable to try again in case the accident had no such meaning. Three times, however, is the max, for three failures is an unambiguous sign that the god does not want to answer that query (or perhaps any query that day). It is generally wise to wait at least twenty-four hours before trying the divination again. As I mentioned in chapter 2, Apollo told Hermes that if mortals persisted in consulting the Delphic Oracle in spite of an inauspicious preliminary divination, then the oracle would be unreliable. Likewise, if you force a divination when the signs are against it, you are unlikely to get a good result.

Sometimes a failed divination portends an unfavorable outcome. Cicero tells of a time when the Spartans came to the Oracle of Zeus at Dodona, which was in the territory of the Molossians.[52] When a monkey, who was a pet of the Molossian king, knocked the lots over and scattered them everywhere, the attending priestess told the Spartans that they should give up hope of victory and attend to their safety instead.

Accepting the Oracle

After you have had time to carefully consider the oracle—to solve the enigma—and have decided on a meaning (which might take days!), you may formally accept it by addressing

---

52. Cicero, *On Divination*, I.76; 70.

the god and saying "I accept the oracle" (Grk., *Lambanô ton khrêsmon*; Lat., *Oraculum accipio*). Think of it as confirming an agreement or understanding. Deliberate wisely! Don't decide in haste!

Divination Journal

To improve your divination skill, I suggest that you keep a divination journal. Whenever you cast the lots, record the oracle question, the oracle response you received, alternative interpretations you might have considered, the final interpretation you accept, and how you intend to act on it. Record related factors, such as miscasts. If you make a supporting talisman (described in later chapters), record what you made and how it was consecrated. Record the actions you actually take relevant to the oracle. Later, as events relevant to the divination unfold, record them as well. You might discover, for example, that one of your alternative interpretations was better or that a completely new interpretation was most appropriate. By reviewing your journal from time to time, you will improve your skill.

Repeating Divinations

It goes without saying, I suppose, that you should not repeat a divination in hopes of getting a more pleasing answer. At the very least, this is disrespectful to the gods and exhibits an unwillingness to accept their advice. On the other hand, it is quite reasonable to ask a follow-up question or to seek clarification. It is also reasonable to ask the same question again after a change in circumstances, which makes it, in effect, a different question. If an oracular response pertains to time (e.g., B (Beta) in the Alphabet Oracle: "Briefly wait; the time's not right for you"), then it is reasonable to ask again, after an appropriate amount of time. The ancients sometimes recommended asking a timing question at most three times before abandoning the intended action.

A good guide is to think of yourself having a brief and valuable audience with a wise sage (or, indeed, with a god!). It would be impolite and foolish to keep asking the same question, but it would be wise to seek clarification or additional information, provided you listen carefully and strive to understand what you hear. (See also appendix B on probability and repeated divinations.)

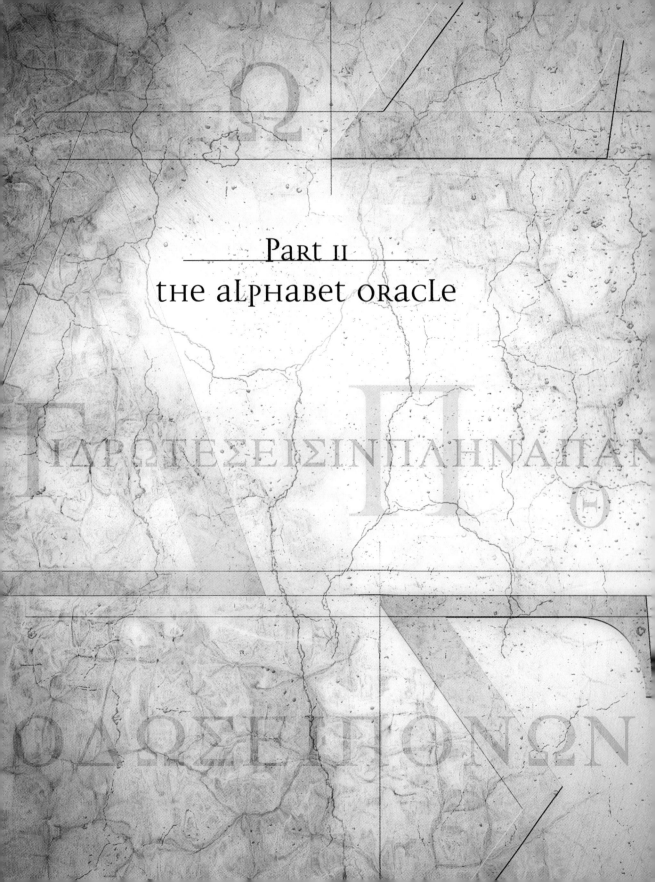

Part II
the alphabet oracle

Chapter 4

Introduction to the Alphabet Oracle

This chapter will introduce you to the Alphabet Oracle. First, you will learn the interesting story of the expedition that discovered it. Next, I will give you a little practical advice on learning the Greek alphabet, in case you don't know it. (Don't worry, it's easy!) Finally, I will say a little about who used the oracle in ancient times and how you can use it now.

Origin of the Alphabet Oracle

Catharine Lorillard Wolfe (1828–1887), heir to the Lorillard Tobacco fortune, art collector, and generous philanthropist, who made significant donations to the Metropolitan Museum of Art, also supported archaeological expeditions. In the summers of 1884 and 1885, she financed the *Wolfe Expedition to Asia Minor*, led by Dr. J. R. Sitlington Sterrett (1851–1914), a young archaeologist, to locate and record ancient inscriptions.[53] The 1885 expedition, which began in May, traveled into the unmapped interior of Turkey on horseback with servants, a cook, tents, and equipment. Mapping along the way, each night they camped near a village (often nothing more than a handful of homes), where they obtained supplies and inquired about inscriptions and other ancient remains in the area.

Many of the archaeological remains were badly damaged; Muslim zealots had destroyed earlier Christian and Pagan buildings and monuments. Many of the stones had been reused to build mosques, fountains, and even private homes; some were used as tombstones. Since the local inhabitants could not read the Greek or Latin inscriptions, they supposed that they showed the way to hidden treasure, and so they were reluctant to

---

53. Information of the Wolfe Expedition is from Sterrett, *The Wolfe Expedition to Asia Minor* and *Leaflets from the Notebook of an Archaeological Traveler in Asia Minor*.

reveal inscriptions on the stones used in their homes. Other locals thought that the treasure was hidden inside the stones themselves, so they broke them up.

If Sterrett couldn't read an inscription due to its position in a wall, he would offer to pay the owner to demolish it. Some stones were partly buried, and Sterrett paid the villagers to dig them up and move them. He reports that sometimes he had to hang upside down in a hole, in the blazing sun, to read an inverted, buried inscription. One time, he had wood brought from several miles away to construct a fifty-foot ladder so that he could totter for two hours on the top rung, a pencil in one hand, a notebook in the other, to copy an inscription off a wall. In another place, he had to jump down into waiting arms from a forty-foot cliff, which he had climbed to copy an inscription. He worked to exhaustion almost every day.

The expedition traveled through wooded country, dry river beds, and mountainous terrain, "for the most part over wild and difficult country," and on September 2 they arrived in the Sigirlik valley. Following "rough and tortuous" paths, they arrived at an immense, ruined monastery on the side of the mountain. They camped by it and the next morning spent two hours climbing to the summit. There they found the Alphabet Oracle, engraved in the stone wall. They expected to find it there, for August Schönborn (1801–1857) had discovered it in May 1842, but Sterrett was the first to make an accurate copy and publish it (1888).

In 1986—nearly a century later—the archaeologist Johannes Nollé traveled to Turkey to inspect the oracle and make a new copy. Sadly, he discovered that shortly before, a treasure hunter had drilled holes in it with a jackhammer, inserted dynamite sticks, and blown it apart, supposing there was treasure behind. As a result, much of the inscription was destroyed, and the only record we have of some parts is the copy Sterrett made a century earlier.[54]

We are fortunate that over the years archaeologists have found a dozen tablets, more or less complete, inscribed with Alphabet Oracles. They have been found at locations in Turkey that correspond to the ancient lands of Phrygia, Pisidia, Lycia, and Pamphylia, and also on Cyprus, and date to the second to third centuries CE. Perhaps surprisingly, the text is very similar among them, and so these tablets represent a coherent tradition of ancient divination. Nollé has gathered the most frequent readings into a *koinê* (Grk., "common")

---

54. Nollé, *Kleinasiatische Losorakel*, 232. Plates 22a and 22b show the vandalized oracle; Plate 21 shows the rough terrain.

text, which is the one I have used. In a few cases I have added readings from the Olympos tablet, and if you want to know why, read the next section.[55]

What About the "Limyran Oracle"?

You might have seen the "Limyran Alphabet Oracle" on the Internet and be wondering how it is related to the Alphabet Oracle presented here. However, if you have not heard of it, I suggest that you go on to the next section, since what I am about to write about it will be irrelevant to you. When I began using the Alphabet Oracle for divination, I used one of the few complete texts available, which was that recorded by the Wolfe Expedition and published in Sterrett's *The Wolfe Expedition to Asia Minor* and in Heinevetter's *Würfel- und Buchstabenorakel in Griechenland und Kleinasien*. The inscribed oracle tablet was reported to be from the ancient city of Limyra. Therefore, when I did my translation and made it available on the Internet in 1995, I called it "The Limyran Alphabet Oracle." In this form it has been used successfully by many people and has been widely copied to other sites (with and without permission). I also published it in several magazines (see bibliography). I have been very pleased that so many people have found it to be a worthwhile divination tool.

In 2004, I learned from Dr. Nollé that there was an error in the original publication and that the pillar was in fact from the ancient city of Olympos in Asia Minor. Therefore, I corrected my website and retitled it "The Greek Alphabet Oracle from Olympos," and you might know it by that name. As it turns out, the Olympos oracle differs in several ways from most of the other surviving alphabet oracles. Therefore, in this book I have used this more common text, which has been reconstructed by Nollé from the surviving fragments.[56] I have not abandoned the Olympos oracle, however, and I provide its text here when it differs from the common text, sometimes with an improved translation compared to my original one. So now you know what has become of the "Limyran Oracle"!

Learning the Greek Alphabet

In order to use the Greek Alphabet Oracle, it helps if you know the Greek alphabet! If you don't know it, however, don't worry, because it's very easy to learn well enough to use the Oracle. It's certainly easier than learning the runes or ogham. First of all, you will be happy to discover that you already know almost half of it, because the following uppercase Greek

---

55. The texts are collected, edited, compared, classified, and translated into German in Nollé, *Kleinasiatische Losorakel*, ch. 4; the Koinê text is on pp. 249–250.

56. Nollé, *Kleinasiatische Losorakel*, 249–250.

letters have approximately the same sounds as the corresponding Roman letters: ABEIK–MNOTZ. They have different names from the Roman letters (*alpha*, *beta*, etc.), but that's not so important (you'll see their names in the tables). Several other letters look like Roman letters, but have different sound values in Ancient Greek. Thus H is called *êta* and stands for the sound AY (which I write ê in transcribed Greek words). P is called *rho* and has an R sound (think of P as a one-legged R). X is called *chi* or *khi* and has an aspirated (breathy) k sound something like *ch* in Scottish "loch" or German "acht." Y is called *upsilon* and is a "close front rounded vowel" (written /y/ in the International Phonetic Alphabet); it is pronounced like ü in German or like French *u* in *tu* or *û* in *sûr*.

The remaining letters look different from Roman letters, but you may be familiar with some of them from the Greek letters of sororities or fraternities, from science or math classes, or other common uses. They are:

- Δ (*delta*) has a D sound and resembles a D; you might know it as a symbol of change in mathematics or from the emblem for Delta Airlines. Or you can think of the Nile or Mississippi River deltas.
- Π (*pi*) is a P sound, and you probably remember the lowercase π from math classes.
- Θ (*theta*) is a soft TH sound; you might remember it from math, since lowercase θ is often used as a symbol for an angle.
- Σ (*sigma*) is an S sound; it stands for "sum" in mathematics and statistics. Ancient Greeks sometimes wrote it C, which might help you to remember its sound if you think of a soft C.
- Λ (*lambda*) is an L sound, and it looks a little like a rotated L.
- Γ (*gamma*) is a G sound.
- Ξ (*xi*) is a KS or X sound, which it resembles, but don't confuse it with *khi*.
- Φ (*phi*) has a PH or F sound.
- Ψ (*psi*) sounds PS and is sometimes used as an emblem in connection with psychology, psi phenomena, etc.
- Ω (*ômega*) is a long-O sound; it looks kind of like an O with a line below it. It is the last letter of the classical Greek alphabet, and we sometimes use A and Ω—Alpha and Omega—to mean the beginning and end of anything, and thus its totality.

This then is the classical Greek alphabet in the alpha-beta order in which children would have learned it:

ΑΒΓΔΕΖΗΘΙΚΛΜΝΞΟΠΡΣΤΥΦΧΨΩ

You do not need to remember this order if you use the charts in this book. Also, you do not need to know the lowercase Greek letters for the purpose of consulting the Oracle, but here they are:

αβγδεζηθικλμνξοπρστυφχψω

We Are All Wayfarers

The engraved tablets containing the alphabet oracles were commonly displayed in the market squares or other public places. They seem to have been intended for answering practical questions from people engaged in some enterprise, and typical querents may have been merchants or pilgrims passing through the town. Their activities were fraught with uncertainty. Of course, they were concerned with the success of their plans, but there were other questions. Would they have an accident or get sick? Would they be robbed or murdered? Would they lose their way? Which was the best way to go?

Sometimes the Oracle makes a straightforward prediction, for example, (A) "All these things, he says, you'll do quite well." In these cases, we should understand the oracle to mean that this will be the outcome if current conditions continue. Make a change, and the outcome could be different (for better or worse). In other cases, the prediction is more conditional, for example, (I) "In everything, thou shalt excel—with sweat!" In other words, success is conditional on hard work. Yet other oracles state a fact, and you are left to determine what to do about it. For example, (H) "Helios, all-watcher, watches thee." Is he watching over you? Or is he witnessing your crime? Or something else? You are left to decide. In such a case, if after careful consideration it is unclear why the god told you this, it might be advisable to present a follow-up query to the Oracle (but remember the warnings in chapter 3 about repeating divinations!).

The Alphabet Oracle in the city of Adada in ancient Pisidia (modern Karabaulo, Turkey) had a sort of prologue, from which I've adapted the following:

> *Apollo, Lord, and Hermes, lead the way!*
> *And thou, who wanders, this to thee we say:*
> *Be still; enjoy this oracle's excellence,*

for Phoebos Apollo has given it to us,
this art of divination from our ancestors.[57]

Although we might not be wandering pilgrims or merchants on business trips, we are all wayfarers on the pilgrimage of life. We have plans, projects, goals, tasks to accomplish, people we want to spend time with, sights to see, and places to go. We also face joys and sorrows, challenges and accomplishments, health and sickness. Even if you never leave your birthplace, you have a long way to go. Therefore, we all can benefit from the advice above as we journey through life: Be still. Consider what you need to know to fulfill your destiny, and ask the gods for guidance. Cast the lots and enjoy the Oracle's excellence!

---

57. Heinevetter, *Würfel- und Buchstabenorakel in Griechenland und Kleinasien*, 33–34.

Chapter 5

Consulting the Alphabet Oracle

There are several ways you can cast the Alphabet Oracle depending on circumstances and your personal preferences. I suggest that you read them all, try a few, and decide which you like best. Really, you only need to learn one!

Alphabet Stones

Since this is an alphabet oracle, the most basic method asks the gods to guide your hand in selecting a letter. One way is to mark twenty-four stones with the letters of the Greek alphabet, like those shown in figure 1.

Figure 1: Greek alphabet stones. Left: Engraved crystal stones.
Right: Engraved pot shards (ostracta). Both are modern.

These stones are like the rune stones used in rune casting. Table 1 shows the Greek letters in their archaic forms, which look rather like runes and are easier to carve or inscribe than the printed forms. Some of the letters look similar to each other (for example, M, Σ), so mark them in some way so that you can tell them apart (e.g., by putting a line under the letter: M̲, Σ̲).

ΛΑ⋗∀	ΒΒ𐌁𐌁	Γ𐌂Λ	△ΔΔ◁	ΕΕƎ	ΖΙΙ
ΗΗΘ	⊙θ⊗	Ι𐌆Ζ	ΚΚ𐌊𐌊	ΛΛ𐌋	ΜΜᴍᴍ
ΝΝᴎ	ΞΞvΧ	Οο☉	ΠΠ𐌐𐌐	Ρϙϙ	ΣΣ𐌔𐌔
Τͳ	ΥΥ𐌖	ϕϕΦΦ	Χ𐌗	Ψͳͳ𐌙Υ	ᘯΩ

Table 1: Archaic forms of Greek letters.

You can paint the letters on small round stones or carve them into pieces of wood. If you are used to working with polymer clays (for instance, Sculpey®), then you can impress the letters into small disks of clay. Often the ancient Greeks and Romans would use pot shards, that is, pieces of broken pottery; you can paint the letters on or scratch them with a large nail.

Although they are not as common as rune stones, you can buy a set of Greek alphabet stones, but it is much better to make your own. A set of stones is a magical tool, and it is most effective if it is psychically attuned to you, and making it yourself is one way to attune it. In other words, turn the making of the stones into a ritual. Keep in your mind your goals and intentions for the stones. Read the meaning of each letter (given in chapter 7) and keep it in mind as you paint or carve that letter. Chant the name of each letter's spirit over it. When your stones are complete, consecrate them as a ritual instrument (see chapter 3 for a sample consecration ritual). Keep your stones in a special jug, box, or bag.

When you want to consult the oracle, invoke the gods (using, for example, a divination ritual from chapter 3), and draw a stone without looking. You can either pick one quickly or rummage among them until one seems to "ask" to be chosen (it may feel warm or just gravitate to your hand). An ancient method of selecting a stone, which also works well, is to shake the stones in a bowl or frame drum until one jumps out. These are just examples, and you may find other ways to let the gods pick a stone for you.

Alphabet Leaves

Another way of consulting the oracle, which was also used in ancient times, is to inscribe the letter and oracle text of each oracle on a card (such as an index card), a flat piece of wood (such as a popsicle stick), or a metal leaf (Lat., *lamella*). These are analogous to *rune staves.* You can draw one in the same ways as drawing a stone and read the oracle text directly. Another technique is to scatter the leaves facedown, mix them around, and then draw one. This technique also works with stones if they are relatively flat. Your set of leaves should be made ritually and consecrated, like alphabet stones.

Such a practice might be the origin of a tradition about the Cumaean Sibyl, "whom the Delian seer/ Inspires with soul and wisdom to unfold/ The things to come." She is supposed to have written her oracles on leaves, which were scattered about by the wind that reveals the divine presence, the physical manifestation of the god's spirit.[58] Perhaps this is how she cast her lots. In any case, Aeneas begs her:

> *Only to leaves commit not, priestess kind,*
> *Thy verse, lest fragments of the mystic scroll*
> *Fly, tossed abroad, the playthings of the wind.*
> *Thyself in song the oracle unroll.*
> —Virgil, *Aeneid* VI.74–6, after Taylor translation

Astragaloi

Two of the most common methods for consulting oracles in ancient times were to use astragaloi and dice, and many of the temples had them available beside a table or dice tray on which they could be cast. The table stood before an image of a god or goddess (often Apollo or Hermes), and so the divination was protected and guided by the deity, to whom the querent would pray for advice. Dice and astragaloi are still convenient today. It's easier to carry a few of them than a whole bag of alphabet stones; in fact, one die or astragalos is enough! In a pinch you can borrow one or more dice for a divination, although they will not be consecrated for your use. I'll talk first about astragaloi, since they are probably the more ancient procedure, and explain the use of dice and other methods as well.

What are astragaloi? True astragaloi (Lat., *tali*) are the pastern bones from the hind legs of goats, cows, and sheep, known in English as *hucklebones* or (less accurately) *knucklebones*. Our ancestors got them for free when they slaughtered livestock for food, and they probably accepted them as a gift from the animal spirit or from the god to whom the animal

---

58. Kerényi, *Apollo*, ch. 2.

was sacred. Astragaloi were not only used for divination but were also used for games, like modern children use dice and jacks, and for gambling.[59]

The ancient historian Herodotus (fifth century BCE) tells a tale about how astragaloi and dice games were invented. There was a famine in the ancient land of Lydia and so the people decided to eat only on every other day. They invented all the games known to the Greeks, including dice and astragaloi, to distract them from their hunger on their fasting days. However, the famine continued for eighteen years, and so they decided that half the people would leave their country and start a colony across the sea. The ones to leave were chosen by lot, perhaps by casting dice or astragaloi. They founded a colony in northern Italy and named it Tyrrhenia after their leader Tyrrhenus. The Tyrrhenians are better known as Etruscans, and were considered masters of divination, who taught the divinatory arts to the Romans. Lydia was located in what is now western Turkey, and so it is interesting that many of the surviving alphabet and dice oracles come from western Turkey. (By the way, Herodotus's story about the origins of the Etruscans is probably inaccurate.)

Historically, in Egypt astragaloi were used in board games as early as the First Dynasty (ca. 3500 BCE), but they do not seem to have been used for divination before the arrival of Ptolemy I (ca. 323 BCE). Astragalos games appeared in Turkey by 1300 BCE and are mentioned in the *Iliad* (eighth century BCE). Astragalos divination is practiced in the Far East, and could have originated in Tibet or India, but the first evidence for it appears after the arrival of Alexander and his army (ca. 324 BCE), so its origin is more likely in the West.

Back to the Alphabet Oracle. The ancient procedure for consulting the oracle was to roll five astragaloi (or, in a pinch, one astragalos five times). Unlike we do with dice, the ancients noted the numerical values of the *downward* faces. (The ancients might have read the downward faces of dice too.[60]) Of course, astragaloi don't come marked with numbers, so you have to learn to tell the faces apart by their shape. If you look at a real astragalos and compare it to figure 2, you won't have much trouble. Or, you can do like the ancients sometimes did, and mark the faces with pips or with Greek or Roman numerals.

Notice that, unlike a die, an astragalos can land on only four different faces. The first face shown in the figure has the value three; its Greek name, *Huptios*, and Latin name *Supinum*, both mean supine. It is one of the broad faces and has a fairly deep pit or depression in the middle. The next face (Grk., *Pranês*; Lat., *Pronum*, prone) has the value four; it is the

---

59. Historical information about astragaloi and dice and their use in divination can be found in David, *Games, Gods, and Gambling* (New York: Hafner, 1962), chs. 1–2.

60. Peck, *Harper's Dictionary of Classical Literature and Antiquities* (New York: Harper & Bros., 1898), s.v. Talus.

rounder, somewhat cylinder-shaped broad face. The next (Grk., *Khios*, Chian; Lat., *Planum*, flat), which has the value one, is the narrow face with a sort of S-shaped depression. While the last (Grk., *Kôios*, Coan; Lat., *Tortuosum*, twisting), with value six, is the narrow face that has a somewhat flat, irregular surface.

Figure 2. Astragalos faces. Huptios/Supinum (3), Pranês/Pronum (4),
Khios/Planum (1), Kôios/Tortuosum (6).

To consult the oracle, you add the numbers for the downward faces of the five astragaloi (or five casts of one astragalos). There are twenty-four possible totals: five to thirty, excepting six and twenty-nine, which are mathematically impossible (that is you can't get them with combinations of five of 1, 3, 4, and 6). We do not have any direct evidence of how astragalos throws might correspond to the letters. Some scholars argue that the highest cast would be associated with Alpha and the lowest with Omega (so Alpha = thirty, Beta = twenty-eight, Gamma = twenty-seven, ..., Psi = seven, Omega = five). However, all the other astragalos oracles from the ancient world arrange the throws in increasing order, and so we would expect Alpha = five, Beta = seven, ..., Psi = twenty-eight, Omega = thirty. For example, if you rolled 3-1-4-1-1, the sum would be 10, which corresponds to Epsilon (**E**) if you use increasing sums, and Upsilon (**Y**) if you use decreasing. See table 6, the *Key for Consulting the Alphabet Oracle* (page 92) if you want to use either method.

You can "roll the bones" with your bare hands or with a dice cup or dice tower. A dice cup (Grk., *phimos*; Lat., *fritillus*) is a cylindrical container about four inches tall and a couple inches in diameter; sometimes it has ribs inside to help tumble the astragaloi. You shake the cup with your hand over its mouth and dump the astragaloi out. Alternatively, you can put the astragaloi into the top of a dice tower (Grk., *purgos*; Lat., *turricula*), in which baffles cause the lots to tumble before they spill out of the bottom. They are not new inventions; examples date from the fourth century CE (the Vettweiss-Froitzheim dice tower). You don't need either of these devices; you can shake the astragaloi in your bare hand (or cupped hands) and throw them so they tumble. Some practitioners recommend blowing into your hand after you pick up the lots to "inspire" the divination.

Of course I have left an important question unanswered: "Where can I get astragaloi?" One answer is to make friends with ranchers who slaughter their own sheep, cows, or goats, and ask for the pastern bones from hind legs. Then you have to clean them up and prepare them. This solution is impractical for most people, so it is fortunate there are other options. One possibility is to use artificial astragaloi made from clay or carved from wood. If you look at some good pictures of astragaloi, you can make acceptable copies. You also can find artificial astragaloi for sale, so look on the Internet. You may be interested to know that artificial astragaloi are traditional and the ancients often used astragaloi made from carved stone, metal, clay, and other materials (see figure 3). The ancients sometimes marked the faces of their astragaloi with numbers, pips, or other signs, and you can too, especially if you have trouble telling the faces apart.

Figure 3. Astragaloi. Clockwise from upper left: two modern natural astragaloi; five modern artificial astragaloi; three ancient astragaloi (bone, stone, lead).

Long Dice

You can also make a kind of dice with four faces (sometimes called "long dice" or "stick dice"), which were also common in ancient Greece and Rome (figure 4). You want to cut a piece of wood that is a few inches long and has a square or rectangular cross-section at most an inch on a side. The idea is that when you cast it, it can land on one of the four long faces, but not on the ends.

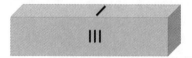

Figure 4. Long die.

You can mark the numbers one, three, four, and six on the long faces. If your pieces have a rectangular cross-section, then mark three and four on the wider faces, and one and six on the narrower, just like the numbering of astragaloi. If it has a square cross section, you should still have three opposite four and one opposite six (opposites add to seven—Apollo's number—on astragaloi as well as on dice). You can mark long dice with Arabic numbers 1, 3, 4, 6, but traditionally they would be marked with Greek numerals A (1), Γ (3), Δ (4), F (6). As will be explained in chapter 6, Greek numerals used the obsolete letter F (*digamma*), which is not in the classical Greek alphabet. On some long dice B is substituted for F, and so we have the four letters ΑΒΓΔ, which are also the Greek numerals for 1, 2, 3, 4. Some long dice are marked with archaic Roman numerals: I, II, III, IIII, or with pips (dots). Long dice marked with dots and rings are known from the Indus Valley civilization 4,500 years ago. The oldest Indian examples are marked 1-2-3-4, but later ones are marked 1-3-4-6 (like astragaloi) or 1-2-5-6. Long dice are sometimes used for consulting the *I Ching*.

You can cast long dice like ordinary dice and astragaloi or by rolling them out of your hand. When divination with astragaloi spread to the East, a new style was developed: a hole was drilled down through four dice (through the faces that would have been marked two and five) and they were strung on a stiff wire. The dice would be spun on the wire, and when it was put down, the uppermost faces would be noted. You can do this too.

Dice

Figure 5. Ancient and modern dice. Clockwise from upper left:
modern gaming dice (4-, 6-, 8-, 10-, 12-, 20-sided);
8-sided brass teetotum; three modern dice;
three ancient dice (stone, bone, lead); ancient 14-sided die.

Another way to consult the oracle is to roll five ordinary dice and to add up the upper-most numbers. Alternately, you can roll one die five times and add up its numbers. Either way, there are twenty-six possible values (five through thirty inclusive). Again, some scholars believe that the numbers corresponded to the letters in decreasing order (so Alpha = thirty, Beta = twenty-nine, Gamma = twenty-eight, …, Psi = six, Omega = five), but most ancient dice oracles are arranged in increasing order (Alpha = five, Beta = six, …, Psi = twenty-nine, Omega = thirty); take your choice. To consult the oracle, you add up the numbers and look in table 6 (page 92) to get the corresponding letter oracle. For example, if you throw 2-1-1-4-1, which add to 9, your oracle is Upsilon (Y) if you use the decreasing method, and Epsilon (E) for the increasing method. The correspondences are given in the *Key for Consulting the Alphabet Oracle* (table 6).

There are only twenty-four letters in the Classical Greek alphabet, and so two of the sums do not have corresponding letter oracles. Some scholars think these sums corresponded to obsolete Greek letters that were eliminated in the classical alphabet (as explained in chapter 6).[61] Given the position of these letters (*digamma* and *qoppa*) in the

---

61. Heinevetter, *Würfel- und Buchstabenorakel*, 35–39.

pre-classical alphabet, they would correspond to the sums thirteen and twenty-five in the decreasing order, and to ten and twenty-two in the increasing order. Perhaps some ancient ancestor of the Alphabet Oracle provided oracles for these sums and their corresponding letters, but the surviving tablets do not. So what should you do if you cast one of these sums? One solution is to recast. However, such a cast may be considered a situation in which the oracle is reluctant to give an answer (see chapter 3 for more information on dealing with miscasts).

Interestingly, both thirteen and twenty-five are uncanny numbers, associated with transgression of cycles or transcendence over them (e.g., twelve months, twenty-four hours). These numbers are often associated with sacrificed and resurrected gods (e.g., Dionysos was the Thirteenth Olympian, and it's reasonable to associate these casts with him). The wholly negative interpretation of thirteen is no older than the Middle Ages, and twenty-five always has been accompanied by connotations of perfection (since it is the square of five).[62]

Dice seem to have evolved from astragaloi, for we have ancient astragaloi that have been sanded to make their faces flatter. (On the other hand, astragaloi are a lot like dice without their two and five faces.) Early dice have their pips in various arrangements, but by about 1370 BCE the common modern arrangement appears in Egypt; that is, opposite numbers add to seven and if you look at three consecutive numbers (1-2-3 or 4-5-6) they increase in a counter-clockwise direction. (This "right-handed" arrangement is standard in the West, but "left-handed" dice are common in the East.) Most ancient dice were marked with pips, like modern dice, but some were marked with Greek numerals (ΑΒΓΔΕF). The word "die" comes ultimately from Latin *datum*, "what is given," which is a good way to understand an oracle. You cast dice with a dice cup, dice tower, or your bare hands (see under the section "Astragaloi").

Teetotums

Closely related to astragaloi and dice are *teetotums*. They survive from the ancient world, and they were used for games such as "Put and Take," but I don't know of evidence that they were used for divination. The teetotum is a kind of top, which can land on one of a few sides; the most familiar modern descendant is the dreidel. It is essentially a long die that can be spun on its axis. The classical teetotum (like the dreidel) had four sides, typically marked "T" for *totum* (meaning "to take all"), "D" for *deponere* ("deposit one"), "N"

---

62. Schimmel, *The Mystery of Numbers* (Oxford: Oxford University Press, 1993), 203–8, 237.

for *nihil* (meaning "do nothing"), and "A" for *auferre* (meaning "to take one"). (In this order, corresponding to the numbers 4-3-2-1, opposites are on opposite sides of the teetotum; that is, "all" is opposite "none" and "put" is opposite "take.") The word "teetotum" comes from "T totum," the best cast. Teetotums (also called "put and takes") can be made with any number of sides. You can order them online from game distributers or make your own.

Instead of an astragalos, you can use a traditional four-sided teetotum. Think of an ordinary die and imagine drilling a whole through its two and five faces. The remaining faces are one, three, four, six, just like an astragalos. Fix a short dowel through the hole for an axle. (Drilling a manufactured die is not such a good idea; you are better off starting with a wooden cube.) Similarly, you can use a six-sided teetotum instead of a die for divination; they are readily available. Ancient ones were marked 1-5-3-6-2-4 in clockwise order (opposites add to seven).

To use a teetotum, you spin it, usually by snapping its axle between your thumb and middle finger. For a good reading, it should spin for at least two seconds and land with one side clearly uppermost; otherwise, spin again. For the Alphabet Oracle, spin a four- or six-sided teetotum five times and interpret like astragaloi or dice, respectively. (For a teetotum with an odd number of sides, such as the three- and seven-sided teetotums for the Oracle of the Seven Sages, read the downward face.)

Twenty-Four–Sided Die

A very direct method of consulting the oracle is to cast a twenty-four–sided die. At least one such die, made of glass paste and marked with the Greek letters, survives from the ancient world and might have been used with the Alphabet Oracle. It can't have been the most common method, or such dice would not be so rare compared to the thousands of surviving astragaloi and six-sided dice. Making a twenty-four–sided die is complicated, but they are used for gaming and can be bought for a few dollars. Try searching for "buy 24 sided dice" or "d24 dice." These dice are labeled with the numbers one through twenty-four, so you will have to use table 6 to determine the correct letter. Alternately you can buy an unmarked die and paint the letters onto its faces.

Alphabet Tablet

There is another way of letting the gods guide you to a letter. We don't know if it was used in ancient Greece or Rome, but it has been traditional in Europe for a long time. Make up a card (Grk., *pinax*; Lat., *tabula*, tablet) with the Greek letters in squares as shown in table

2. It is best to carefully make a nice tablet and consecrate it, but in a pinch you can draw it on any sheet of paper or even mark it in the sand.

A	B	Γ	Δ
E	Z	H	Θ
I	K	Λ	M
N	Ξ	O	Π
P	Σ	T	Y
Φ	X	Ψ	Ω

Table 2. Alphabet Tablet.

To consult the oracle, close your eyes and place your finger on the tablet. Where you are pointing is your oracle. Or you can toss a small stone or coin on the tablet and see where it lands. If it bounces off the tablet or lands on a line, try again, but at most three times (see chapter 3 on miscasts). A more modern device is a disk with the letters inscribed around the edge and a spinning arrow in the center.

Coin Methods

I don't know if the ancients used this method, but it is similar to casting an ancient Chinese oracle called the *Ling Ch'i Ching*, which dates back to the Wei-Chin period (222–419 CE). This technique uses coins or other disks with distinct sides, which I'll call the head and tail. There are several different ways to use this method, and I'll begin with the simplest, which uses five coins of four different types. For clarity, I'll assume we have two quarters and one dime, nickel, and penny. To cast the oracle, you shake up the coins, allow them to fall on a flat surface, and observe the heads and tails.

To explain reading the oracle, I will use "O" for a head (considered feminine) and "I" for a tail (considered masculine); they kind of look like their meaning. If the quarters show one head and one tail, the throw represents the number 1, for in Pythagorean numerology the monad is androgynous. If they are both heads, then write down 2, for even numbers are feminine and this throw is purely feminine. If they are both tails, write down 3, for odd numbers are masculine. Next observe whether the other three coins were heads or tails, and write O or I for each in order. For example, suppose both quarters were tails, the dime shows its head, and the nickel and penny are tails. We would write "3.OII," where for clarity I have put a point between the quarters and the other coins. To determine the oracle, look up this cast in the *Key for Consulting the Alphabet Oracle* (table 6, page 92), and you will see it is Upsilon (Y). Similarly, if the quarters were mixed (a head and a tail), and the dime, nickel, and penny were tail, head, head, respectively, we would write down "1.IOO," which is Epsilon (E). (Of course, you don't actually have to write down anything; you can look at the pattern of heads and tails and directly consult table 6.)

As with dice and astragaloi, you don't have to have five coins to use this method; you can do it by casting one coin five times. For the first two casts, you are concerned only with the number of heads and tails, not the order in which they occur. Mark 1, 2, or 3 as before. For the next three casts, record O (head) or I (tail) in order.

This coin method can be used easily to find the corresponding letter in the Alphabet Tablet with six rows and four columns shown in table 2. Notice that there are three pairs of rows, upper (A–Θ), middle (I–Π), and lower (P–Ω). (These correspond to the units (1–9, omitting 6 = digamma), tens (10–90, omitting 90 = qoppa), and hundreds (100–900, omitting 900 = sampi) of the ancient Greek numeration system used in Greek gematria, described in chapter 6.) Depending on whether the quarters represent 1, 2, or 3, you pick the upper, middle, or lower pair of rows. If the dime shows a head, you pick the upper row of four, or if tails, the lower. Within the row, if the nickel is a head, take the left pair of letters, otherwise the right pair. Finally, if the penny is a head, choose the left letter in the pair, otherwise the right letter. For example, suppose that the quarters were mixed, and the dime, nickel, and penny were tail, head, head, respectively. Since the quarters represent 1, we take the upper pair of rows (A–Θ). The dime was a tail, so we take the lower row (E–Θ); the nickel was a head, so take the left pair (EZ); the penny is a head, so take the left letter (E).

If you have a set of alphabet stones, you can use them with the coin method as follows. Arrange your letter stones in six rows of four as in the Alphabet Tablet (table 2). Cast two coins, or one coin twice (corresponding to the quarters), and based on the throw (OI or IO = 1, OO = 2, II = 3), eliminate the unneeded double rows. Cast again (corresponding to the dime) and eliminate the upper or lower row of four. Another cast (the nickel) tells you whether to eliminate the left or right pair of letters. The final cast (the penny) selects the oracle letter. You might wonder why you would want to use the slower coin method if you have a full set of alphabet stones, since you can simply draw one for the oracle. The reason is that the slower method better focuses the attention and helps to induce a meditative state, which may give a more accurate reading. (This is the reason that some *I Ching* readers, including me, prefer the complicated yarrow-stalk method to the easier coin method.) In divination, faster is not necessarily better.

Now a few words about the divinatory disks themselves. For clarity, I have explained the procedure in terms of ordinary coins, and they can be used effectively, but for spiritual purposes such as divination, ordinary coins may not be the best choice. You can, of course, use coins with some spiritual significance, such as ancient Greek or Roman coins bearing the image of a god (or inexpensive reproductions), I Ching coins, etc. You can also make a set of disks especially for divination. As we have seen, a complete set is five coins of four types with distinct heads and tails. For example, you can mark the head side and leave the tail side blank. Or you can mark both sides, either with abstract symbols (for example, O and I), or with something more concrete. For example, you can put a goddess on one side and a god on the other; you can use either an image of the deity or write their name. (Traditionally, O is female and I is male.) There are many other symbolic possibilities. Of course, as you have seen, you can do the procedure sequentially with just one disk.

You can make your disks out of a variety of material; wood was traditional in Taoist divination, because it is receptive. In Ancient Greek the words for *matter*, *matrix* (the heart-wood, but also the womb), and *mêtêr* (mother) are all related; so wood symbolizes well the matter or substance of the divination. Nevertheless, clay, pottery, and metal are also good choices. Since there are four kinds of disks, they could be colored and made out of materials associated with the four elements. (You could mark the element's symbol on the head side and leave the other blank.) Obviously, your disks should be flat enough that they can't land on their edges!

Geomantic Method

Since all that is required to use the coin method is a sequence of fives heads or tails, many other traditional divination procedures can be adapted to this method. For example, as is done in geomancy, you can make five long rows of marks on a piece of paper or in the soil while keeping the query clearly in mind. The idea is to make each row long enough and quickly enough that you cannot immediately see how many marks you have made (a dozen is the minimum). Then you count off the marks in each row by twos to see if there is an even or odd number of marks. If it is even, you mark an O for that row, if odd, an I. Proceed to read the oracle the same way as the coin method.

A related technique comes from West African *Ifa* divination. String five two-sided objects on a thread (cowry shells are traditional). When you toss this device on the ground or a divining cloth, some of the objects will show their head side, others their tail side. Of course you need to know where to start reading, and the easiest way to do this is make one of the objects different from the rest (bigger, a different color, etc.); alternately, you can make the first two (corresponding to the quarters) distinct.

Bead Methods

A Tibetan procedure uses a long string of prayer beads (a *mala*); they were also used for prayer and meditation in the ancient Pagan West. Grab the string of beads with both hands in two random places, spaced well apart. Then count off by twos from each end (alternating your hands) until there are only one or two beads left between your hands. If there is one, mark I, and if two, mark O. Repeat this four more times to get a sequence of five Is and Os, and read them in the usual way. A slight variation requires you to count off only four times. The first time you count off by threes, alternating your hands, until there are one, two, or three beads between them. You interpret the number of beads like the number represented by the quarters. The remaining three times you count off by twos, as before, to get an I or O each for the dime, nickel, or penny. You may find these techniques convenient if you are accustomed to wearing a long string of prayer beads. (This method does not work so well with rosaries or other strings of beads that are divided into groups.)

Pebble Methods

A similar method uses a container, such as a bag or a jug, of any small objects, such as pebbles, marbles, beans, or unstrung beads. Take out a fairly large handful and count them back into the container by threes until one, two, or three are left, as in the coin method. Take another handful, and put them back two at a time until one or two are left. Repeat twice more to get the oracle. Alternately, count down to one or two pebbles five times, as in the geomantic method.

You can also use a container of beans, marbles, or other small objects of two kinds (colored or marked differently, etc.), and interpret one kind as heads and another as tails. Obviously, the objects of different kinds should be similar in feel so that you cannot tell them apart by touch. Draw five from the container one at a time and interpret them as heads and tails as in the coin method. Perhaps one of these methods is the "divination by pebbles" that the Thriai taught Hermes (as told in chapter 2). We know that divination with beans was conducted at Delphi, and that a two-bean method was used there, but perhaps other bean methods were used as well. Large numbers of colored pebbles can be found in archaeological sites, sometimes with astragaloi.

Mixed Dice Methods

One simple method of consulting the Alphabet Oracle uses the Alphabet Tablet (table 2, page 67) with one ordinary die and two coins or other disks. Toss one coin and use it to pick either the left or right double column. Toss the second coin and use it to pick the left or right column out of the two. Finally, roll the die to pick one of the six rows. You can use a similar technique with the following tablet for the Three-Out-of-Four Method (see table 3), which is more useful if you are interested in the correspondences to the letters that will be discussed in chapter 6. Use the coins to pick the row and the die to pick the column.

You can also use special dice in a variant of the coin method. Instead of the quarters, you use a three-sided long die, which is a triangular prism. You can mark the faces 1, 2, 3 and read the face that is down. However, some of these long dice have the numbers near the edges, in which case you read the upmost edge. In addition, you need an eight-sided die or teetotum. A cast of these two dice is most easily interpreted by arranging the alphabet in six rows of four columns, as in the Alphabet Tablet (table 2, page 67). Based on the cast of the three-sided long die, consult the first, second, or third double-row of four. This narrows it down to eight letters, and you pick one of these by casting the eight-sided die or spinning the eight-sided teetotum.

Three-Out-of-Four Method

I'll give you one final, convenient method for consulting the oracle, although I don't know of any evidence that it was used in ancient times. In this case, you need only four distinctly marked objects. They could be marked with four symbols (such as the four elements) or painted four colors. To cast the oracle, you draw the objects at random from a container, and their sequence determines the oracular letter. (Of course, once you see the first three, you know what the fourth will be, so the first three are sufficient to reveal the oracle.)

For convenience, I will use 1, 2, 3, 4 for the token's markings, and in the Key for Consulting the Alphabet Oracle (table 6, page 92) I show just the first three tokens drawn. So 123 =

Alpha, 124 = Beta, 132 = Gamma, ..., 432 = Omega. You will be able to understand the correspondence better if you write the alphabet in a square with four rows and six columns (see table 3): (1) each row has the same first number, (2) within a row, each pair of columns have the same second number, and (3) within each pair, the third numbers are in increasing order.

A	B	Γ	Δ	E	Z
123	124	132	134	142	143
H	Θ	I	K	Λ	M
213	214	231	234	241	243
N	Ξ	O	Π	P	Σ
312	314	321	324	341	342
T	Y	Φ	X	Ψ	Ω
412	413	421	423	431	432

Table 3. Three-Out-of-Four Method.

How to Choose a Method

With all these different methods for consulting the Alphabet Oracle, you may be wondering which you should use. Should you learn them all? Probably not. The simplest and most authentic method is to use a full set of alphabet stones, so I suggest that you plan on purchasing or (preferably) making a set. However, it's also useful to learn at least one of the other methods. You can use this until you get your alphabet stones, but it is also useful to know an alternative method in case you don't have your alphabet stones with you, or if it's inconvenient to carry them. For example, you can get by with a single coin, astragalos, or die. So I suggest that you read through all the alternative methods, maybe give them a try, and if one appeals to you, learn it. You can learn other methods later, but I don't think it's necessary (or even useful) to know them all. It is better to know a couple methods well, than all of them poorly.

Chapter 6

The Esoteric Greek Alphabet

In this chapter, you will learn some of the hidden secrets of the Greek alphabet. I will begin with its origin in history and myth and explain the magical correspondences of the letters. This allows you to use them as theurgic *symbols*, as explained in chapter 2. The Greek letters also have numerical values, and this allows hidden correspondences among Greek words and names to be discovered (called *isopsephy* or Greek gematria). Finally, I will explain how to use the Greek alphabet for magic following a divination (analogous to rune magic). You don't need to know any of this to use the Alphabet Oracle, so if lore and magic is not your thing, feel free to move on to chapter 7, where you will learn to use the Oracle. You might be inclined to come back to this chapter later, after you experience for yourself the Oracle's power.

Alphabet Lore

The Greek alphabet is one of the sacred alphabets of the West, and there is much esoteric lore associated with it. This information can be useful in more detailed divination and for alphabet magic (discussed in the next section). For example, suppose you cast (Θ) "Thou hast gods as comrades and as aides." That is good to know, but you might want to know who these gods are. To find out, you can do a second divination asking, "Which god is my comrade and aid?" Suppose you cast Φ; the god associated with this cast is Artemis, and so you should expect help from her.

There are many stories of the origin of the Greek alphabet. Historians tell us it is based on a Phoenician alphabet that was derived from Egyptian hieroglyphics and was brought to Greece around 800 BCE. Legends credit this to the Phoenician prince Cadmus, who founded the Greek city Thebes, but he is dated to around 2000 BCE, and so the story is a bit muddled (perhaps he brought the earlier Linear B writing system, which does go back to the second millennium BCE). The twenty-two–letter Phoenician alphabet contained only consonants, and one of the Greek innovations was to add vowels by repurposing unneeded consonants or inventing completely new letters. The result was the first true alphabet. However, it existed in many different versions in the Greek cities, in part to accommodate the different Greek dialects and pronunciations. In 403 / 402 BCE, Athens standardized the twenty-four–letter Greek alphabet presented in chapter 4, which was adopted throughout Greece and is still used today.

Mythology credits the alphabet to several gods, including Prometheus (as mentioned in chapter 2) and Hermes, who was said to have been inspired by observing cranes (his sacred bird) flying in letter-like formations; this is especially obvious in the fourth letter (Δ), because the number four is sacred to Hermes. He brought the alphabet to Egypt, where he is known as Thoth and the ibis is his bird. Later, Cadmus brought a sixteen-letter alphabet from Egypt to Greece, and Euander (the son of Hermes and Carmenta, a goddess) took it from Greece to Italy, where it became the Etruscan alphabet. Subsequently, Carmenta adapted fifteen Etruscan letters for Latin, which was the ancestor of the Roman alphabet that we still use for English and many other languages.[63]

Some say that the Moirai (Three Fates) themselves invented the first seven letters, and that certain men later increased the number to twenty-four. Hyginus (ca. 64 BCE–17 CE), in his *Fables*, says that Moirai invented five vowels and two consonants, but I think he is incorrect. He is not a very reliable source; his modern editor described him (in Latin) as "an ignorant youth, semi-learned, stupid."[64] It is much more likely that they invented the seven vowels, which as pure sounds are akin to the heavenly spheres; they are spiritual, compared to the materiality of the consonants. In particular, the vowels correspond to the seven planetary spheres in the Ptolemaic / Chaldean order: A Moon, E Mercury, H Venus, I Sun, O Mars, Y Jupiter, Ω Saturn.[65] They also correspond to the seven pitches of the Phrygian mode (e.g., E, F, G, a, b, c, d), and thus to the music of the spheres. Vowel chants are common in the invocations of the Greek Magical Papyri.

There is esoteric significance to twenty-four, the number of letters in the classical Greek alphabet. For example, two letters are assigned to each of the Twelve Olympians

---

63. Hyginus, *Hygini Fabulae,* (Cambridge, MA: Harvard University Press, 1963), 277.

64. H. J. Rose in Hyginus, *Hygini Fabulae*. See also page 277.

65. Godwin, *The Mystery of the Seven Vowels* (Grand Rapids, MI: Phanes, 1991), ch. 3.

and to each sign of the zodiac. (In the Alphabet Tablet, table 2, the letters in the first column correspond to the fire signs, those in the second to earth, in the third to air, and in
the fourth to water.) Marcus the Gnostic (second century CE) had a vision of a goddess
called *Alêtheia* (Grk., Truth), who revealed a correspondence between these pairs of letters
and twelve parts of her body. The ancient Greeks divided many things into twenty-four
parts and labeled them with their letters. For example, Homer's *Iliad* and *Odyssey* are each
divided into twenty-four books, which are labeled with the letters of the alphabet. They
divided the day into twenty-four hours, but differently than we do. The time between sun-
rise and sunset was divided into twelve equal hours, each ruled by one of the *Twelve Hôrai*
(Grk., Hours), daughters of Helios (the Sun), and the night was similarly divided. Each
Hôra oversees an activity, such as was common in Pythagorean communities.[66] The Egyp-
tians also had a twenty-four–character alphabet of sorts: hieroglyphs that represented
single consonants, which they used to transcribe Greek and Roman names.[67] (All these
correspondences are given with the individual oracles, below.)

   The Renaissance mage Henry Cornelius Agrippa (ca. 1486–1535) provides a different
system of correspondences between the letters and the planets, signs of the zodiac, and
five elements. (I don't know if it goes back to ancient times.) He says the seven vowels
are assigned to the planets, but he doesn't specify the order. However, in the accompanying table they are assigned in the opposite order to that given above, that is, he uses the
order of descent (A Saturn, E Jupiter, H Mars, I Sun, O Venus, Y Mercury, Ω Moon). This
disagrees with every ancient source we have (see, for example, Godwin, *The Mystery of
the Seven Vowels*, chapter 3), and so I give the standard correspondences with Agrippa's in
parentheses with an asterisk. I have found the standard correspondences to work best, but
you might prefer to use Agrippa's. Next, he says the twelve *single consonants* are assigned
to the zodiac signs in order (ΒΓΔΖΚΛΜΝΠΡΣΤ = Aries to Pisces). The remaining five
consonants are *double* in that they combine two consonant sounds (Θ *th*, Ξ *ks*, Φ *ph*, Χ *kh*,
Ψ *ps*); they are assigned to the elements in the order of increasing subtlety (Θ Earth, Ξ

---

66. Hyginus, *Hygini Fabulae*, fab. 183, gives the names of the Twelve Hôrai; Iamblichus (*On the Pythagorean
    Way of Life*, ch. 21, ¶¶95–100; pp. 120–123) described the Pythagorean day.

67. Since hieroglyphs do not generally represent vowels, some of the hieroglyphs for consonants not needed
    in Greek were repurposed to write Greek vowels, but this was not always done consistently. See Gardner,
    Egyptian Grammar (Cambridge: Oxford University Press, 1957), 18–20, and Budge, *An Egyptian Hieroglyphic
    Dictionary* (New York: Dover, 1978), xi–xv. To avoid complications, I have regularized the correspondences.

Water, Φ Air, X Fire, Ψ Spirit).[68] These correspondences between the Greek letters and the terrestrial and celestial elements can be used for many purposes.

In one of Plutarch's dialogues, we read that the twenty-four letters are divided into seven voiced (vowels), eight half-voiced (semivowels), and nine voiceless (consonants).[69] The seven vowels ΑΕΗΙΟΥΩ are associated with Apollo, for seven is his sacred number, and as the god of music, he increased the strings on Hermes's lyre from four to seven (the diatonic scale).[70] On the other hand, nine is the number of his Muses, who oversee the arts and sciences (which address everything on earth and in the heavens). The nine voiceless consonants are divided into three groups of three: smooth (ΚΠΤ), middle (ΒΓΔ), and rough (ΘΦΧ).[71] The Muses oversee nine cosmic spheres: the earth, the seven planetary spheres, and the sphere of fixed stars; Apollo rules over them all as the tenth. He is the source of their harmony and unity (and so his name was explained as *a-pollon* = not many, i.e., one). Finally, since the half-voiced letters (ΖΛΜΝΞΡΣΨ) partake of the power of both the voiced and the voiceless, their number, eight, is the mean of seven and nine; according to Pythagorean principles, a mean is required to bind the extremes together. Pythagoreans call the octad (number eight) "Embracer of all Harmonies" and "Cadmean" because Harmonia was the wife of Cadmus.[72]

---

68. Agrippa, *Three Books of Occult Philosophy* (St. Paul, MN: Llewellyn, 1993), I.74, pp. 223–5. The following is a little complicated, and I advise you to ignore it unless you are a language geek! In the classical period ΘΦΧ were aspirated (pronounced $t+h$, $p+h$, $k+h$), and so they are double consonants according to Agrippa. Classical grammarians, however, classified Ξ (pronounced *ks*), Ψ (pronounced *ps*), and Z (classically pronounced *zd*) as double consonants, the rest as simple (Goodwin, *A Greek Grammar*, Cambridge: Oxford University Press, 1892, §18). Nevertheless, in support of Agrippa's classification, there is evidence that at other times they were pronounced Ξ (*khs*), Ψ (*phs*), and Z (*z*). (Allen, *Vox Graeca*, Cambridge: Cambridge University Press, 1968, 53–7; Goodwin, *A Greek Grammar*, §28(3); Woodard, *Greek Writing From Knossos to Homer*, Oxford: Oxford University Press, 1997, §6.5). Therefore, Z could be considered simple, and Agippa's five double consonants (ΘΞΦΧΨ) have aspiration "h" in common. The ancients called them *dasu* (rough, hairy, bushy, not bare or smooth), and this "roughness" seems appropriate for the elements that constitute material nature.

69. Plutarch, *Plutarch's Complete Works* (New York: The Wheeler Publ. Co, 1909), *Symposiacs* ix.3.

70. On the strings of the lyre in Greek esoteric music theory, see Opsopaus, "Greek Esoteric Music Theory" at http://omphalos.org/BA/GEM.

71. Stanford, *The Sound of Greek* (Berkeley, CA: University of California Press, 1967), 51–55. They fall into three classes: labial (ΠΒΦ), palatal (ΚΓΧ), and lingual (ΤΔΘ), thus forming a three-by-three matrix.

72. Iamblichus, *The Theology of Arithmetic* (Grand Rapids, MI: Phanes, 1988), 102.

We also read in Plutarch that the Cadmean alphabet had sixteen letters, because it is four times four, and four is Hermes's number.[73] Later, Simonides and Palamedes each added four more letters, therefore bringing it to completion at twenty-four; that is, six fours. For, according to Pythagoreans, the triad is the first perfection, for it has beginning, middle, and end, and the hexad (number six) is the second perfection for it is the sum of its divisors ($6 = 1 + 2 + 3$, $6 = 1 \times 2 \times 3$). Moreover, twenty-four is also the product of the first perfection (the triad) and the first cube (the octad, for eight is two cubed, $8 = 2^3 = 2 \times 2 \times 2$). They also call the octad "Mother," for it is the extension into three dimensions of the dyad (number two), which they call "Rhea," the Mother of the Gods.

As you can see, there is hidden significance to the fact that the classical Greek alphabet has twenty-four letters, but for some esoteric purposes we use an older twenty-seven–letter Greek alphabet, which included three obsolete letters that were retained from pre-classical Greek alphabets although unneeded for writing classical Greek. The three obsolete letters are F (called *digamma* or *wau*, which looks like our F and is its ancestor), Q (called *qoppa*, the ancestor of our Q), and) (called *sampi* because it looks like pi, Π). From at least the fifth century BCE, this twenty-seven–letter alphabet was used for numerals in ancient Greece; the letters *alpha* through *theta* stood for one to nine, the letters *iôta* through *qoppa* for ten to ninety, and the letters *rho* through *sampi* for one hundred to nine hundred (see table 4). Since twenty-seven is the cube of three (that is, three to the third power: $27 = 3^3 = 3 \times 3 \times 3$), it is an especially holy number (for some of the meaning of the cubes eight and twenty-seven, see my *Pythagorean Tarot*, pages 406–11 and 433–8).

	1	2	3	4	5	6	7	8	9
× 1	A	B	Γ	Δ	E	F	Z	H	Θ
× 10	I	K	Λ	M	N	Ξ	O	Π	Q
× 100	P	Σ	T	Y	Φ	X	Ψ	Ω	)

Table 4. Numerical Values of Greek Letters.

Therefore, for example, the ancients might write **XIB'** for 612 (the prime ' indicates a number). This correspondence implies, however, that every Greek word has a numerical value; for example, **ZEYΣ** (Zeus) also has the value 612 (**ZEYΣ** $= 7 + 5 + 400 + 200 = 612$). The study of the numerological significance of Greek words is called *isopsephy* from *iso-* (equal) and *psêphos* (pebble), since the ancients calculated with pebbles. Sometimes it's

---

73. Plutarch, *Plutarch's Complete Works, Symposiacs* ix.3.

called "Greek gematria," but the art seems to have originated with the Greek alphabet and was only later applied to the Hebrew alphabet. Two words with the same numerical value (or differing by only one) are called *isopsephic* (Grk., *isopsêphos*) and are numerologically linked. One explanation for ignoring differences of one (called *colel*) is that The Inexpressible One is in everything. For example, 1138 = ΛΗΤΩ (Leto), the mother of Apollo, which is isopsephic with 1139 = ΔΕΛΦΥΣ (*delphus*, "womb"), from which Delphi is named (recall chapter 2). Further, "The god Apollo" (Ο ΘΕΟΣ ΑΠΟΛΛΩΝ = 1415) is isopsephic with twice the value of "The god Hermes" (Ο ΘΕΟΣ ΕΡΜΗΣ = 707), which links them together (Hermes is Apollo's younger brother, see chapter 2). Finally, **ΤΟ ΑΡΡΗΤΟΝ ΕΝ** (The Inexpressible One) and ΑΓΝΩΣ (*agnôs*, "unknown," "obscure," "unintelligible") both equal 1054, for The Inexpressible One is beyond rational grasp. Isopsephy can reveal hidden connections between the meanings of Greek words.

As explained in chapter 2 (under "Theory of Divination"), Neoplatonists understand the Cosmos to be an emanation from The Inexpressible One, through the Cosmic Mind and Cosmic Soul into the Cosmic Body, which is the material world. Marcus the Gnostic illustrated this with an analogy. Take a Greek letter, such as Ι (*iôta*). In Greek its name is spelled ΙΩΤΑ, which we can think of as its emanation and unfolding on a lower level, Ι ⇒ ΙΩΤΑ. But each of the letters of ΙΩΤΑ has its own emanation on a yet lower level: Ι ⇒ ΙΩΤΑ, Ω ⇒ ΩΜΕΓΑ (*ômega*), Τ ⇒ ΤΑΥ (*tau*), Α ⇒ ΑΛΦΑ (*alpha*). Each letter in these names has further emanations in lower levels, and so on to generate the infinite multiplicity of the cosmos.

I've chosen *iôta* as an example for a particular reason, for this vowel corresponds to the Sun among the planets and is therefore in the most direct line of emanation from The One: One ⇒ Apollo ⇒ Helios (Sun). Now consider the name ΙΩΤΑ. It includes the Gnostic divine name ΙΑΩ, which among other things, symbolizes the Sun (Ι) as ruler over all the other planets, from the Moon (Α), the nearest, most changeable planet, to Saturn (Ω), the farthest and slowest moving planet. They are like bookends: the Moon's period is 29 ½ days, and Saturn's is 29 ½ years. In Greek, the god Saturn is called Kronos, who was the father of Zeus and the other Olympians with Rhea, Mother of the Gods. Plato interpreted his name to mean Pure Intuiting Mind (from *koreô*, "to purify," and *nous*, "intuiting mind"). Plotinus interpreted it as the fullness (*koros*) of the intuiting mind, which includes all the Platonic Ideas (symbolized by the myth that Kronos ate all his children before Zeus brought them forth into the light). Therefore, Saturn is sometimes called the Occult Sun, because it is the hidden source of illumination, the illumination sought by sages. The *Chal-*

dean Oracles inform us that the Moon is associated with Hekatê, the goddess of theurgy, whose womb brings the Ideas into manifestation in the material world.

What of *tau*? It was the last letter of the Phoenician alphabet, in which it was written as an X cross and had the name *tâw*, which means a mark or sign. Therefore, ΙΩΤΑ is a sacred sign.[74] By isopsephy its value is 1111, which symbolizes the emanation of The One through four levels of reality increasing in multiplicity (1 ⇒ 10 ⇒ 100 ⇒ 1000). It has the same value as ΑΠΛΩΣ (*haplôs*), which means "singly, in one way, simply, absolutely" (characteristics of The One), and with Ο ΜΑΡΤΥΣ (*ho martus*, the witness). By *colel* it is isopsephic with Ο ΣΟΦΟΣ (*ho sophos*, the wise man), ΜΑΘΗΜΑ ΟΡΜΑΩ (*mathêma hormaô*, "I incite learning"), and Ο ΜΙΚΡΟΣ ΚΟΣΜΟΣ (*ho mikros kosmos*, the microcosm), all with the value 1110, and it is isopsephic with twice ΦΗΜΗ (*phêmê*, heavenly or prophetic voice). All of these words and phrases point to The One as the source of wisdom and oracular knowledge.

There is also an esoteric connection between the alphabet and the daily phases of the moon. There are approximately 29½ days from one new moon to the next (the *synodic month*), and many ancient cultures around the world associated twenty-nine or thirty animals or other symbols with each of these phases. Remarkably, the ABC order of our alphabet (or ΑΒΓ of Greek) is preserved in many ancient scripts, the oldest of which is the Ugaritic script, used 1400–1200 BCE. This script had thirty letters and seems to have been based on an earlier twenty-seven–letter script extended to accommodate all the moon's phases. In fact, some authors think that the letters were originally signs for the thirty lunar animals, and that only later were they used to represent sounds. The Phoenicians selected twenty-two of these letters to write their language, preserving the order found in the Ugaritic script. The twenty-seven–letter Greek alphabet restores some of the omissions and adds new letters at the end. The twenty-seven Greek letters correspond to the days when the moon is visible, from new moon (first visible crescent) to old moon (last visible crescent); the dark of the moon has no letters in Greek.[75]

---

74. Franklin, *Origins of the Tarot Deck: A Study of the Astronomical Substructure of Game and Divining Boards* (Jefferson, NC: McFarland and Company, 1988), 132, adds that ΙΟΤΑ represents the quarters of the year, starting with the summer solstice.

75. Gordon, "The Accidental Invention of the Phonemic Alphabet, *Journal of Near Eastern Studies* 29 (1970): 193–197; Kelley, "Calendar Animals and Deities," *Southwestern Journal of Anthropology* 16 (1960): 317–337; Moran and Kelley, *The Alphabet and the Ancient Calendar Signs* (Palo Alto, CA: Bell's, 1969); Weinstock, "Lunar Mansions and Early Calendars," *The Journal of Hellenic Studies* 69 (1949): 48–69.

We know that as early as the sixth century BCE the ancient Orphics associated animals with the days of the lunar month, but their correspondences have not survived. On the other hand, we have a list of twenty-seven correspondences from an invocation of the Moon (*Mênê*) in the *London Magical Papyrus*: ox, vulture, bull, cantharus-beetle, falcon, crab, dog, wolf, dragon, horse, she-goat, asp, goat, he-goat, baboon, cat, lion, leopard, field mouse, deer, multiform maiden (a description of the goddess Hekatê), torch, lightning, garland, caduceus (herald's wand), child, and key. The last seven, associated with the last week of the waning moon's visibility, are all symbols associated with Hekatê as a goddess of the underworld. These twenty-seven lunar symbols correspond to the letters of the Greek alphabet, and are given in the correspondences in the Alphabet Oracle text (chapter 7).[76]

Alphabet Magic

If you are familiar with runes, you know that they can be used for magic as well as for divination, and the Greek Alphabet Oracle can be used in a similar way. The runes represent forces, and so it is natural to use them singly or in combination to achieve some purpose. In contrast, the Alphabet Oracles are answers to questions, and so the normal way to use them is to make a talisman to strengthen a positive response or to weaken a negative response. The oracles tell you what will happen if the current conditions continue, or they give you conditions under which an outcome will occur, but a talisman can help to change or reinforce these conditions.

For example, suppose you have asked about the success of a project and you cast Π (Pi) "Passing many tests, you'll win the crown." The oracle predicts that your project will eventually succeed in spite of difficulties along the way, so your talisman could invoke the god's aid in passing those trials. You might invoke Apollo or Heracles (who founded the Olympic games and was later deified) to empower a success talisman. On the other hand, suppose you cast M (Mu) "Make no haste; in vain you press ahead." In this case you might make a talisman to help restrain yourself and to request insight as to when progress is possible (as discovered, perhaps, by another divination). You could invoke Athena to grant you prudence so you act wisely.

For each of the Alphabet Oracles, I suggest qualities to infuse into your talismans and suggest gods to invoke to empower them (see table 5, *Information for Alphabet Oracle Talismans*, pages 84–87). Of course, as previously mentioned, the ancients had gods corre-

---

76. Weinstock, "Lunar Mansions and Early Calendars"; PGM VII.780–785. The obsolete letters FQ⟨⟩, which are not used in the Alphabet Oracle, have the correspondences: F crab, Q leopard, ⟨⟩ key.

sponding to each Greek letter, but the gods I've listed in table 5 are especially appropriate to the specific oracles. These are just suggestions, however, so please use your own judgment in choosing the intent of your talisman and the god(s) to invoke.

Usually your talisman will be a flat object (a *lamella*), such as a disk of metal, wood, or even paper. You can also use self-hardening clay or a polymer clay (such as Sculpey®), which has to be baked. You can inscribe it (carefully!) with an awl or a craft knife, or write or paint your inscription on it.

Inscribe one side with the *vox magica* for the oracle in a "grapelike figure," that is, in a downward triangle, eliminating the first letter in each line. Make sure you have enough space for all the lines! For example, for Π (Pi), which has the *vox magica* ΠΥΡΟΒΑΡΥΠ, inscribe:

ΠΥΡΟΒΑΡΥΠ

ΥΡΟΒΑΡΥΠ

ΡΟΒΑΡΥΠ

ΟΒΑΡΥΠ

ΒΑΡΥΠ

ΑΡΥΠ

ΡΥΠ

ΥΠ

Π

This invokes and concentrates the power of the letter into the talisman. While you are inscribing it, focus on the purpose of your talisman. Keep positive: concentrate on the goal and avoid thinking about negative outcomes. You can use the other correspondences to the letter (given with the oracles) in the design of your talisman or in the consecration ritual. For example, each letter has a numerical value, a hieroglyph, and astrological associations. In fact, you can write the *vox magica* in hieroglyphs (given with the individual alphabet oracles). Arrange them artistically, ordered generally, but not exclusively, left to right or top to bottom. Don't forget to surround the name with a *cartouche* (⬭ for left-to-right writing, vertical for vertical writing).

When you have constructed your talisman, you can consecrate it as follows. Prepare yourself and your ritual space as I described for the consecration ritual in chapter 3. That ritual invoked Apollo, but you might want to invoke a different deity more appropriate to the purpose of your talisman. The following is the consecration ritual adapted to talismans:

The Operation:

1. If you are not working in consecrated space, then cast a circle or create sacred space in your accustomed way.

2. Light the incense.

3. *Invocation:* While pouring libations and making offerings, invoke the god selected to empower your talisman:

Hear me, (name of god)!

(burn incense while saying:)

I offer Thee this spice, (name of god),

(names and epithets of the god)

Or by whatever name is thy delight,

approach and come thou to this sacred rite.

If ever I've fulfilled the vows I've made,

then hear me now and grant to me thine aid.

Accomplish now this deed, and as I pray

give heed to me, and to these words I say.

4. *Purification:* Hold your talisman to be consecrated in the incense smoke and pray:[77]

I have called on thee, the greatest god,

and through thee on all other gods

to purify this charm of every taint.

Protect this charm today and for all time,

and give it strength supreme, divine.

Give power, truth, and fortune to this charm.

For this consecration I beseech you,

gods of the heavens,

gods under the earth,

gods residing in the middle,

masters of the living and the dead,

you who hear the needs of gods and mortals,

---

77. Essentially the same as in the chapter 3 consecration, see there for source notes.

> *you who reveal what's been concealed!*
> *Immortal gods! Attend my prayers and grant*
> *that I may fill with spirit this, my charm.*

5. *Potentiation:* For additional strength, the remainder of the consecration up to the release can be repeated seven times with increasing force and power:

> *Empower this talisman with (the qualities and powers you desire).*

While concentrating on your talisman's intent, intone sonorously the *vox magica* for the letter as given in chapter 3 (e.g., *Pü-raw-bah-rüp* for Π).

6. Continue the empowerment as follows:

> *I conjure Earth and Heaven!*
> *I conjure Light and Darkness!*
> *I call the god who hath created all,*
> *Complete this sacred consecration now!*
> *The Gates of Earth are opened!*
> *The Gates of Sea are opened!*
> *The Gates of Sky are opened!*
> *The Gates of Sun and Moon*
> *and all the Stars are opened!*
> *My spirit has been heard by all the gods,*
> *So give now spirit to this mystery*
> *that I have made, O gods whom I have named,*
> *O gracious gods on whom I've called.*
> *Give breath to this, the mystery I've made!*
> *Esto!*

7. *Release:* Bring the ritual to a definite end by making final thanks offerings and libations while reciting a dismissal such as this:

> *Depart, O Master/Mistress, to thy realm,*
> *to thine own palace, to thy throne.*
> *Restore the order of the world.*
> *Be gracious and protect me, Lord/Lady.*
> *I thank thee for thy presence here.*
> *Depart in peace and joy. Farewell!*

8. If you do not need to use it right away, leave your talisman on the altar until the next day. To protect it from stray influences, you may want to wrap it in silk or put it in a special box.

9. Your talisman will keep its charge better if each morning when you get up and each night before you retire, you repeat the potentiation, step (5) above, stating your intent and intoning the *vox magica* seven times. Keep your talisman protected when it's not in use.

You can string your talisman on a thong or chain and wear it around your neck, or you can carry it in a small cloth or leather bag. The ancients sometimes wrote the spell on a piece of papyrus, which they rolled up and put in a closed metal tube strung around their neck. In Ancient Greek a talisman is called a *períapton*, which means "something tied on."

When you no longer need your talisman, you should "retire" it by burning it (if paper or wood) or by burying it (if metal, ceramic, etc.). Thank the gods for their aid and fulfill any vows that you have made.

Letter	Vox Magica	Oracle Verse	Talisman Goals	Relevant Gods
A (Alpha)	ΑΒΛΑΝΑΘΑΝΑΛΒΑ	All these things, he says, you'll do quite well!	Guidance, good fortune	Apollo
B (Beta)	ΒΟΥΛΟΜΕΝΤΟΡΕΒ	Briefly wait; the time's not right for thee. (Both Apollo, Fortune bring thee aid.)	Patience, good timing (Divine aid)	Hermes (Apollo, Tychê)
Γ (Gamma)	ΓΕΝΙΟΜΟΥΘΙΓ	Gaia gives thee ripe fruit from thy work.	Good results, help in work	Gaia

Letter	Vox Magica	Oracle Verse	Talisman Goals	Relevant Gods
Δ (Delta)	ΔΗΜΟΓΕΝΗΔ	Dodge the dreadful deeds, avoiding harm. (Drive ill-timed is weak before the rules.)	Prudence, caution (Appropriateness)	Athena (Hermes)
E (Epsilon)	ΕΝΚΥΚΛΙΕ	Eager art thou for right wedding's fruits.	Guidance, children, love	Zeus, Hera
Z (Zeta)	ΖΗΝΟΒΙΩΘΙΖ	Zealously avoid the harmful storm!	Protection	Poseidon
H (Eta)	ΗΣΚΩΘΩΡΗ	Helios, all-watcher, watches thee.	Protection, truth	Helios
Θ (Theta)	ΘΩΘΟΥΘΩΘ	Thou hast gods as comrades and as aides. (Thou hast gods as helpers on this path.)	Divine aid and protection	Athena, Ares, or any others
I (Iota)	ΙΑΕΟΥΩΙ	In all things, thou shalt excel—with sweat!	Strength	Hephaistos
K (Kappa)	ΚΟΡΚΟΟΥΝΟΩΚ	Contests with the waves are hard; endure!	Endurance	Poseidon

Letter	Vox Magica	Oracle Verse	Talisman Goals	Relevant Gods
Λ (Lambda)	ΛΟΥΛΟΕΝΗΛ	Leave off grief, and then await delight. (Lovely bodes the widespread word all things.)	Relief, joy (Good omen)	Aphrodite (Apollo, Tychê)
M (Mu)	ΜΟΡΟΘΟΗΠΝΑΜ	Make no haste; in vain you press ahead. (Mandatory toil: the change is good.)	Patience, prudence (Strength, energy)	Athena (Hephaistos)
N (Nu)	ΝΕΡΞΙΑΡΞΙΝ	Now springs forth the fitting time for all. (Nike's gift enwreathes the oracle.)	Opportunity, timing (Victory, prize)	Hermes (Nike)
Ξ (Xi)	ΞΟΝΟΦΟΗΝΑΞ	Xanthic Dêô's ripened fruit awaits. (You can pick no fruit from withered shoots.)	Good results (Timing, prudence)	Demeter (Demeter)
O (Omicron)	ΟΡΝΕΟΦΑΟ	Out of sight are crops that are not sown.	Effort, foresight	Demeter
Π (Pi)	ΠΥΡΟΒΑΡΥΠ	Passing many tests, you'll win the crown.	Victory	Apollo, Heracles

Letter	Vox Magica	Oracle Verse	Talisman Goals	Relevant Gods
P (Rho)	ΡΕΡΟΥΤΟΗΡ	Rest awhile; you'll go more easily.	Patience, ease	Aphrodite
Σ (Sigma)	ΣΕΣΕΝΜΕΝΟΥΡΕΣ	"Stay thou, friend," Apollo plainly says.	Patience, steadfastness	Apollo
T (Tau)	ΤΑΥΡΟΠΟΛΙΤ	Take release from present circumstance.	Deliverance	Ares, Artemis
Y (Upsilon)	ΥΠΕΦΕΝΟΥΡΥ	Useless toil: this wedding isn't thine! (Undertaking fine is held by deed.)	Prudence (Courage)	Athena, Hera (Athena)
Φ (Phi)	ΦΙΜΕΜΑΜΕΦ	Forthwith Plant! For Dêô fosters well. (Faultily you act, and blame the gods.)	Divine guidance and support (Responsibility)	Demeter (Athena)
X (Khi)	ΧΕΝΝΕΟΦΕΟΧ	"Happily press on!" says Zeus himself. (Happy end fulfills this golden word.)	Energy, confidence (Good luck, success)	Zeus (Hermes)
Ψ (Psi)	ΨΥΧΟΜΠΟΙΑΨ	Proper is this judgment from the gods.	Justice	Zeus, Dikê
Ω (Omega)	ΩΡΙΩΝ	Otiose the fruit that's plucked unripe.	Patience, timing	Demeter

Table 5. Information for Alphabet Oracle Talismans.

Chapter 7

Text of the Alphabet Oracle

This chapter presents the text of the Greek Alphabet Oracle with additional aids to help you use it. The bulk of the chapter is devoted to the oracles for each of the twenty-four letters, and this is what you will consult when you do divinations. Since each of the oracles is organized in the same way, the next section explains this organization. Some of you may want to memorize the oracular text (it's only twenty-four lines), and so the following section gives a few hints on how to do so. Next comes table 6, which is the key to consulting the oracle by means of dice, astragaloi, beads, etc., as described in chapter 5. The remainder of the chapter comprises the twenty-four oracles with their interpretive aids. They are preceded by figure 6, which shows how the Oracle would appear engraved on a stone tablet.

Interpreting the Oracles

On the following pages you will find the texts of the alphabet oracles along with additional information to help you interpret them. Since I will be explaining the format of the oracles, you may want to look at the oracle for Alpha, which follows this explanation (page 94).

You will see that each oracle is headed by a Greek letter and its name, for example, "A (Alpha)." Following this is a verse translation that begins with a similarly sounding letter of the Roman alphabet, or one that suggests the Greek letter. For example, for Alpha the verse is: "All these things, he says, you'll do quite well!" (These verses are collected in table 7, which follows the oracles.) I suggest that you eventually memorize these verses so that you don't need this book to read the oracle, but it's best to work with the book until you are very familiar with the oracles and their meanings (see "Memorizing the Alphabet Oracle," on page 91).

Although I have tried to capture the essence of the oracles in these verses, the translations are somewhat free, in order to fit the meter and to have the verse begin with an appropriate Roman letter. Therefore, following the verse translation I provide my own literal translation of the oracle, for example, "The god [Apollo] says you will do everything {Ἅπαντα} successfully." The Greek word in {curly braces} is the first word of the Greek oracle, for example, Ἅπαντα (*hapanta*), which I have translated "everything." You don't need to know anything about Ancient Greek to use the oracle, but I have provided this information for those who want to know the Greek word that begins with the relevant letter (also shown in table 7). If you're not interested, ignore the text in curly braces.

Like English words, Ancient Greek words have a range of meanings, which any Greek reader would have known. Moreover, the enigmatic character of an oracle often arises from these different meanings. Since the English words I have used to translate the Greek might not have the same range of meanings, I have provided the meanings of the Greek word for the English reader. For example, the translation of the Alpha oracle is followed by "*successfully*: prosperously, luckily, with good fortune," which means that the Greek word I have translated "successfully" can also be translated "prosperously," "luckily," or "with good fortune." Read over these alternate meanings to get an understanding of the possible interpretations of the oracle. This is especially useful if an oracle does not seem to apply to the question asked. By looking at these alternate meanings, you will often find a fitting answer. I've added to these a "key phrase," which is suggested by the first word of the oracle in Greek, and can be thought of as the essence of its meaning. (These are collected in table 7 on pages 134–135.)

Following these word definitions, I have supplied several paraphrases of the oracle, which state common interpretations. One of these, for the Alpha oracle, is "You will have good luck in all your activities, or prosperous business transactions and negotiations." As you can see, this is just an alternate, more specific interpretation of the primary translation. These alternate interpretations are not intended to be exhaustive, and no doubt you will find your own. You may want to write them in this book.

Next, I provide a more open-ended discussion of the oracle and what it means to me in divination. Sometimes I add cultural or esoteric lore, which you may find useful for interpreting the oracle or for explaining readings to others. I might suggest talismans corresponding to the letters, as described in chapter 6.

Finally, I give a few useful correspondences: the letter's numerical value; its Olympian god; its zodiac sign; the part of the Body of Truth according to Marcus; its correspondence (planet, zodiac sign, or element) according to Agrippa; its lunar phase and day of month; its hieroglyph; its hour of the day; and finally its *vox magica* (the name of its spirit).

This may all seem a bit overwhelming, but it is just to help you get started. Just as with tarot reading or rune casting, with time and practice you will acquire an intuitive understanding of the oracles, which will be enriched by your own experience using them for divination.

I should also mention that in nine cases (ABΔΛMNΞOY) the text of the Olympos oracle differs from the Common Alphabet Oracle text. Therefore, under the heads for those letters I have also included the Olympos text in the same format. You can ignore it if you like, but it sometimes will provide a more meaningful answer if the Common text does not. In general, however, I think it is better to pick either the Olympos Oracle or the Common Oracle and stick with it (otherwise, you might be tempted to pick the most appealing reading).

Memorizing the Alphabet Oracle

As I mentioned, I do not recommend that you bother memorizing the Alphabet Oracle verses right away. As you learn the Alphabet Oracle, it is best to consult this book so you can see the range of Ancient Greek meanings of each verse. Before long, you will develop an intuitive grasp of the meanings, and you will be able to interpret readings without looking them up. Then, you may find it worthwhile to memorize the verses, but it is by no means necessary to do so. (You will probably learn many of them just by using them.)

If you do want to learn them, I recommend that you use the ancient "art of memory," which was invented by Simonides of Ceos (ca. 556–468 BCE) and has been practiced ever since. To apply it to the Alphabet Oracle, you imagine a memorable, vivid, ridiculous, exaggerated, action-packed vignette that incorporates the letter and suggests its verse. For example, to remember the verse for A (Alpha), "All these things, he says, you'll do quite well," I picture Apollo stabbing a giant awl (for "All") into a giant stack of paper ("thesis," suggesting "these") and throwing them into an old-fashioned water well (for "well"). A large wooden "A" stands over the well with a bucket hanging from its crossbar. Therefore, the image associates the letter "A" with the first couple words of the verse ("All these") and also picks up another word ("well"). The image of Apollo helps me remember "he says," since in this case Apollo is the speaker. This is just an example, and I suggest you come up with your own images. First, include the Greek letter, either its shape (e.g., the wooden "A" in the example) or, if you know it, the letter's name (e.g., a pie for Pi). In addition, try to encode the first few words of each verse. (In principle, you can encode the whole verse, but that is usually impractical and unnecessary.) Try also to include the key phrase. Make the image vivid and include some action. Practice visualizing the entire image in your mind's eye. When you have all twenty-four verses encoded, rehearse them from time to time in order to keep the memories secure. Test yourself by drawing alphabet stones (or otherwise casting lots) and seeing if you can remember the corresponding verse. As I said before, however, you can use the Alphabet Oracle quite well without memorizing it at all.

Letter	Astragaloi		Coin	24-Sided Die	Three-Out-of-Four	Dice	
	Sum of 5 Increasing	Sum of 5 Decreasing				Sum of 5 Increasing	Sum of 5 Decreasing
A	5	30	1.OOO	1	123	5	30
B	7	28	1.OOI	2	124	6	29
Γ	8	27	1.OIO	3	132	7	28
Δ	9	26	1.OII	4	134	8	27
E	10	25	1.IOO	5	142	9	26
Z	11	24	1.IOI	6	143	11	24
H	12	23	1.IIO	7	213	12	23
Θ	13	22	1.III	8	214	13	22
I	14	21	2.OOO	9	231	14	21
K	15	20	2.OOI	10	234	15	20
Λ	16	19	2.OIO	11	241	16	19
M	17	18	2.OII	12	243	17	18
N	18	17	2.IOO	13	312	18	17
Ξ	19	16	2.IOI	14	314	19	16
O	20	15	2.IIO	15	321	20	15
Π	21	14	2.III	16	324	21	14
P	22	13	3.OOO	17	341	23	12
Σ	23	12	3.OOI	18	342	24	11
T	24	11	3.OIO	19	412	25	10
Y	25	10	3.OII	20	413	26	9
Φ	26	9	3.IOO	21	421	27	8
X	27	8	3.IOI	22	423	28	7
Ψ	28	7	3.IIO	23	431	29	6
Ω	30	5	3.III	24	432	30	5

Table 6. Key for Consulting the Alphabet Oracle.

ΑΠΑΝΤΑΠΡΑΞΕΙΣΕΥΣΤΟΧΩΣΘΕΟΣΛΕΓΕΙ

ΒΡΑΧΥΠΕΡΙΜΕΙΝΟΝΚΑΙΡΟΣΟΥΓΑΡΕΣΤΙΣΟΙ

ΓΗΣΟΙΤΕΛΕΙΟΝΚΑΡΠΟΝΑΠΟΔΩΣΕΙΠΟΝΩΝ

ΔΕΙΝΩΝΑΠΟΣΧΟΥΠΡΑΓΜΑΤΩΝΜΗΤΙΒΛΑΒΗΙΣ

ΕΡΑΙΣΔΙΚΑΙΩΝΕΚΓΑΜΩΝΙΔΕΙΝΣΠΟΡΑΝ

ΙΑΛΗΝΜΕΓΙΣΤΗΝΦΕΥΓΕΜΗΤΙΚΑΙΒΛΑΒΗΙΣ

ΗΛΙΟΣΟΡΑΙΣΕΛΑΜΠΡΟΣΟΣΤΑΠΑΝΘΟΡΑΙ

ΘΕΟΥΣΑΡΩΓΟΥΣΚΑΙΠΑΡΑΣΤΑΤΑΣΕΧΕΙΣ

ΙΔΡΩΤΕΣΕΙΣΙΝΠΛΗΝΑΠΑΝΤΩΝΠΕΡΙΕΣΗΙ

ΚΥΜΑΣΙΜΑΧΕΣΘΑΙΧΑΛΕΠΟΝΑΝΑΜΕΙΝΟΝΒΡΑΧΥ

ΛΙΠΗΣΠΕΠΑΥΣΟΠΡΟΣΔΕΧΟΥΛΟΙΠΟΝΧΑΡΑΝ

ΜΑΤΗΝΕΠΕΙΓΗΙΜΗΤΑΧΥΝΟΥΣΥΜΦΕΡΕΙ

ΝΥΝΕΙΣΑΠΑΝΤΟΚΑΙΡΟΣΑΡΜΟΙΩΝΕΦΥ

ΞΑΝΘΗΣΣΕΔΗΟΥΣΚΑΡΠΟΣΩΡΙΟΣΜΕΝΕΙ

ΟΥΚΕΣΤΙΜΗΣΠΕΙΡΑΝΤΑΘΕΡΙΣΑΙΚΑΡΠΙΜΑ

ΠΟΛΛΟΥΣΑΓΩΝΑΣΔΙΑΝΥΣΑΣΛΗΨΗΙΣΤΕΦΟΣ

ΡΑΙΟΝΔΙΑΞΕΙΣΕΤΙΒΡΑΧΥΝΜΕΙΝΑΣΧΡΟΝΟΝ

ΣΑΘΩΣΟΦΟΙΒΟΣΕΝΝΕΠΕΙΜΕΙΝΟΝΞΕΝΕ

ΤΩΝΝΥΝΠΑΡΟΥΣΩΝΣΥΜΦΟΡΩΝΕΞΕΙΣΛΥΣΙΝ

ΥΜΗΝΟΔΟΥΣΟΣΕΣΤΙΜΗΜΑΤΗΝΠΟΝΕΙ

ΦΥΤΕΥΕΔΗΩΠΑΝΤΑΓΑΡΘΡΕΨΕΙΚΑΛΩΣ

ΧΑΙΡΩΝΕΠΕΙΓΟΥΙΕΥΣΤΑΔΑΥΤΟΣΕΝΝΕΠΕΙ

ΨΗΦΟΝΔΙΚΑΙΑΝΤΗΝΔΕΠΑΡΑΘΕΩΝΕΧΕΙΣ

ΩΜΗΝΟΠΩΡΑΝΗΝΛΑΒΗΙΣΟΥΧΡΗΣΙΜΟΝ

Figure 6. Text of the Alphabet Oracle as it would appear engraved on a stone tablet.

A (Alpha)

All these things, he says, you'll do quite well!
"The god [Apollo] says you will do everything {"Απαντα} successfully."

Do: achieve, bring about, effect, accomplish, make, manage, negotiate, transact, practice, fare. *Successfully*: prosperously, luckily, with good fortune.

Key Phrase: All things.

Your entire project will turn out well and you will meet all your goals. You will have good luck in all your activities, or prosperous business transactions and negotiations. Your management activities or practice will result in success.

In the oracle, "the god" says that you will be successful, and in this context "the god" must be understood as Apollo, the deity who oversees all prophecy and divination, and in particular this Alphabet Oracle. In effect, all the oracles are oracles of Apollo.

This in an entirely positive oracle. The implication is that there is some activity or project that you have underway, and that you will succeed in all aspects of it. You may have asked the oracle about this project specifically, in which case you have a welcome answer. Remember too that the oracle is addressed to pilgrims who are engaged in some enterprise, quest, or adventure. You are in the midst of a long journey (perhaps a lived life), and this oracle tells you that it will be brought to a successful conclusion. If you did not ask about some project, then the oracle may be providing an answer to a question you did not ask. Because the gods know more than we do, they sometimes answer the questions we *should have* asked, or provide information that we did not know we needed. In this case, the oracle is telling you that you will succeed in some (probably significant) activity that you have underway or are contemplating. This is important information, even if you expect to succeed, but especially if you're pessimistic or have some doubts about it. You have this added guarantee from Apollo. So if you have not asked about some project, then ask yourself (or the querent) what important activities are in progress or being contemplated. See if this oracle from the god is helpful.

For a talisman to reinforce this good oracle, you might invoke Apollo to guide you so that you achieve the beneficial outcome he has predicted.

Numerical value = 1

Planet: Moon

Olympian: Athena

Zodiac: Aries

Body: Head

Agrippa: Moon (*Saturn)

Lunar symbol: Ox (1)

Hieroglyph: (Egyptian vulture: a symbol of divine power)

First hour of the day (Augê, Daybreak): Salute to King Helios

Vox magica: ΑΒΛΑΝΑΘΑΝΑΛΒΑ[78]

---

78. PGM, CI.23 has AKPAMMAXAMAPI, but I have substituted this *vox magica*, which has similar beneficial force, but begins and ends with the appropriate letter like the other *voces magicae*. For additional information, see the note in the Consecration Ritual in chapter 3.

B (Beta)

Briefly wait; the time's not right for thee.

"Wait a little {Βραχύ}; it's not opportune for you."

Wait: abide. *Opportune*: the right time, the critical time, the season, opportunity, advantage, fitness, due measure (see discussion of *kairos* below).

Key Phrase: Brief delay.

Patience is recommended. A little delay, and the time will be right. Timing is everything. Stay where you are until it's time. It's to your advantage to wait, but be alert for the opportune moment. Wait until matters are appropriate for you. There is a time for everything, and everything has its season.

This oracle cautions you to wait just a little, because it's not the right time *for you* (it might be right for someone else). The implication seems to be that your *kairos* will arrive soon. *Kairos* is an important word in Ancient Greek, but it is difficult to translate. The general meaning is a circumstance that is just right, fit, or in proper measure. It commonly, as here, refers to a time or moment that is perfect or advantageous. It is the moment or season when it's best to do something, the opportunity that will come and then be gone. Wise action consists in knowing the *kairos*. Pythagoras said, "Nothing is better than *kairos*," and Hesiod said, "*Kairos* is best in everything." Chilon (ca. 500 BCE), one of the Seven Sages, said, "All good things belong to *kairos*," [79] and attention to *kairos* is recommended in several of the Oracles of the Seven Sages (10, 98, 111; see chapter 10). The Pythagoreans said that recognizing *kairos* is "a complex and many-faceted art," which is "to some extent teachable and subject to calculation (*technologia*)," but is better learned through sensitive practice and experience. [80]

"Kairos" was also a Pythagorean name for the number seven, because many processes come to completion in the seventh stage; Iamblichus called it "the most critical number." [81]

---

79. Pythagoras quoted in Iamblichus, *On the Pythagorean Way of Life* (¶49; pp. 72–3); Hesiod, *Hesiod, the Homeric Hymns*, "Works & Days," line 692; Chilon in de Vogel, *Pythagoras and Early Pythagoreanism* (Assen: van Gorcum,1966), 115.

80. The quotations are from Iamblichus, *On the Pythagorean Way of Life*, ¶¶181–2; pp. 190–1. For more on *kairos*, see de Vogel, *Pythagoras and Early Pythagoreanism*, 113–123.

81. Iamblichus, *Theoulogumena Arithmeticae* (Suttgarg: Teubner, 1975), ¶50; p. 67, line 15; and Iamblichus, *The Theology of Arithmetic*, 88 and 89–100 for other characteristics of the heptad discussed here.

The heptad (number seven) is considered the second monad—that is, an image of The One—because it is not a product of any other number but The One. Nor does it produce any numbers in the decad (the manifestation of the monad), so it defines a critical juncture between potentiality and actuality. It is irrational (not subject to reason), for it is neither a product nor a divisor of the other numbers in the decad. (See also the discussion of the number seven in chapter 8.)

For a talisman appropriate to this oracle, I suggest you invoke Hermes to grant you patience and the wisdom to perceive the *kairos*. I think Hermes is especially helpful in matters of timing and opportunity.

The Olympos Oracle has this text:

Both Apollo, Fortune bring thee aid.

"You will have Tychê [Fortune] and the Pythian [Apollo] as a helper {Βοηθόν}."

Helper: assistant, auxiliary, one who hastens (*theô*) to the battle cry or other call for help (*boê*).

Key Phrase: Helper.

You are at a critical point, but if you are fortunate, Apollo the Far-shooter will help you if you call on him. Even with luck, the god will only assist; ultimate responsibility is yours. "Pythian" refers to Apollo as the god at Delphi (which was in Pytho), one of the most important oracular sites (see chapter 2). Therefore, the help to be expected might be of a prophetic nature.

It would be very appropriate to invoke Tychê and/or Pythian Apollo to bring you the divine aid offered in this oracle.

Numerical value = 2

Olympian: Aphrodite

Zodiac: Taurus

Body: Neck

Agrippa: Aries

Lunar symbol: Vulture (2)

Hieroglyph: ⫝ (leg: movement)

Second hour of the day (Anatolê, Rising): Solitary walk in nature

Vox magica: **ΒΟΥΛΟΜΕΝΤΟΡΕΒ**

Γ (Gamma)

Gaia gives thee ripe fruit from thy work.

"Gaia [the Earth] {Γῆ} will give you the ripe fruit of your labors."

Ripe: complete, final. *Fruit*: produce, returns, profits, results.

Key Phrase: Gaia.

You will have a successful harvest, or you will reap all your profits from the Earth. The Mother of All will bring your labors to a fruitful conclusion. Gaia will give you your just deserts.

The concrete meaning of this oracle is that Mother Earth will grant a good harvest as a reward for your hard work, but this is a metaphor with much broader meaning. More broadly it seems to say that we will get what we have worked for, whether crops, a good yield, profits, or other desired results. Notice, however, that the oracle does not guarantee a desirable outcome. Rather, it says Gaia will give you the final results that are a consequence of your work. That is, she will give you what you have earned. The implication is that if you have not worked very hard, you will not have a good return. Thus it can be read as a law of consequences or even of retribution. "As ye sow, so shall ye reap" is a wisdom saying in many cultures. For example, a well-known ancient Hindi proverb, *Jaise karni, waise bharni*, has the same meaning. It is like karma, but in this oracle it is Mother Earth who metes out justice.

One can hardly avoid seeing global climate change as an instance of this oracle. Gaia is bringing us the consequences, the final results, of our industry. However, the oracle balances this prediction with a more hopeful one: If we work diligently to use less and recycle more, and strive for conservation and recovery of the environment, then Gaia will reward our efforts. Just as farmers who care for their land will be rewarded by fruitful harvests.

A talisman for this oracle could invoke Gaia to aid you in your work and to grant you the good results that you deserve.

Numerical value = 3

Olympian: Apollo

Zodiac: Gemini

Body: Shoulder and hands

Agrippa: Taurus

Lunar symbol: Bull (3)

Hieroglyph: ⌧ (jar-stand)

Third hour of the day (Mousikê, Music): Spiritual practices in temples and similar places

Vox magica: ΓΕΝΙΟΜΟΥΘΙΓ

Δ (Delta)

Dodge the dreadful deeds, avoiding harm.
"Desist from dreadful {Δεινῶν} deeds, so that you avoid harm."

Desist: keep away, abstain. *Dreadful*: fearful, terrible, strange, wonderful, mighty, powerful, skillful, clever. *Deeds*: affairs (public or private), matters, circumstances, expediencies, annoyances, troubles. *Harm*: damage, hurt.

Key Phrase: Dreadful.

Avoid matters that are terrible, fearful, or uncanny. Beware of the excessively wonderful, skillful, or clever. Don't commit terrible deeds. Stay away from strange circumstances and affairs. Don't make bad choices for the sake of expediency. In these ways you may escape harm.

The basic meaning of this oracle is, I think, clear and common sense: you will be at less risk if you avoid terrible or bizarre behavior. So if you were contemplating such things, this oracle would be a warning. However, the word *deinos* has a wide range of meanings that encompasses things that inspire dread and awe, including some that we value, such as power, skill, and cleverness. I think that this oracle is warning us that their overuse, or use in the wrong circumstances, can backfire and harm us.

A talisman for this oracle might be directed toward bolstering your willpower in order to abstain from these harmful activities. Athena is a good god to invoke for prudence and good sense. Like Ares she is a war god, but whereas he is aggressive and rash, she is defensive and smart; she often prevails.

The Olympos Oracle has this text:

Drive ill-timed is weak before the rules.
"In customs, inopportune strength {Δύναμις} is weak."

Customs: rules, laws, allotments. *Inopportune*: ill-timed, unreasonable, importunate, undue, not *kairos* (fit, in due measure, exact, at the appropriate or critical time, etc.). *Strength*: power, ability, authority.

Key Phrase: Strength.

Ill-timed force will be ineffective; act with precision; timing is everything. Knowing where and when to strike is more important than strength; misapplied ability is disability. Blind conformity to customs is spineless; overly strict adherence to rules is self-defeating. Unreasonable or undue force will defeat itself; a tyrant must fall.

See the discussion of *kairos* under the oracle for **B** (Beta). A talisman might invoke Hermes to show you the *kairos* to exercise your strength. Alternatively, Athena can grant the practical wisdom to know what strength is appropriate.

Numerical value = 4

Olympian: Hermes

Zodiac: Cancer

Body: Breast

Agrippa: Gemini

Lunar symbol: Cantharus-beetle or scarab (4)

Hieroglyph: ⬭ (hand)

Fourth hour of the day (Gymnastikê, Gymnastics): Exercise and massage as suited to the individual

Vox magica: ΔΗΜΟΓΕΝΗΔ

E (Epsilon)

Eager art thou for right wedding's fruits.

"You desire {Ἐρᾷς} to see the offspring of righteous marriages."

Desire: love, are in love with. *Offspring*: seed, sowing. *Righteous*: fitting, well-balanced, legitimate.

Key Phrase: Desire.

This is a statement of fact, not a command or prediction. The obvious meaning is that the querent wants children or grandchildren from suitable marriages. However, it can also mean he or she is in love with seeing this, that is, obsessed by the idea. The "rightness" of the marriage admits many interpretations; it could be a terrible marriage if that was fitting and righteous (i.e., deserved). The oracle may also refer to seeds, other than children, sown by the marriage (e.g., family alliances, marrying into wealth or influence, status). Or to other benefits of marriage, such as love, companionship, support, and sex. Finally, marriage may be taken metaphorically to refer to any alliance or union.

E (Epsilon) is the Greek numeral for five, and in Pythagorean numerology, the pentad (number five) is called "Marriage" (Grk., *Gamos*) and "Androgyny" (Grk., *Androgynia*), for it unites the female (2) with the male (3).[82] In the context of ancient Greek homosexual relations, it would refer to the lover (3, Grk., *erastês*) and the beloved (2, Grk., *erômenos*).

An appropriate talisman could provide guidance on marital affairs or strengthen a future with children. Appropriate deities to invoke are Zeus, "Father of Gods and Mortals," and Hera, who rules lawful marriage.

Numerical value = 5

Planet: Mercury

Olympian: Zeus

Zodiac: Leo

---

82. Iamblichus, *The Theology of Arithmetic*, 65, 74; and Iamblichus, *Theoulogumena Arithmeticae*, ¶¶24, 31–32; p. 30, line 19, p. 41, line 14.

Body: Diaphragm

Agrippa: Mercury (*Jupiter)

Lunar symbol: Falcon (5)

Hieroglyph: ∤ (reed)

Fifth hour of the day (Nymphê, Nymph or Bride): Morning ablutions

Vox magica: ΕΝΚΥΚΛΙΕ

Z (Zeta)

Zealously avoid the harmful storm!
"Flee the very great storm {Ζάλην}, lest you be disabled in some way."

Storm: surge, distress. *Disabled*: hindered.

Key Phrase: Storm.

Don't make a sea voyage in bad weather. It is futile to fight the force of the ocean; likewise, bucking the inevitable will weaken you and hinder your progress. Avoid raging storms of any kind; save your energy for when it can be effective. Escape from the chaos or controversy. Sometimes flight is wiser than fight. Go with the flow.

Although a literal interpretation might apply, usually you will want to interpret the storm metaphorically. It could be an argument or controversy, or some *groundswell*, for example. The predicted consequences of allowing yourself to become involved are that you will be hindered or disabled in some way. This could, of course, refer to physical injury but more generally that you will be disempowered or perhaps prevented from achieving your aims.

Poseidon is a storm god; invoke him for a talisman to protect you from this storm, whatever it might be.

Numerical value = 7

Olympian: Demeter

Zodiac: Virgo

Body: Back

Agrippa: Cancer

Lunar symbol: Dog (7)

Hieroglyph: —⧓— (door bolt: closure, secret)

Sixth hour of the day (Mesêmbria, Midday): Lunch

Vox magica: ΖΗΝΟΒΙΩΘΙΖ

H (Eta)

Helios, all-watcher, watches thee.

"Bright Helios [Sun] {Ἥλιος}, who watches everything, watches you."

The life-giving Sun will care for you. He is the divine overseer. Helios is an enforcer of oaths and promises, and he knows the deceit in your heart.

Key Phrase: Helios.

Because he witnesses everything that takes place on earth, Helios enforces oaths and is especially concerned with truth. He witnessed the abduction of Persephone by Hades and revealed her fate to her mother Demeter. Neoplatonists teach that Helios is in the line or series of emanation from Apollo, who oversees oracles and divination.

You can reinforce Helios's oversight with a talisman to invoke his protection, to reveal or guard the truth, or to guarantee a promise.

Numerical value = 8

Planet: Venus

Olympian: Hephaistos

Zodiac: Libra

Body: Belly

Agrippa: Venus (*Mars)

Lunar symbol: Wolf (8)

Hieroglyph: ⳤ (forearm: offering pose)

Seventh hour of the day (Spondê, Libation): Libations and other offerings to the gods

Vox magica: ΗΣΚΩΘΩΡΗ

Θ (Theta)

Thou hast gods as comrades and as aides.
"You have the gods {Θεούς} as assistants and defenders."

Assistant: helper, aide, advocate, defender. *Defender*: one who stands by, comrade, supporter.

Key Phrase: Gods.

You have divine assistance at hand. The gods will aid and defend you. Call on the gods for help, and they will be there for you. Have confidence!

This oracle offers divine aid and protection, so you could construct a talisman for those purposes. You might invoke Athena, Ares, or any other defensive gods, including gods who oversee the issues for which you need aid.

The Olympos Oracle has this text:

Thou hast gods as helpers on this path.
"You have the gods {Θεούς} as assistants of this path."

Assistant: helper, aide, advocate, defender. *Path*: road, course, way.

Key Phrase: Gods.

The "path" may be an actual road, a plan of action, a spiritual path, a way of life, etc. In any case, the gods who oversee this path will help and defend you, so you may go forward with confidence; you are under divine care because you are following your destiny.

Hermes is the god who most frequently aids people on the path, and he would be a good choice to invoke for a talisman for assistance and protection. However, the oracle tells you that multiple gods are helping you, so you can invoke others, such as Athena or Ares for defense. Think about where you need aid or assistance.

Numerical value = 9

Olympian: Ares

Zodiac: Scorpio

Body: Thighs

Agrippa: Earth

Lunar symbol: Dragon (*drakôn*) (9)

Hieroglyph: ⟐ (tethering rope or hobble: restraint)

Eighth hour of the day (Êletê): Prayer and civic affairs

Vox magica: ΘΩΘΟΥΘΩΘ

I (Iota)

In all things thou shalt excel—with sweat!

"There is sweat {Ἰδρῶτες}, but you will surpass everything."

Sweat: gum, exudation of trees. *Surpass*: excel, be superior to, outlive, survive.

Key Phrase: Sweat.

Although you are working hard, you will accomplish everything. Hard work is the surest means of success. When you have lost all other possessions, you still have your labor as an asset. The oracle recommends elbow grease. If you work hard, you will succeed in the end. You are sweating it now, but you will prevail. Although you are worried, you will survive and do well.

I (Iota) is the Greek numeral for ten (see chapter 6), which is the end of the archetypal numbers, according to the Pythagoreans, and thus limits and completes them. Therefore, they call the decad (number ten) "Power" (Grk., *Kratos*), "All-fulfiller" (Grk., *Panteleia*), and "Atlas," because this Titan god holds aloft the heavens that encompass all the planetary spheres.[83]

When I think of sweat, I think of Hephaistos pounding away on his anvil, beating red-hot bronze into beautiful forms. You could make a talisman to ask him to grant you strength and energy so that you succeed.

Numerical value = 10

Planet: Sun

Olympian: Artemis

Zodiac: Sagittarius

Body: Knees

Agrippa: Sun (*Sun)

---

83. Iamblichus, *The Theology of Arithmetic*, 111, 114; and Iamblichus, *Theoulogumena Arithmeticae*, ¶¶61, 63; pp. 82, 86.

Lunar symbol: Horse (10)

Hieroglyph: 𓇌 or \\ (pair of reeds)

Ninth hour of the day (Aktê, Grain; Cypris): Pleasant dining in small groups with libations and offerings before and after

Vox magica: ΙΑΕΟΥΩΙ

K (Kappa)

Contests with the waves are hard; endure!

"To fight with the waves {Κύμασι} is difficult; endure, friend."

Waves: swells, floods. *Difficult*: hard to bear, do, or deal with; painful, grievous, dangerous. *Endure*: delay.

Key Phrase: Waves.

In time, the force of ocean waves can grind down anything; they can be a metaphor for repetitive, unstoppable processes. It is difficult, dangerous, and painful to try to resist them; the sensible thing to do is to wait until they abate, or if that is impossible, then to endure the inevitable with courage.

The letter **K** is isopsephic with **BIH** (*biê*, "force, strength") and **AΔEIA** (*adeia*, "freedom from fear"). For a talisman, you could invoke Poseidon to grant endurance and fearlessness.

Numerical value = 20

Olympian: Hestia

Zodiac: Capricorn

Body: Legs

Agrippa: Leo

Lunar symbol: She-goat (11)

Hieroglyph: ⌒ (basket with handle)

Tenth hour of the day (Hesperis, Evening): Public readings by the young as directed by the elders

Vox magica: **KOPKOOYNOΩK**

Λ (Lambda)

Leave off grief, and then await delight.
"Make an end of grief {Λύπης}; hereafter expect joy.

Make an end of: stop, hinder, leave off, cease from. *Grief:* sorrow, distress, mental or bodily pain. *Hereafter:* in the future, for the rest, finally. *Expect:* await, accept, receive favorably. *Joy:* delight.

Key Phrase: Grief.

You have grieved long enough. Although you have been sad, you will be happy soon. Stop worrying, and prepare to be pleased. Turn your attention from your pain to the things that give you joy. Pain will yield to happiness. You have been through dark times, but the sun will rise again.

The letter Λ is isopsephic with **HKA** (êka, "gently, softly, smoothly"). For a talisman you might invoke Aphrodite, who oversees delight and pleasure, to grant you relief from sorrow and eventual joy.

The Olympos Oracle is unique in having this verse:[84]

Lovely bodes the widespread word all things.
"The spreading word {Λόγος} bodes all things well."

Word: oracle, prophecy, divine word, maxim, saying. *Spreading:* traveling, passing, arriving, widespread. *So:* oft-repeated, well-known. *Also:* going through, narrative. *Bodes:* shows, indicates, gives a sign, signifies, declares. *Well:* rightly, beautifully, happily, fortunately.

Key Phrase: Word.

This oracle predicts a favorable outcome, good fortune, a happy event. The circulating saying is a good indicator; the current prophecy or story is accurate. Con-

---

84. My previous translation of the Olympos (née Limyra) Oracle was based on an incorrect reading of the inscription reported in Heinevetter, *Würfel- und Buchstabenorakel*, 35. The present translation is based on the corrected text in Nollé, *Kleinasiatische Losorakel*, 241–2.

ventional wisdom gives good advice; pay attention to the wise maxim, story, or explanation.

This oracle is pregnant with ambiguity. First, it may say either that this "word" *signifies* all things well, or that all things *will go* well. Second, the word (saying) may refer to this very oracle or to some other saying, prophecy, or maxim that is current. In the Greek it is possible to take "all things" as the object of "spreading," so the meaning is "The word that spreads out (explicates, recounts) all things is the word that bodes well." That is, it is a more detailed account that signifies well or favorably.

The practical advice of this verse may be this: It tells you primarily that things will turn out well. But it also advises that you keep your eyes and ears open. For if you encounter a wise maxim, pithy saying, story, or other such words, you should pay attention, since it may beautifully, clearly, or accurately indicate the situation or the answer to your question. Be sensitive to synchronicity.

A talisman might invoke Apollo or Tychê to bring you a favorable omen or good tidings.

Numerical value = 30

Olympian: Hera

Zodiac: Aquarius

Body: Ankles

Agrippa: Virgo

Lunar symbol: Asp (12)

Hieroglyph: (lion)

Eleventh hour of the day (Dusis, Sunset): Libations with exhortations from the elders

Vox magica: ΛΟΥΛΟΕΝΗΛ

M (Mu)

Make no haste; in vain you press ahead.

"You press on in vain {Μάτην}; don't hurry; it's not useful."

Press on: press hard, drive on, urge on, hasten. *In vain*: fruitlessly, idly, falsely, at random, without reason. *Hurry*: make haste. *Useful*: beneficial, profitable, expedient.

Key Phrase: Vainly.

Don't keep busy at what you are doing, it's pointless. Haste makes waste. *Festine lente* (Lat., "Hurry slowly"). You are rushing around and working hard, but randomly and thoughtlessly. You are putting a lot of energy into wasting time. Pressing on now will be futile; wait for a better time.

The letter **M** is isopsephic with **AIKH** (*aikê*, "rush," "rapid flight") and **AΛH** (*alê*, "wandering," "distraction"). For a talisman, invoke Athena to bring you patience and prudence, to help you make slow but steady progress toward your goal.

The Olympos Oracle has this text:

Mandatory toil: the change is good.

"It is necessary to be weary with toil {Μοχθεῖν}, but the change will be admirable."

Necessary: necessary due to laws of nature, logic, fate, destiny, constraint, compulsion, duress, distress, anguish, pain, physical force, blood ties. *Be weary with toil*: labor, be weary, be distressed. *Change*: exchange. *Admirable*: fair, beautiful, good, noble.

Key Phrase: Toil.

Through toil and distress a change will be made for the better. Hard work will result in a good return. It is your fate to be weary with labor, but there will be a beautiful or noble transformation. You yourself will be ennobled. You are obliged to work hard, but the change will be good. Circumstances will cause distress, but there will be a good change or exchange. Pain will force an admirable change.

In support of this oracle, you could make a talisman invoking Hephaistos to grant you the strength and energy to bring about a change for the better.

Numerical value = 40

Olympian: Poseidon

Zodiac: Pisces

Body: Feet

Agrippa: Libra

Lunar symbol: Goat (13)

Hieroglyph: (owl: penetrating vision)

Twelfth hour of the day (Arktos, Bear): Salute to the setting Sun

Vox magica: ΜΟΡΟΘΘΟΗΠΝΑΜ

N (Nu)

Now springs forth the fitting time for all.
"Now {Νῦν} the fitting opportunity for everything arises."

Fitting: suitable, harmonious, joining, adapting, ordering. *Opportunity*: right time, critical time, season, advantage, profit, fruit, fitness, due measure (see discussion of *kairos* under **B**, Beta). *Arises*: springs up, is born, grows.

Key Phrase: Now.

Now is the suitable time for anything; the right time begins now. You are entering into a harmonious season, a time when everything is well ordered and bears fruit. An appropriate opportunity or profit is at hand; it is developing. Orderly profits are growing. The most suitable situation is now. Seize the moment; you can accomplish anything! You are entering a synchronistic period when anything is possible.

The time is right for some opportunity, but for what? Hermes is the god who brings us the wit to seize sudden, unexpected opportunities, so you could make a talisman invoking him to bring you the opportunity and the recognition of the right time to act.

The Olympos Oracle has this text:

Nike's gift enwreathes the oracle.
"A victory-bearing {Νεικηφόρον} gift enwreathes the oracle."

Victory-bearing: victory-bringing, victorious. *Gift*: anything given. *Enwreathes*: crowns, encircles, surrounds. *Oracle*: oracular response.

Key Phrase: Nike's gift.

Something will be given (to you, by you, or from one to another) that brings victory with it and will crown this oracle. The import seems to be that this gift will be the answer to the question asked of the oracle. So, for example, if the querent asked when something will happen, the gift is the sign that it's immanent.

If you want to make a talisman, invoke Nike to bring you victory or whatever the prize might be.

Numerical value = 50

Olympian: Athena

Zodiac: Aries

Body: Feet

Agrippa: Scorpio

Lunar symbol: He-goat (14)

Hieroglyph: ∿∿∿ (ripple of water)

First hour of the night

Vox magica: ΝΕΡΞΙΑΡΞΙΝ

Ξ (Xi)

Xanthic Dêô's ripened fruit awaits.

"The seasonable fruit of Dêô the golden {Ξανθῆς} awaits you."

Fruit: produce, returns, profits, results. *Golden:* yellow, golden-haired, xanthic. *Awaits:* waits for, expects.

Key Phrase: Golden.

The fruit that is due now is available for you. The ripe grain is yours for the cutting. The gifts of the goddess are yours for the taking. She has brought you the profits, results, or returns that are due. I think that the oracle is telling you that the goddess Dêô (a name for Demeter, the Grain Mother) has brought you some benefit, so perhaps you should accept the gift.

See also the oracles for Γ (Gamma) and O (Omicron), which are somewhat complementary to this one, for they warn that you will reap nothing if you do not sow. See Φ (Phi) for more on Dêô. The letter Ξ is isopsephic with ΜΑΓΕΙΑ (*mageia*, magic).

For a talisman, invoke Dêô to bring you the good results that are waiting.

The Olympos Oracle has this text:

You can pick no fruit from withered shoots.

"There is no fruit to take from a dry {Ξηρῶν} shoot."

Fruit: produce, returns, profits, results. *Take:* grasp, pick, seize, receive. *Dry:* withered, lean, harsh, haggard. *Shoot:* branch.

Key Phrase: Dry.

Don't wait too long to harvest or to take your profit. There is no good to be gained from an angry or tired young man or woman. The frayed end of a good line. Harshness and stinginess will achieve nothing. There is no advantage to overworking people or animals. You can't get blood from a turnip; you can't get water from a stone. Don't polish a turd.

This oracle advises that you not wait too long to reap your rewards, so you could make a talisman for timing and prudence. Demeter would be an appropriate goddess to invoke.

Numerical value = 60

Olympian: Aphrodite

Zodiac: Taurus

Body: Ankles

Agrippa: Water

Lunar symbol: Baboon (15)

Hieroglyph: ⬛ (lake, basin, pool)

Second hour of the night

Vox magica: ΞΟΝΟΦΟΗΝΑΞ

O (Omicron)

Out of sight are crops that are not sown.

"There are no {Οὐκ} crops to be reaped that were not sown."

Crops: fruit trees, cornfields, croplands. *Reap*: mow, cut off. *Sown*: engendered, begotten, scattered.

Key Phrase: No crops.

You reap what you sow. You will get nothing because you have given nothing. If you do not work now, there will be no reward later. If you want apples, plant apple seeds. What we spread about comes back to us. What goes around comes around. You must plan ahead in order to achieve anything. There will be no return if you do not invest. What has not been created cannot be destroyed. What has not been born cannot die.

In some ways this oracle is complementary to the previous one, Ξ (Xi), which says that the Grain Goddess has brought the fruits of your previous sowing. See also the oracle for Γ (Gamma), which promises the fruits of your labor.

For a talisman, invoke Demeter to help you exert the effort and have the foresight to make the investment now so that you will have your reward later.

Numerical value = 70

Planet: Mars

Olympian: Apollo

Zodiac: Gemini

Body: Legs

Agrippa: Mars (*Venus)

Lunar symbol: Cat (16)

Hieroglyph: 𓎛 (lasso: hunting, capturing)

Third hour of the night

Vox magica: ΟΡΝΕΟΦΑΟ

Π (Pi)

Passing many tests, you'll win the crown.
"Completing many {Πολλούς} contests, you will seize the crown."

Contests: struggles, trials, dangers. *Crown*: wreath, garland.

Key Phrase: Many tests.

If you persist in your struggles, after many trials you will succeed. Perseverance through adversity. Keep striving and victory will come. After much competition, you will emerge the winner.

The letter Π is isopsephic with ΛΗΜΑ (*lêma*, will, desire, courage, resolve, purpose). This oracle can be reinforced with a victory talisman; invoke Apollo or Heracles (founder of the Olympics) to empower it. Or invoke another god more appropriate to the contests or prize at hand.

Numerical value = 80

Olympian: Hermes

Zodiac: Cancer

Body: Knees

Agrippa: Sagittarius

Lunar symbol: Lion (17)

Hieroglyph: ☐ (reed mat or stool)

Fourth hour of the night

Vox magica: ΠΥΡΟΒΑΡΥΠ

P (Rho)

Rest awhile; you'll go more easily.

"You will go on more easily {Pᾷον} if you wait a short time."

Go on: live, continue. *Easily*: willingly, recklessly, thoughtlessly. *Wait*: stand fast, remain, stay.

Key Phrase: Easily.

If you will hold your ground for only a short time, you will be able to proceed (more easily or with greater cooperation). You'll live more easily if you take a break. You will go faster by waiting than by going now; on the other hand, delaying *too* long may provoke reckless action. By standing fast you live recklessly. By remaining where you are, you live life thoughtlessly.

The plain meaning is that everything will go more easily if you wait a bit. However, oracles are ambiguous, and you should also consider the possibility that hesitating is the easy way out—the thoughtless path. Perhaps the harder path is to be preferred. Socrates told the story of the "Choice of Heracles," in which the hero comes to two goddesses at a Y in a road. Vice (*Kakia*) entices him to a life of ease, but Virtue (*Aretê*) leads him down the harder path leading to the blessed life of the gods.[85] This led to his eventual deification. The letter P is isopsephic with ΕΓΚΑΙΝΙΑ (*engkainia*, a feast of renewal).

You might want to make a talisman for patience. Aphrodite is an appropriate goddess to invoke, for she grants ease and relaxation.

Numerical value = 100

Olympian: Zeus

Zodiac: Leo

Body: Thighs

Agrippa: Capricorn

---

85. Xenophon (II.i.21–33) in Lindsay, *Socratic Discourses by Plato and Xenophon* (London: J. M. Dent, 1910), 41–45; see also Hesiod, *Hesiod, the Homeric Hymns, and Homerica* (*Works & Days*, ll. 287–92) and Opsopaus, *The Guide to the Pythagorean Tarot* (St. Paul, MN: Llewellyn, 2001), 15–16.

Lunar symbol: Field mouse (19)

Hieroglyph: (mouth: opening, cleft, division; vagina; organ of creation)

Fifth hour of the night

Vox magica: **PEPOYTOHP**

Σ (Sigma)

"Stay thou, friend," Apollo plainly says.
"Phoibos [Apollo] speaks plainly {Σαφῶς}, 'Stay, friend.'"

Plainly: distinctly, certainly. *Stay*: wait, stand fast, remain.

Key Phrase: Plainly.

Neither advance nor retreat; wait or hold your ground, as appropriate; the best action is inaction. Don't travel. Stay firm; don't let yourself be swayed. "Phoibos" refers to Apollo as Bright and Pure, which also characterizes the clarity of his advice in this oracle.

A talisman could invoke Phoibos Apollo for patience and steadfastness.

Numerical value = 200

Olympian: Demeter

Zodiac: Virgo

Body: Belly

Agrippa: Aquarius

Lunar symbol: Deer (20)

Hieroglyph: ⌐ (folded cloth)

Sixth hour of the night

Vox magica: ΣΕΣΕΝΜΕΝΟΥΡΕΣ

T (Tau)

Take release from present circumstance.

"You will have release from the {Tῶν} present circumstances."

Release: deliverance, setting free, ransoming, means of release, parting. *Present*: nearby. *Circumstances*: events, mishaps, misfortune, conjunction. *Rarely*: good luck, happy issue.

Key Phrase: The events.

You will be rescued! Your misfortune will come to an end. You will be given a way out of present circumstances. You are between a rock and a hard place, but you will get out. All your mishaps will come to an end. Leave present events behind. If you have been having good luck, that too may be departing.

You can make a talisman for deliverance from the current situation. Pray to the warrior gods Ares and Athena for their aid.

Numerical value = 300

Olympian: Hephaistos

Zodiac: Libra

Body: Back

Agrippa: Pisces

Lunar symbol: Multiform maiden [86] (21)

Hieroglyph: ⌓ (bun or bread loaf: food, offering)

Seventh hour of the night

Vox magica: ΤΑΥΡΟΠΟΛΙΤ

---

86. Grk., *polymorphos parthenos*, a name for the goddess Hekate.

Y (Upsilon)

Useless toil: this wedding isn't thine!

"This wedding {Ὑμήν} is not yours; do not labor in vain."

Wedding: Hymên, wedding hymn, membrane. *Labor*: toil. *In vain*: fruitlessly, idly, falsely, at random, without reason.

Key Phrase: Wedding.

The person whom you are trying to woo will not be yours. This romance or relationship will not be permanent. Give it up. Be sensible. You have not made a good choice of someone to pursue. Do not pretend that you are interested in marriage. Don't pursue the partnership (of any kind); you are wasting your time. The Oracle advises you to abandon some alliance or union that you have been pursuing.

The letter Y is isopsephic with ΚΑΙΡΟΣ (*kairos*, "opportune time"), on which, see the discussion for B (Beta). For a talisman, invoke Athena for prudence in dealing with the situation or Hera for marriage issues specifically.

The Olympos Oracle has this text:

Undertaking fine is held by deed.

"The affair holds a noble undertaking {Ὑπόσχεσιν}."

Affair: deed, act, issue. *Holds*: involves, implies, gives cause for, holds fast, hinders, guides, steers. *Noble*: high-born, high-minded, excellent, notable. *Undertaking*: engagement, promise, profession.

Key Phrase: Undertaking.

There is some issue to be resolved, or some action is under consideration; it involves high-mindedness, either in commitment, deed, or professional pursuit. The oracle may tell us that the affair is admirable due to this noble element, or that the situation may guide us to seek the appropriate noble undertaking or profession. The hero's quest. On the other hand, the oracle may mean that the situation hinders this fine undertaking. Thus you should try to understand the situation: does it demand an excellent undertaking or impede it?

For a talisman, you might invoke Athena to grant you high-minded courage for this noble undertaking.

Numerical value = 400

Planet: Jupiter

Olympian: Ares

Zodiac: Scorpio

Body: Diaphragm

Agrippa: Jupiter (*Mercury)

Lunar symbol: Torch (22)

Hieroglyph: (quail chick)

Eighth hour of the night

Vox magica: ΥΠΕΦΕΝΟΥΡΥ

Φ (Phi)

Forthwith plant! For Dêô fosters well.

"Plant {Φύτευε}! For Dêô will nourish everything beautifully."

Plant: beget, engender, produce, bring about, cause. *Nourish*: cause to grow, cause to increase, rear, educate, develop, form, tend, guard, foster, cherish, maintain, support, keep, thicken. *Beautifully*: well, happily, rightly, deservedly, nobly, honorably, thoroughly.

Key Phrase: Plant.

Plant your crops or vegetable garden, and the Grain Mother will make them grow well. Start your project, for the goddess will bring it to fruition. She will care for it, and it will come out very well. Plant your seeds (of any sort), and the goddess will help you to cultivate them productively. Make a baby, for it will grow up beautiful and noble, for the goddess will foster the child's development.

Dêô is a name for Demeter, the Grain Mother; see also under Ξ (Xi). I believe this oracle is advising you to have faith in the goddess. In the myth of the Eleusinian Mysteries, the disguised goddess Demeter secretly puts the infant Demophoön, who is under her care, in the fire each night, burning away his mortality so that he will become godlike. When the child's mother discovers what is being done, she cries out in alarm and ruins the alchemical process. "Ye mortals are unknowing and thoughtless," admonishes the goddess, "ye know not whether good or evil comes your way." Make a beginning and have faith that Dêô will bring forth something beautiful. The letter Φ is isopsephic with ΤΟ ΠΑΝ (*To Pan*, The All).

Invoke Dêô to empower a talisman for divine guidance and support to bring this wonderful enterprise to fruition.

The Olympos Oracle has this text:

Faultily you act, and blame the gods.

"Having done something carelessly {Φαύλως}, you will thereafter blame the gods."

Done: caused, accomplished, made, managed, negotiated, transacted, practiced, fared. *Carelessly*: thoughtlessly, indifferently.

Key Phrase: Faultily.

Take responsibility for your actions (or inactions); don't blame the gods (or the universe, or fate, or society, or nature) for your own failings, for your thought- less or careless actions. The ancient Greeks said, "Hermes will help you get your wagon unstuck, but only if you push on it." Another old story told of a ship that was wrecked. Everyone was in the water, and one man was desperately calling on Athena. Another said, "Sure, pray to Athena, but don't forget to move your arms!"

You might want to make a talisman to help you be more responsible and to have a greater sense of responsibility. Pray to Athena to grant you this strength and wisdom.

Numerical value = 500

Olympian: Artemis

Zodiac: Sagittarius

Body: Breast

Agrippa: Air

Lunar symbol: Lightning (23)

Hieroglyph: ✍ (horned viper: a manifestation of Horus)

Ninth hour of the night

Vox magica: ΦΙΜΕΜΑΜΕΦ

X (Khi)

"Happily press on!" says Zeus himself.
"'Rejoicing {Χαίρων}, press on!' Zeus himself says this."

Rejoicing: being glad, delighted, joyful, faring well, safely. *Press on*: press hard, drive on, urge on, hasten. *Says*: bids you do.

Key Phrase: Rejoicing.

Charge ahead! Keep working with joy in your heart. Zeus urges you forward, even commands you! Act with the confidence that you will fare well and be safe. With joy, hasten the matter or yourself forward. Lean hard on it, but stay happy.

This oracle is quite clear: you should act with decision and haste, not stressed out or anxious, but with joy and confidence. I think of someone doing what they are trained and skilled at doing. The expert healer starts the treatment; the warrior charges into the fray; the witch or wizard starts the spell. However, the oracle definitely implies that you will have to work hard, while taking pleasure in the effort. That Zeus himself speaks may imply that the matter involves leadership, authority, or some other activity in which Zeus is involved, such as parenting. Note that the oracle does not guarantee success, only that you will fare well in your effort. The letter X is isopsephic with ΚΟΣΜΟΣ (Cosmos) and ΕΥΠΡΑΓΙΑ (*eupragia*, well-being, welfare, success).

Zeus has brought you this good news, so invoke him for a talisman bringing the energy and confidence to press on joyfully.

The Olympos Oracle says:

Happy end fulfills this golden word.
"Succeeding, wanderer, you will fulfill this golden {Χρυσοῦν} oracle."

Succeeding: gaining your end, hitting the mark, meeting someone. *Fulfill*: bring to pass, cause, accomplish. *Golden*: magnificent, splendid.

Key Phrase: Golden.

"Golden" may be a metaphor for rich, noble, excellent, etc. This admirable oracle will be fulfilled by you attaining your ends, or a mere chance meeting could constitute the golden event. Rejoice, you will succeed!

The oracle does not specify the goal at which you'll succeed, and if it is not obvious, your interpretation will need to consider the possibilities and pick the wisest choice. The letter X is isopsephic with ΚΟΣΜΟΣ (Cosmos) and ΕΥΠΡΑΓΙΑ (*eupragia*, "well-being," "welfare," "success").

Hermes is the god of the happy happenstance, so invoke him in a talisman to bring good luck and success.

Numerical value = 600

Olympian: Hestia

Zodiac: Capricorn

Body: Shoulders and hands

Agrippa: Fire

Lunar symbol: Garland (24)

Hieroglyph: ◉ (placenta, sieve, or ball of string?)

Tenth hour of the night

Vox magica: ΧΕΝΝΕΟΦΕΟΧ

Ψ (Psi)

Proper is this judgment from the gods.
"You have this righteous judgment {Ψῆφον} from the gods."

Righteous: just, fitting, meet, fair. *Judgment*: resolve, decree, vote.

Key Phrase: Judgment.

Literally, a *psêphos* (Lat., *calculus*) is a stone used for divination, voting, counting, and similar purposes, so this oracle refers to collective judgment rather than individual judgment. This implies that the majority of the gods concur in this judgment, and that this judgment is appropriate, fair, and righteous, though there is no implication that the result is that desired by the querent. Accept it and move on.

This oracle is enigmatic; the puzzled querent might ask, "What judgment?" In some cases the answer will be obvious, because the querent will have been subject to some decision or is facing one in the near future. The oracle tells you that it's just and comes from the gods. In the absence of an obvious judgment affecting the querent, you may look for any recent significant occurrence, which might be understood as divine judgment. The oracle tells you to see it this way. If you can't solve the enigma, do another divination asking for clarification. The letter Ψ is isopsephic with ΚΡΙΤΟΣ (*kritos*, "chosen," "selected," "excellent").

You might make a talisman to strengthen justice, for which Zeus and Dikê are appropriate patrons.

Numerical value = 700

Olympian: Hera

Zodiac: Aquarius

Body: Neck

Agrippa: Spirit

Lunar symbol: Herald's wand (caduceus) (25)

Hieroglyph: ▢⃒ (reed mat or stool + folded cloth)

Eleventh hour of the night

Vox magica: ΨΥΧΟΜΠΟΙΑΨ

Ω (Omega)

Otiose the fruit that's plucked unripe.

"If you take unripe {Ὠμήν} fruit, it won't be useful."

Take: grasp, pick, seize, receive. *Unripe*: savage, cruel, rough, untimely, uncooked. *Fruit*: fruit time, autumn, summer bloom, bloom of youth. *Useful*: suitable, apt, profitable, good, serviceable, fit.

Key Phrase: Unripe fruit.

If you pick your fruit too soon, you will have a bad harvest. More abstractly, too early grasping of the fruits of your labor (whether the taking is voluntary or necessary) will yield a poor return; the rewards will not be suitable for their purpose. Don't be impatient, or the results will be inferior. If someone has a rough youth, he or she won't be a well-adjusted adult.

The letter Ω is isopsephic with ΚΥΡΙΟΣ (*Kurios*, "Lord"), a title that is often applied to the Greek gods. Invoke Demeter, the Grain Mother, in a talisman for patience and good timing.

Numerical value = 800

Planet: Saturn

Olympian: Poseidon

Zodiac: Pisces

Body: Head

Agrippa: Saturn (*Moon)

Lunar symbol: Child (26)

Hieroglyph: ℚ (coil of rope or cursive quail chick)

Twelfth hour of the night

Vox magica: ΩΡΙΩΝ

Letter	Oracle Verse	Initial Word	Key Phrase
A (Alpha)	All these things, he says, you'll do quite well!	Ἅπαντα	All [things]
B (Beta)	Briefly wait; the time's not right for thee. (Both Apollo, Fortune bring thee aid.)	Βραχύ (Βοηθόν)	Brief [delay] (Helper)
Γ (Gamma)	Gaia gives thee ripe fruit from thy work.	Γῆ	Gaia
Δ (Delta)	Dodge the dreadful deeds, avoiding harm. (Drive ill-timed is weak before the rules.)	Δεινῶν (Δύναμις)	Dreadful (Strength)
E (Epsilon)	Eager art thou for right wedding's fruits.	Ἐρᾷς	Desire
Z (Zeta)	Zealously avoid the harmful storm!	Ζάλην	Storm
H (Eta)	Helios, all-watcher, watches thee.	Ἥλιος	Helios
Θ (Theta)	Thou hast gods as comrades and as aides. (Thou hast gods as helpers on this path.)	Θεούς (Θεούς)	Gods (Gods)
I (Iota)	In all things, thou shalt excel—with sweat!	Ἱδρῶτες	Sweat
K (Kappa)	Contests with the waves are hard; endure!	Κύμασι	Waves
Λ (Lambda)	Leave off grief, and then await delight. (Lovely bodes the widespread word all things.)	Λύπης (Λόγος)	Grief (Word)
M (Mu)	Make no haste; in vain you press ahead. (Mandatory toil: the change is good.)	Μάτην (Μοχθεῖν)	Vainly (Toil)

Letter	Oracle Verse	Initial Word	Key Phrase
N (Nu)	Now springs forth the fitting time for all. (Nike's gift enwreathes the oracle.)	Νῦν (Νεικηφόρον)	Now (Nike's gift)
Ξ (Xi)	Xanthic Dêô's ripened fruit awaits. (You can pick no fruit from withered shoots.)	Ξανθῆς (Ξηρῶν)	Golden (Dry)
O (Omicron)	Out of sight are crops that are not sown.	Οὐκ	No [crops]
Π (Pi)	Passing many tests, you'll win the crown.	Πολλούς	Many [tests]
Ρ (Rho)	Rest awhile; you'll go more easily.	Ρᾷον	Easily
Σ (Sigma)	"Stay thou, friend," Apollo plainly says.	Σαφῶς	Plainly
Τ (Tau)	Take release from present circumstance.	Τῶν	The [events]
Υ (Upsilon)	Useless toil: this wedding isn't thine! (Undertaking fine is held by deed.)	Ὑμήν (Ὑπόσχεσιν)	Wedding (Undertaking)
Φ (Phi)	Forthwith Plant! For Dêô fosters well. (Faultily you act, and blame the gods.)	Φύτευε (Φαύλως)	Plant (Faultily)
Χ (Khi)	"Happily press on!" says Zeus himself. (Happy end fulfills this golden word.)	Χαίρων (Χρυσοῦν)	Rejoicing (Golden)
Ψ (Psi)	Proper is this judgment from the gods.	Ψῆφον	Judgment
Ω (Omega)	Otiose the fruit that's plucked unripe.	Ὠμήν	Unripe [fruit]

Table 7. Alphabet Oracle Verses.

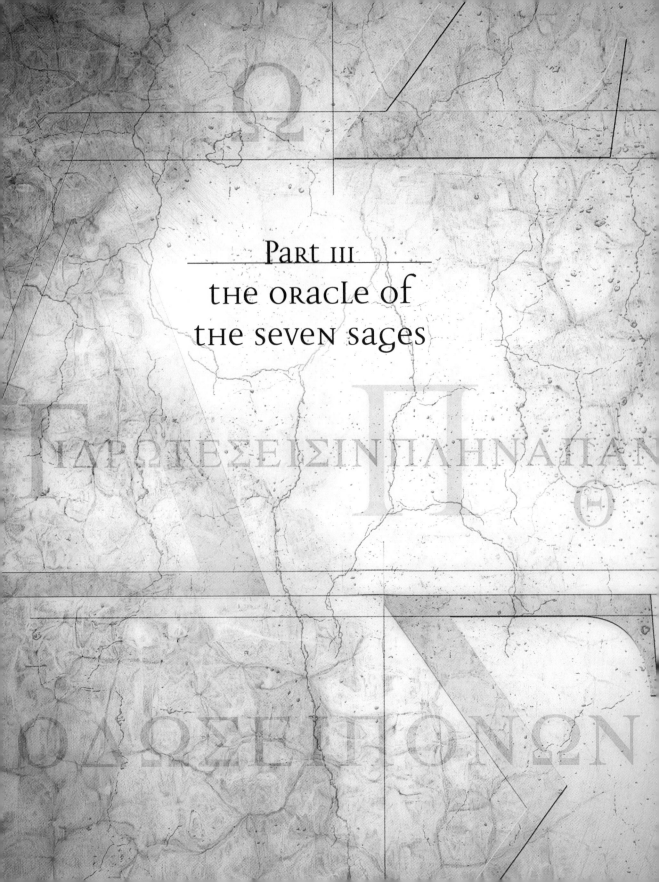

Part III
the oracle of
the seven sages

Chapter 8

The Counsels of the Seven Sages

In this chapter, you will learn about the Counsels of the Seven Sages, an ancient collection of 147 pithy and enigmatic sayings, which were inscribed on a tablet at the Temple of Apollo at Delphi. They are the text for the Oracle of the Seven Sages. You will learn the story of their origin and the significance of the number 147. I will also explain a meditative practice of daily divination by which you can absorb the wisdom of the Seven Sages, and how to make talismans to help you to live by this wisdom. This information will help you to use the Oracle of the Seven Sages more effectively.

The Origin of the Counsels of the Seven

Plutarch of Chaeronea (ca. 46–ca. 120 CE), who was High Priest of Apollo at Delphi and an expert in sacred lore, tells an interesting tale.[87] One day in the sixth century BCE, some fishermen from the island of Cos hauled in their nets, and some young men of Miletus, who were there, offered to buy their catch, sight unseen. When they inspected the contents, they found a heavy golden tripod that had belonged to Helen of Troy.

Before continuing with the story, let me say a little about tripods, which were important in Greek culture from the earliest times.[88] They were three-legged stands, generally made of bronze or other metals, and often supported a built-in cauldron or shallow dish. They were used for many ordinary purposes, such as cooking, but also as altars for making

---

87. The story exists in several versions. I have supplemented Plutarch's version (*Life of Solon*, ch. 4) with details from Diogenes Laertius, *Lives of the Eminent Philosophers* (I.28–34), and Stanley, *The History of Philosophy Containing the Lives, Opinions, Actions, and Discourses of the Philosophers of Every Sect* (London: A. Millar, 1743), 4.

88. Papalexandrou, *Warriors, Youths, and Tripods in Early Greece* (Lanham, MD: Lexington Books, 2005), 47–51.

offerings to the gods. They were often awarded as prizes in athletic games and dramatic contests, given by guests to their hosts, or dedicated by worshippers to the gods. In mythology, the craft god Hephaistos is supposed to have made magical tripods that moved about by themselves and brought food to the gods in their banquets. However, tripods are most closely associated with Apollo. For example, Aeneas, the hero who escaped fallen Troy and founded Rome, received oracles from the tripod at the temple of Apollo in Delos. To prophesy, the Pythia, the High Priestess of Apollo at Delphi, sat on a slab supported by a tripod over a cleft in the earth, from which emerged the trance-inducing spirit of Pythôn (*pneuma Puthônos*). One of the earliest myths depicted in Greek art tells how Heracles (half-brother of Apollo) stole the Delphic tripod after he was denied advice on how he could be purified of bloodguilt. They fought over it until Zeus separated them with a lightning bolt; the tripod was returned to Delphi, and Heracles was purified.

The ancients disagreed about the origin of Helen's Tripod. Some said it was a sacred heirloom in the family of her husband Menelaos, which was originally given to his grand-father Pelops by Hephaistos as a wedding gift, and that Helen had taken it when she ran away with Paris. Others said that it was booty from the sack of Troy, where perhaps it stood in the temple beside the Palladion—the statue of Pallas Athena—that guarded the city. In any case, Helen threw it into the ocean when she was being brought back to Sparta from Troy.

The tripod is a symbol of wisdom, especially practical wisdom, such as the Seven Sages possessed, and in particular the ability to deliver wisdom in short maxims. Therefore the Pythia sat upon a tripod to deliver her oracles from the god. But why did Helen throw her tripod overboard? Perhaps because of her dishonest behavior or her conflicted loyalties to Sparta and Troy. In any case, *her* explanation was that the tripod would be a source of conflict, and so it was.

Back to our story. True to Helen's prophecy, a fight broke out about who would keep such a precious artifact. The Milesians said they had bought everything fair and square; the Coans said that they were selling only the fish. Soon the dispute escalated into a war between the cities. They sent a delegation to the Temple of Apollo at Delphi to consult the Oracle. "Who should possess the tripod?" the Milesians asked, and the Pythia replied:

> *Com'st thou Milesian to consult my shrine?*
> *The Tripod to the wisest I assign.*[89]

---

89. Translation from Stanley, *The History of Philosophy*, 4.

The Coans received this reply:

> *No end of strife, until it reach the Seer*
> *Whose presence makes Past, Present, Future clear.*[90]

After much discussion, the Milesians and Coans agreed that the god meant the Milesian philosopher Thales, known for his mathematical and scientific knowledge, including the ability to predict eclipses and the weather. He was also an expert in divine matters and said "all things are full of gods." Therefore, they presented the tripod to him. But Thales said, "I am not the wisest. That honor belongs to Bias of Priene, for no judge is wiser" and so he sent the tripod to Bias. But Bias likewise judged himself to be unworthy of the honor, and sent the tripod on to Pittacus of Mytilene, who had brought democracy to Lesbos. And so the tripod was passed on, to Chilon of Sparta, to Cleobulus of Lindus, who had studied philosophy in Egypt, to Periander of Corinth, known for his justice, each Sage humbly sending it on to another, whom he deemed more worthy, until it came to Solon of Athens, who had instituted the Athenian constitution. Solon thought, "I am a mere statesman; the prize should go to someone with knowledge of the natural and the divine," and so he sent the tripod to Thales.

Thus the tripod made the circuit of the Seven Sages. They consulted among themselves and realized that whatever wisdom they had, they owed to Apollo, who is the wisest god, and that the tripod should be dedicated in his temple. The Seven traveled together to Delphi, where they erected a marble stele (Grk., *stêlê*), a tablet on which they engraved their wisdom.[91] Thales contributed "Know thyself." Solon contributed "Nothing too much." Together they had 147 wise maxims engraved on the stele. Thus they offered the fruit of their wisdom to the god.

What were these gems of ancient wisdom? They might have been lost in the ruins of Delphi, but a certain Johannes Stobaeus, who lived in Macedonia in the fifth century CE, kept extensive notes on everything that he read. Among them is "Sosiades's Counsels of the Seven Sages," which lists 147 short maxims.[92] There is no explanation, but a reasonable

---

90. Diogenes Laertius, *Lives of the Eminent Philosphers*, I.33.

91. Plato, *The Dialogues of Plato* (New York: Scribners, 1899), *Protagoras*, 343a–b. Plato's list of the Seven Sages has Myson of Chen instead of Periander.

92. "Counsels of the Seven Sages" is *Tôn Hepta Sophôn Hypothêkai* in Ancient Greek and *Septem Sapientum Sententiae* in Latin.

assumption is that the (otherwise unknown) philosopher Sosiades copied them down from the Tablet at Delphi.

Many scholars were skeptical about the existence of this Tablet of the Seven Sages; after all, there are many legends about engraved tablets containing ancient wisdom. This changed in 1966 when archaeologists found the base of a stele in present-day Afghanistan. It was engraved with a dedication by Klearchos, one of Aristotle's students in the fourth century BCE, who traveled throughout the ancient world, even as far as India. In his dedication he says that he has very carefully copied the Wise Sayings of the Men of Old in the most holy Pythian Shrine, and has set them up in that faraway place so that their wisdom could illuminate the people there. Unfortunately, the stele that the base supported, which contained the maxims, has been lost except for a small fragment, but we have a good idea what they were, thanks to a happy accident. Apparently the stone cutter ran out of room on the stele and had to squeeze the last five lines on the base next to the dedication. (I imagine Klearchos was pretty unhappy with this sloppy carving job, and I hope he didn't pay the full amount in advance!) These five lines are also the last five lines in Stobaeus's text, and the surviving fragment of the stele contains two maxims in Stobaeus's order. This is good evidence that Stobaeus's text is the correct one, and therefore it is the text I have used in the following Oracle of the Seven Sages.[93]

The Importance of 147

Why 147, you ask? It seems to be an unusual and arbitrary number, but it's not. For 147 is 3 times 49, and there is evidence that the tablet was engraved in three columns of text: some of the surviving manuscript copies are arranged in three columns, and some of the errors in the others can be explained if the scribe were copying from an original in three columns. (See figure 7, page 154, for a depiction of how it might have looked.) In addition, we know that Solon's Laws, oracle collections, and other important texts were inscribed on three-sided pillars.[94] Moreover, 49 is 7 times 7. There were, of course, Seven Sages, and

93. For the history of the Stobaeus's text and Klearchos's stele, see Oikonomides, "Records of 'The Commandments of the Wise Men' in the 3rd c. B.C.," *Classical Bulletin* 63 (1987), who also describes several third century BCE fragmentary pillars and a papyrus fragment that record many of the Counsels of the Seven in the same order as Sosiades, but there are minor differences in text and order. On this basis, he constructs a partial "new text," which I have not used because it is too fragmentary.

94. These were called *kurbeis* (sing., *kurbis*) and usually made of three wooden tablets, joined side-by-side and tapered, something like an obelisk, set in a stone base (Davis, "Axones and Kurbeis," *Historia* 60, 1, 2011: 1–35).

seven is Apollo's sacred number. In the ancient Greek sacred lunar month, the seventh day (that is, the first quarter moon) is consecrated to Apollo and celebrated as his birthday (recall chapter 2). The number seven is especially appropriate to divination, as the Pythagorean *Theology of Arithmetic* explains:

> Since everything comes together and is distinguished by coincidence and in a critical manner at the place of the *hebdomad* (number 7), Pythagoreans called it "critical time" (*kairos*) and "Fortune" (*Tychê*).[95]

Moreover, the *Theology of Arithmetic* tells us that "Athena" is a Pythagorean name for the number 7, for it is not a product of any of the other numbers of the decad, except one (considered neither odd nor even), as Athena was born of neither mother (even number) nor father (odd number), but from The Inexpressible One (identified with the mind of Zeus). The name of the related Roman goddess, Minerva, comes from *mens* (Lat., for "mind"; Grk., *nous*) and symbolizes central or innermost thought. Furthermore, like Athena, the number seven is a virgin and unwed, for it does not produce any other numbers in the decad and has a masculine character (odd number). Finally, the third day is sacred to Athena as her birthday, and Pythagoreans call the triad (number 3) "Prudence" and "Wisdom" (*Phronêsis*), for prudence is when people act correctly in the present, look ahead to the future, and gain experience from the past, and wisdom has knowledge (*gnôsis*) of the three parts of time. Bernardus Silvestris says perfect wisdom arises from three powers: wit (the power of discovery: future), reason (the power of discerning what has been discovered: present), and memory (the power of retention: past).[96] [See the Alphabet Oracle under (B) Beta for a discussion of *kairos*, chapter 6 for the number seven, and the Oracle of the Seven Sages for *phronêsis* (Oracle 17 [1-3-3] "Practice prudence") and *Tychê* (Oracle 68 [2-3-5] "Acknowledge Fortune").]

In summary, 147 is a symbolic number closely connected with Apollo and his Seven Sages, but also with Athena, goddess of wisdom.

---

95. Translation adapted from Iamblichus, *The Theology of Arithmetic,* 99; see also Iamblichus, *Theoulogumena Arithmeticae,* ¶53; p. 70, lines 22–4.

96. Iamblichus, *The Theology of Arithmetic,* 51; and Iamblichus, *Theoulogumena Arithmeticae,* ¶14; p. 16, lines 17–22. On Minerva and wisdom, see Bernardus, *Commentary on the First Six Books,* ¶68; p. 47; and Watkins, *The American Heritage Dictionary of Indo-European Roots* (Boston, MA: Houghton Mifflin, 2000), s.v. men-[1].

Meditating on the Counsels of the Seven

I know of no evidence that the Counsels of the Seven were used for divination in the ancient world, but it's not an unreasonable supposition. The engraved Counsels were venerated. Socrates is said to have bowed down before them. People came to Delphi seeking oracles from Apollo. Might they not, while contemplating the Tablet, have felt that one of the maxims especially spoke to them, and have taken that as a sign from the god? Perhaps, as with the alphabet and dice oracles, a table stood nearby with dice or some other means of letting the god choose an oracle for the querent. Or an attendant priest might have cast the lots. Chilon himself said, "Do not hate divination." In any case, I think *you* will find the Oracle of the Seven Sages to be a valuable guide.

Plato and other ancient philosophers recommended the Counsels of the Seven as a basis for Greek education. (It is still a good way to learn Ancient Greek. Most of the maxims are two words long, and the rest are three or four. The grammatical forms are simple.) As the distilled wisdom of the Seven Sages, the Counsels are good advice for living your life. They are terse: wisdom in concentrated form. "Say not few things in many words," Pythagoras advised, "but much in few words." [97] Because of their brevity, they also tend to be ambiguous, more like Zen koans. Therefore, they invited discussion and interpretation. In this way ancient Greeks refined their own wisdom. (I explained the importance of enigmatic oracles in chapter 2.)

Contemplation on the Counsels of the Seven can be a valuable spiritual practice for you, too. If you meditate on one per day, it will take you thrice seven weeks to get through all 147 of them. This is precisely five of the sacred lunar months of the ancient Greeks. A little explanation is in order. Normally "hollow months" of twenty-nine days alternated with "full months" of thirty days to approximate the lunar month of about 29 ½ days (occasionally an extra full month was inserted to keep the lunar calendar in harmony with the sun). Therefore, five alternating months, starting with a hollow month, is exactly 147 days (147 = 29 + 30 + 29 + 30 + 29). Start on the new moon, which according to ancient practice is the first sighting of the young moon, which typically occurs a day or two after her conjunction with the sun.

Alternately, instead of working through them in order, you can allow the Oracle to choose your daily meditation. Simply cast the Oracle while asking a question such as,

---

97. Guthrie, *The Pythagorean Sourcebook and Library* (Grand Rapids, MI: Phanes, 1987), 273, #158.

"What is it best for me to contemplate today?" or "What is the best advice for today?" This is one of my daily practices. It's amazing how relevant the advice can be!

Either way, as you go through your day, think about the chosen oracle from time to time and what it means to you. This will deepen your understanding of the oracle and how it can be applied to all sorts of questions.

Although you do not need to know Ancient Greek to use the Oracle of the Seven Sages, I have provided the original Greek and a Latin translation for each of the oracles. So if you are studying either of these languages, you can use your daily meditation as an opportunity to learn the day's oracle in Greek or Latin.

Talismans for the Counsels of the Seven

The Oracle of the Seven Sages offers you advice, which you would be wise to take, but it sometimes takes willpower to follow this advice. A talisman can help by bringing you the strength to obey the Oracle's guidance; at the very least, it serves as a reminder. To create such as talisman, you can use the procedures and rituals for alphabet talismans (see the section "Alphabet Magic" in chapter 6). Inscribe or paint the Greek text of the oracle on a *lamella* (flat object). You can find the Greek with the individual oracles in chapter 10, or if you want it to be more authentic looking, you can copy the archaic Greek from figure 7 (page 154). You can add the English or Latin translations, if you like. For potentiation (step 5), speak aloud and concentrate on the text of the oracle or your interpretation of it.

Chapter 9

Consulting the Seven Sages

In this chapter, you will learn how to cast the Oracle of the Seven Sages. As with the Alphabet Oracle, there are a variety of methods, and I suggest you read them all and then pick one or two to try out and practice. After the methods, I will explain the interpretive aids I've provided with the oracle texts. As in the Alphabet Oracle, they will help you to understand the range of meanings of the Greek words so that you can use the text more effectively for divination. The chapter ends with table 8, *Key for Consulting the Oracle of the Seven Sages*.

Methods for Consulting the Seven Sages

The Oracle of the Seven Sages can be consulted using beads or pebbles, coins or other disks, special dice and teetotums, and even dominoes. All of them depend on casting three numbers, which I call the Column (C), Heptad (H), and Maxim (M), abbreviated C-H-M.

Bead and Pebble Methods

The easiest way to consult the Oracle of the Seven Sages is by the bead method, which uses a long string of beads such as a mala. Pick up the string with both hands, spaced well apart. Let the god guide where you place them. Count off three beads at a time, alternating your hands. Continue until there are one, two, or three beads remaining between your hands; the number determines the "suit," that is, the group of forty-nine, which would be one of the three columns on the engraved tablet; call it C. If we suppose that each column was divided into seven *heptads* (groups of seven), then you can determine the heptad H by starting again and counting off beads seven at a time until between one and seven are left. To determine the maxim M within the heptad, count off by sevens one last time. Use these three numbers, *C-H-M*, to find the oracle in table 8. For example, suppose that when you count by threes, you end up with one left (so $C = 1$). When you count by sevens the first time, you end up with four left (so $H = 4$), and when you count by sevens the second time, two remain ($M = 2$). Look up 1-4-2 in the table and you will find Oracle (23) "Desire wisdom." If you want, you can calculate the oracle's number directly by $49 \times (C{-}1) + 7 \times (H{-}1) + M$. In this case $49 \times (1{-}1) + 7 \times (4{-}1) + 2 = 23$.

You can use a similar method with a container of beans, pebbles, unstrung beads, marbles, or other small objects. Take out a large handful and count them back into the container three or seven at a time to get *C-H-M*.

By the way, I will tell you a little trick that I use when counting the beads or pebbles by sevens, since you may get confused counting 1-2-3-4-5-6-7 while you are holding other numbers (*C*, *H*) in your head. Instead of counting to seven, I move or deposit three beads, then a single one, then another three. You can see these numbers visually without counting. (Esoterically, this 3-1-3 pattern corresponds to the three planets below the Sun [Moon, Mercury, Venus], the Sun in the center, and the three planets above the Sun [Mars, Jupiter, Saturn]. These are also the Seven Vowels, AEH–I–OYΩ.)

Coin Methods

If you don't have beads available, then you can use a variant of the coin method that I explained for the Alphabet Oracle (see chapter 5). You will need fourteen coins or disks of three kinds: two of one kind and six each of the other two kinds. For an example, I will use two quarters, six nickels, and six pennies. Toss the coins. The number of quarter tails *plus one* is the column *C*, the number of nickel tails *plus one* is the heptad *H*, and the number of penny tails *plus one* is the maxim *M*. Look up oracle *C-H-M*. For example, suppose we cast the coins and both quarters are heads, three nickels are tails, and one penny is a tail. Write down the number of tails *plus one* for each coin, separated by dashes: 1-4-2, which is Oracle (23) "Desire Wisdom."

Of course, you actually only need six coins or disks to use the coin method. Cast two of them to determine the column *C*, then cast all six to determine the heptad *H*, and finally cast all six again to determine the maxim *M*. In fact, you can do it with one coin, tossed fourteen times! (But you are likely to lose count unless you write the numbers down.) You can also use a vessel containing a few dozen beans, pebbles, or beads of two colors (interpreted as heads and tails). Draw out two to determine *C*, six to determine *H*, and six more to determine *M*.

Dice and Teetotum Methods

You can use special dice, with three sides and seven sides, to consult the Seven Sages. You can buy these dice, made for games—search for them online—or make your own. For a three-sided long die, make a triangular prism that is several times longer than it is wide (so it won't land on its triangular ends). Mark the three faces of the prism (with pips, for example) to indicate the column C. A seven-sided die has the form of a pentagonal (five-sided) prism with a length about equal to its width. Therefore, it will be about equally likely to land on each of its seven sides. You can use two of these dice, or cast one twice, to determine the heptad H and the maxim M. Since these dice can land with an edge upmost, you should always read the face that lands down. Manufactured three- and seven-sided dice sometimes have the numbers by the edges, in which case you can read the upmost edge.

Instead of dice, you can use three- and seven-sided teetotums, which you will have to make yourself. Since they have an odd number of sides, you read the side that faces down. The teetotum method is perhaps the most symbolically significant method, since both three and seven are sacred numbers (the third day of the lunar month is sacred to Athena, and the seventh to Apollo), and teetotums represent the cosmos revolving on the Spindle of Destiny.

Dominoes Method

Another way to consult the Oracle of the Seven Sages is with ordinary dominoes. A typical set of dominoes contains twenty-eight tiles, called "bones" or "stones," each with two squares containing six or less pips. Spread the bones out facedown on a smooth surface and mix them up. Then let the god guide you to pick two, and arrange them side by side with their long sides horizontal. Turn over the left bone. If one square is odd (masculine) and the other even (feminine), then the cast is androgynous, which refers to the first column, for according to Pythagorean numerology, the number 1 is neither odd nor even (it is the unity preceding duality). Therefore, write down 1. If both squares have an even number of spots, it is wholly feminine, and we interpret it as the second column (write down 2). If both are odd, then it is completely masculine, which is the third column (write down 3). (A blank square is even.) Now turn over the second bone. The square on the left determines the heptad and the square on the right determines the maxim within the heptad; *add one* in each case. If C is the number you wrote down for the column, H is the number of spots in the left square *plus one*, and M is the number on the right square *plus one*, then use C-H-M to find the oracle, as already described. For example, suppose you draw the following bones:

The left bone is even + odd, therefore androgynous, so $C = 1$. The right bone is 3-1, so $H = 4$ and $M = 2$. Therefore, the oracle is 1-4-2, (23) "Desire Wisdom."

Interpretation

Most of the Counsels are two words long in Ancient Greek, the rest are three or four words long. Plato commented on their Spartan terseness. Even to the ancient Greeks they were ambiguous, which meant that they were topics for discussion and contemplation. What does it mean to "know thyself"? They are literally *enigmas*, that is, oracular riddles meant to be puzzled out. As explained in chapter 2, it is a characteristic of divine oracles to be enigmas. The Neoplatonic philosopher Porphyry (ca. 234–ca. 305 CE) said that the gods deliver oracles as enigmas to exercise our minds and to hide their meaning from the foolish. Oracles express truths that cannot be adequately expressed in words, and so their meanings must be grasped through contemplation.

The Counsels are like spells, divine inspirations prescribed by the Sages as medicine for the soul. They must be taken in and chewed over in order to have their effect. Digest them and they will be absorbed in your soul to make it strong and healthy.

The ambiguity of oracles also reflects the openness of the future. Like the properties of a particle in quantum mechanics, the meaning of an oracle is not fixed until it is interpreted, and so it is critically important that its first interpretation be the best one. The oracle is given by the gods, but by deciding on an interpretation you are deciding on your future. Choose wisely! (See chapters 2 and 3 for more on interpreting oracles and accepting them.)

How can English speakers, who might have no Ancient Greek, hope to understand these ambiguous, enigmatic oracles? Ultimately the gods, if you pray to them, will help you, but I have provided some aids in the following translation of the Oracle of the Seven Sages. Glance at the first oracle (page 155) while I describe their presentation.

Each oracle is numbered in the order it was listed by Stobaeus, which is followed by its *C-H-M* code in brackets. Next is a simple, literal translation of the oracle, for example, Oracle 1 [1-1-1] "Follow the god." Often I have sacrificed literary elegance in order to capture the central or most general meaning. Following my translation is the original Greek, which is not necessary to use the oracle, but some Hellenic Pagans will find it useful. "Used as a first school book for the Greek world from the sixth century BC down to the fall of the Byzantine Empire (1453 AD) and some centuries beyond it,"[98] the Counsels of the Seven Sages is a useful vehicle for learning some Ancient Greek vocabulary and syntax. For Roman Pagans who might want it, I have also added the Latin translations of Conrad Gessner (1516–1565), a Swiss classicist and naturalist who published an edition of Stobaeus.[99] Of course, his Latin translations, like my English ones, capture only some of the meanings of the Ancient Greek text.

Therefore, the translations are followed by a list of alternative meanings for the key Greek words in the oracle. If you look over this list, and try some of the alternatives in the translation of the oracle, you will get some idea of its range of meanings. In time, my translation will become a sort of code for all the possibilities. For example, in "Follow the god," the word I have translated "follow" can also mean accompany, attend, obey, submit to, or understand (and, incidentally, "the god" can also mean the goddess or divinity in general). Occasionally, I provide a citation to Peters's *Greek Philosophical Terms* in case you are interested in exploring how a word is used in ancient Greek philosophy.[100] Following the list of words, I have provided some key interpretations in the context of divination. For example, one of the interpretations I suggest is "Imitate the god." These are just starting points. Remember that you, the diviner, are responsible for interpreting the oracle, for you are communicating with the god who has guided your hand. If you are reading for a querent, then they may be able to help you find the best interpretation. Finally, these interpretations may be followed by some discussion if there is something useful I can say about the oracle. In this case of Oracle 1, I say a little about the meaning of *theos* in Ancient Greek.

---

98. Oikonomides, "Records of 'The Commandments of the Wise Men' in the 3rd c. B.C."

99. Stobaeus, *Sententiae ex Thesauris Graecorum*, translated by Conrad Gessner (Tiguri [Zurich]: Christophorum Frosch, 1559).

100. The standard lexicon of Ancient Greek, which I have used, is Liddell, Scott, and Jones, *A Greek-English Lexicon, with Supplement* (Oxford: Clarendon Press, 1968), which is available online at www.perseus.tufts.edu.

H-M	C = 1	C = 2	C = 3
1-1	1 Ἕπου θεῷ	50 Γνοὺς πρᾶττε	99 Πόνει μετ᾿ εὐκλείας
1-2	2 Νόμῳ πείθου	51 Φόνου ἀπέχου	100 Πρᾶττε ἀμετανοήτως
1-3	3 Θεοὺς σέβου	52 Εὔχου δυνατά	101 Ἁμαρτάνων μετανόει
1-4	4 Γονεῖς αἰδοῦ	53 Σοφοῖς χρῶ	102 Ὀφθαλμοῦ κράτει
1-5	5 Ἡττῶ ὑπὸ δικαίου	54 Ἦθος δοκίμαζε	103 Βουλεύου χρόνῳ
1-6	6 Γνῶθι μαθών	55 Λαβὼν ἀπόδος	104 Πρᾶττε συντόμως
1-7	7 Ἀκούσας νόει	56 Ὑφορῶ μηδένα	105 Φιλίαν φύλαττε
2-1	8 Σαυτὸν ἴσθι	57 Τέχνῃ χρῶ	106 Εὐγνώμων γίνου
2-2	9 Γαμεῖν μέλλε	58 Ὅ μέλλεις, δός	107 Ὁμόνοιαν δίωκε
2-3	10 Καιρὸν γνῶθι	59 Εὐεργεσίας τίμα	108 Ἄρρητον κρύπτε
2-4	11 Φρόνει θνητά	60 Φθόνει μηδενί	109 Τὸ κρατοῦν φοβοῦ
2-5	12 Ξένος ὢν ἴσθι	61 Φυλακῇ πρόσεχε	110 Τὸ συμφέρον θηρῶ
2-6	13 Ἑστίαν τίμα	62 Ἐλπίδα αἴνει	111 Καιρὸν προσδέχου
2-7	14 Ἄρχε σεαυτοῦ	63 Διαβολὴν μίσει	112 Ἔχθρας διάλυε
3-1	15 Φίλοις βοήθει	64 Δικαίως κτῶ	113 Γῆρας προσδέχου
3-2	16 Θυμοῦ κράτει	65 Ἀγαθοὺς τίμα	114 Ἐπὶ ῥώμῃ μὴ καυχῶ
3-3	17 Φρόνησιν ἄσκει	66 Κριτὴν γνῶθι	115 Εὐφημίαν ἄσκει
3-4	18 Πρόνοιαν τίμα	67 Γάμους κράτει	116 Ἀπέχθειαν φεῦγε
3-5	19 Ὅρκῳ μὴ χρῶ	68 Τύχην νόμιζε	117 Πλούτει δικαίως
3-6	20 Φιλίαν ἀγάπα	69 Ἐγγύην φεῦγε	118 Δόξαν μὴ λεῖπε
3-7	21 Παιδείας ἀντέχου	70 Ἁπλῶς διαλέγου	119 Κακίαν μίσει
4-1	22 Δόξαν δίωκε	71 Ὁμοίοις χρῶ	120 Κινδύνευε φρονίμως
4-2	23 Σοφίαν ζήλου	72 Δαπανῶν ἄρχου	121 Μανθάνων μὴ κάμνε
4-3	24 Καλὸν εὖ λέγε	73 Κτώμενος ἥδου	122 Φειδόμενος μὴ λεῖπε
4-4	25 Ψέγε μηδένα	74 Αἰσχύνην σέβου	123 Χρησμοὺς θαύμαζε
4-5	26 Ἐπαίνει ἀρετήν	75 Χάριν ἐκτέλει	124 Οὕς τρέφεις ἀγάπα
4-6	27 Πρᾶττε δίκαια	76 Εὐτυχίαν εὔχου	125 Ἀπόντι μὴ μάχου
4-7	28 Φίλοις εὐνόει	77 Τύχην στέργε	126 Πρεσβύτερον αἰδοῦ
5-1	29 Ἐχθροὺς ἀμύνου	78 Ἀκούων ὅρα	127 Νεώτερον δίδασκε
5-2	30 Εὐγένειαν ἄσκει	79 Ἐργάζου κτητά	128 Πλούτῳ ἀπίστει
5-3	31 Κακίας ἀπέχου	80 Ἔριν μίσει	129 Σεαυτὸν αἰδοῦ

H-M	C = 1	C = 2	C = 3
5-4	32 Κοινὸς γίνου	81 Ὄνειδος ἔχθαιρε	130 Μὴ ἄρχε ὑβρίζειν
5-5	33 Ἴδια φύλαττε	82 Γλῶτταν ἴσχε	131 Προγόνους στεφάνου
5-6	34 Ἀλλοτρίων ἀπέχου	83 Ὕβριν ἀμύνου	132 Θνῇσκε ὑπὲρ πατρίδος
5-7	35 Ἄκουε πάντα	84 Κρῖνε δίκαια	133 Τῷ βίῳ μὴ ἄχθου
6-1	36 Εὔφημος ἴσθι	85 Χρῶ χρήμασιν	134 Ἐπὶ νεκρῷ μὴ γέλα
6-2	37 Φίλῳ χαρίζου	86 Ἀδωροδόκητος δίκαζε	135 Ἀτυχοῦντι συνάχθου
6-3	38 Μηδὲν ἄγαν	87 Αἰτιῶ παρόντα	136 Χαρίζου ἀβλαβῶς
6-4	39 Χρόνου φείδου	88 Λέγε εἰδώς	137 Μὴ ἐπὶ παντὶ λυποῦ
6-5	40 Ὅρα τὸ μέλλον	89 Βίας μὴ ἔχου	138 Ἐξ εὐγενῶν γέννα
6-6	41 Ὕβριν μίσει	90 Ἀλύπως βίου	139 Ἐπαγγέλλου μηδενί
6-7	42 Ἱκέτας αἰδοῦ	91 Ὁμίλει πρᾴως	140 Φθιμένους μὴ ἀδίκει
7-1	43 Πᾶσιν ἁρμόζου	92 Πέρας ἐπιτέλει μὴ ἀποδειλιῶν	141 Εὖ πάσχε ὡς θνητός
7-2	44 Υἱοὺς παίδευε	93 Φιλοφρόνει πᾶσιν	142 Τύχῃ μὴ πίστευε
7-3	45 Ἔχων χαρίζου	94 Υἱοῖς μὴ καταρῶ	143 Παῖς ὢν κόσμιος ἴσθι
7-4	46 Δόλον φοβοῦ	95 Γυναικὸς ἄρχε	144 ἡβῶν ἐγκρατής
7-5	47 Εὐλόγει πάντας	96 Σεαυτὸν εὖ ποίει	145 μέσος δίκαιος
7-6	48 Φιλόσοφος γίνου	97 Εὐπροσήγορος γίνου	146 πρεσβύτης εὔλογος
7-7	49 Ὅσια κρίνε	98 Ἀποκρίνου ἐν καιρῷ	147 τελευτῶν ἄλυπος

Table 8. Key for Consulting the Oracle of the Seven Sages.

ΕΠΟΥΘΕΩΙ
ΝΟΜΩΙΠΕΙΘΟΥ
ΘΕΟΥΣΣΕΒΟΥ
ΓΟΝΕΙΣΑΙΔΟΥ
ΗΤΤΩΥΠΟΔΙΚΑΙΟΥ
ΓΝΩΘΙΜΑΘΩΝ
ΑΚΟΥΣΑΣΝΟΕΙ

ΣΑΥΤΟΝΙΣΘΙ
ΓΑΜΕΙΝΜΕΛΛΕ
ΚΑΙΡΟΝΓΝΩΘΙ
ΦΡΟΝΕΙΘΝΗΤΑ
ΞΕΝΟΣΩΝΙΣΘΙ
ΕΣΤΙΑΝΤΙΜΑ
ΑΡΧΕΣΕΑΥΤΟΥ

ΦΙΛΟΙΣΒΟΗΘΕΙ
ΘΥΜΟΥΚΡΑΤΕΙ
ΦΡΟΝΗΣΙΝΑΣΚΕΙ
ΠΡΟΝΟΙΑΝΤΙΜΑ
ΟΡΚΩΙΜΗΧΡΩ
ΦΙΛΙΑΝΑΓΑΠΑ
ΠΑΙΔΕΙΑΣΑΝΤΕΧΟΥ

ΔΟΞΑΝΔΙΩΚΕ
ΣΟΦΙΑΝΖΗΛΟΥ
ΚΑΛΟΝΕΥΛΕΓΕ
ΨΕΓΕΜΗΔΕΝΑ
ΕΠΑΙΝΕΙΑΡΕΤΗΝ
ΠΡΑΤΤΕΔΙΚΑΙΑ
ΦΙΛΟΙΣΕΥΝΟΕΙ

ΕΧΘΡΟΥΣΑΜΥΝΟΥ
ΕΥΓΕΝΕΙΑΝΑΣΚΕΙ
ΚΑΚΙΑΣΑΠΕΧΟΥ
ΚΟΙΝΟΣΓΙΝΟΥ
ΙΔΙΑΦΥΛΑΤΤΕ
ΑΛΛΟΤΡΙΩΝΑΠΕΧΟΥ
ΑΚΟΥΕΠΑΝΤΑ

ΕΥΦΗΜΟΣΙΣΘΙ
ΦΙΛΩΙΧΑΡΙΖΟΥ
ΜΗΔΕΝΑΓΑΝ
ΧΡΟΝΟΥΦΕΙΔΟΥ
ΟΡΑΤΟΜΕΛΛΟΝ
ΥΒΡΙΝΜΙΣΕΙ
ΙΚΕΤΑΣΑΙΔΟΥ

ΠΑΣΙΝΑΡΜΟΖΟΥ
ΥΙΟΥΣΠΑΙΔΕΥΕ
ΕΧΩΝΧΑΡΙΖΟΥ
ΔΟΛΟΝΦΟΒΟΥ
ΕΥΛΟΓΕΙΠΑΝΤΑΣ
ΦΙΛΟΣΟΦΟΣΓΙΝΟΥ
ΟΣΙΑΚΡΙΝΕ

ΓΝΟΥΣΠΡΑΤΤΕ
ΦΟΝΟΥΑΠΕΧΟΥ
ΕΥΧΟΥΔΥΝΑΤΑ
ΣΟΦΟΙΣΧΡΩ
ΗΘΟΣΔΟΚΙΜΑΖΕ
ΛΑΒΩΝΑΠΟΔΟΣ
ΥΦΟΡΩΜΗΔΕΝΑ

ΤΕΧΝΗΙΧΡΩ
ΟΜΕΛΛΕΙΣΔΟΣ
ΕΥΕΡΓΕΣΙΑΣΤΙΜΑ
ΦΘΟΝΕΙΜΗΔΕΝΙ
ΦΥΛΑΚΗΙΠΡΟΣΕΧΕ
ΕΛΠΙΔΑΑΙΝΕΙ
ΔΙΑΒΟΛΗΝΜΙΣΕΙ

ΔΙΚΑΙΩΣΚΤΩ
ΑΓΑΘΟΥΣΤΙΜΑ
ΚΡΙΤΗΝΓΝΩΘΙ
ΓΑΜΟΥΣΚΡΑΤΕΙ
ΤΥΧΗΝΝΟΜΙΖΕ
ΕΓΓΥΗΝΦΕΥΓΕ
ΑΠΛΩΣΔΙΑΛΕΓΟΥ

ΟΜΟΙΟΙΣΧΡΩ
ΔΑΠΑΝΩΝΑΡΧΟΥ
ΚΤΩΜΕΝΟΣΗΔΟΥ
ΑΙΣΧΥΝΗΝΣΕΒΟΥ
ΧΑΡΙΝΕΚΤΕΛΕΙ
ΕΥΤΥΧΙΑΝΕΥΧΟΥ
ΤΥΧΗΝΣΤΕΡΓΕ

ΑΚΟΥΩΝΟΡΑ
ΕΡΓΑΖΟΥΚΤΗΤΑ
ΕΡΙΝΜΙΣΕΙ
ΟΝΕΙΔΟΣΕΧΘΑΙΡΕ
ΓΛΩΤΤΑΝΙΣΧΕ
ΥΒΡΙΝΑΜΥΝΟΥ
ΚΡΙΝΕΔΙΚΑΙΑ

ΧΡΩΧΡΗΜΑΣΙΝ
ΑΔΩΡΟΔΟΚΗΤΟΣΔΙΚΑΖΕ
ΑΙΤΙΩΠΑΡΟΝΤΑ
ΛΕΓΕΕΙΔΩΣ
ΒΙΑΣΜΗΕΧΟΥ
ΑΛΥΠΩΣΒΙΟΥ
ΟΜΙΛΕΙΠΡΑΙΩΣ

ΠΕΡΑΣΕΠΙΤΕΛΕΙΜΗ
ΑΠΟΔΕΙΛΙΩΝ
ΦΙΛΟΦΡΟΝΕΙΠΑΣΙΝ
ΥΙΟΙΣΜΗΚΑΤΑΡΩ
ΓΥΝΑΙΚΟΣΑΡΧΕ
ΣΕΑΥΤΟΝΕΥΠΟΙΕΙ
ΕΥΠΡΟΣΗΓΟΡΟΣΓΙΝΟΥ
ΑΠΟΚΡΙΝΟΥΕΝΚΑΙΡΩΙ

ΠΟΝΕΙΜΕΤΕΥΚΛΕΙΑΣ
ΠΡΑΤΤΕΑΜΕΤΑΝΟΗΤΩΣ
ΑΜΑΡΤΑΝΩΝΜΕΤΑΝΟΕΙ
ΟΦΘΑΛΜΟΥΚΡΑΤΕΙ
ΒΟΥΛΕΥΟΥΧΡΟΝΩΙ
ΠΡΑΤΤΕΣΥΝΤΟΜΩΣ
ΦΙΛΙΑΝΦΥΛΑΤΤΕ

ΕΥΓΝΩΜΩΝΓΙΝΟΥ
ΟΜΟΝΟΙΑΝΔΙΩΚΕ
ΑΡΡΗΤΟΝΚΡΥΠΤΕ
ΤΟΚΡΑΤΟΥΝΦΟΒΟΥ
ΤΟΣΥΜΦΕΡΟΝΘΗΡΩ
ΚΑΙΡΟΝΠΡΟΣΔΕΧΟΥ
ΕΧΘΡΑΣΔΙΑΛΥΕ

ΓΗΡΑΣΠΡΟΣΔΕΧΟΥ
ΕΠΙΡΩΜΗΙΜΗΚΑΥΧΩ
ΕΥΦΗΜΙΑΝΑΣΚΕΙ
ΑΠΕΧΘΕΙΑΝΦΕΥΓΕ
ΠΛΟΥΤΕΙΔΙΚΑΙΩΣ
ΔΟΞΑΝΜΗΛΕΙΠΕ
ΚΑΚΙΑΝΜΙΣΕΙ

ΚΙΝΔΥΝΕΥΕΦΡΟΝΙΜΩΣ
ΜΑΝΘΑΝΩΝΜΗΚΑΜΝΕ
ΦΕΙΔΟΜΕΝΟΣΜΗΛΕΙΠΕ
ΧΡΗΣΜΟΥΣΘΑΥΜΑΖΕ
ΟΥΣΤΡΕΦΕΙΣΑΓΑΠΑ
ΑΠΟΝΤΙΜΗΜΑΧΟΥ
ΠΡΕΣΒΥΤΕΡΟΝΑΙΔΟΥ

ΝΕΩΤΕΡΟΝΔΙΔΑΣΚΕ
ΠΛΟΥΤΩΙΑΠΙΣΤΕΙ
ΣΕΑΥΤΟΝΑΙΔΟΥ
ΜΗΑΡΧΕΥΒΡΙΖΕΙΝ
ΠΡΟΓΟΝΟΥΣΣΤΕΦΑΝΟΥ
ΘΝΗΣΚΕΥΠΕΡΠΑΤΡΙΔΟΣ
ΤΩΙΒΙΩΙΜΗΑΧΘΟΥ

ΕΠΙΝΕΚΡΩΙΜΗΓΕΛΑ
ΑΤΥΧΟΥΝΤΙΣΥΝΑΧΘΟΥ
ΧΑΡΙΖΟΥΑΒΛΑΒΩΣ
ΜΗΕΠΙΠΑΝΤΙΛΥΠΟΥ
ΕΞΕΥΓΕΝΩΝΓΕΝΝΑ
ΕΠΑΓΓΕΛΛΟΥΜΗΔΕΝΙ
ΦΘΙΜΕΝΟΥΣΜΗΑΔΙΚΕΙ

ΕΥΠΑΣΧΕΩΣΘΝΗΤΟΣ
ΤΥΧΗΙΜΗΠΙΣΤΕΥΕ
ΠΑΙΣΩΝΚΟΣΜΙΟΣΙΣΘΙ
ΗΒΩΝΕΓΚΡΑΤΗΣ
ΜΕΣΟΣΔΙΚΑΙΟΣ
ΠΡΕΣΒΥΤΗΣΕΥΛΟΓΟΣ
ΤΕΛΕΥΤΩΝΑΛΥΠΟΣ

Figure 7. How the Tablet of the Seven Sages might have looked.

Chapter Ten

The Oracle of the Seven Sages

This chapter presents the text of the oracles and aids for their divinatory interpretation (alternate meanings of the Greek words, etc.), which was explained in chapter 9.

I. [I-I-I] Follow the god.

Grk.: Ἕπου θεῷ.

Lat.: Sequere deum.

Follow: accompany, attend, obey, submit to, understand. *God*: goddess, divinity.

Obey the god or goddess. Follow the god's lead. Attend to the god by way of honor. Walk with the god. Imitate the god. Understand the god. Obey divinity. Live in accord with divine Providence. The oracle directs you to align yourself with the divine.

Of course the common translation of *theos* is "god," and the ordinary word for "goddess" is *thea*. Nevertheless, *theos* can be used as a feminine noun to mean "goddess." This usage is similar to English, where the term "actor," for example, includes actresses. Although I have included the article "the" in the translation, it is omitted in the Greek, and so the gender of *theos* is left ambiguous, leaving us to ponder its meaning, as we should. We should not suppose that the oracle means "Follow God" in only a monotheistic sense (although that is one possible interpretation), as the Sages were polytheist Pagans.

Follow *the* god. Which god? This is where interpretation enters. It could be the god overseeing the oracle, most likely Apollo. It could also be a god with whom you have some special relationship, such as your patron deity. *Theos* might also mean abstract divinity, that is, the gods in general. The oracle is compatible with many theologies, but invites you to ponder how you (or the querent) can follow the god.

The first principle taught by the Pythagoreans is to live in accordance with divinity, to follow the gods, from whom all goodness comes, and that this is the purpose of philosophy (see Oracle 48 [1-7-6] "Become the philosopher"). How is this accomplished? By listening to the gods (inspired divination), by learning from those who have heard the gods (that is, from sages and oracles), or by divine skill (technical divination).[101]

2. [1-1-2] Trust in Custom.
Grk.: *Νόμῳ πείθου.*
Lat.: *Pareto legi.*

Trust in: be persuaded by, be won over by, rely on, have confidence in, obey, listen to.
Custom: habitual practice, convention, law, divine law, your lot, allotment, province.

Depend on the laws or customs of your community. Don't try something unconventional or illegal. Take the customary action. Do what you usually do. Trust in your habits. Obey the law. Obey the dictates of the gods above or the gods within.

Nomos (custom) is often contrasted with *physis* (nature) as being either more arbitrary (convention) or more divine (whether transcendent or immanent). It depends on whether you suppose the origin of customs to be cultural habit or the gods.[102]

3. [1-1-3] Worship the gods.
Grk.: *Θεοὺς σέβου.*
Lat.: *Cole deos.*

Worship: honor, respect, feel religious awe for, fear, do homage to.

Continue or increase your devotion to the gods. Worship the gods and make offerings to them. Don't forget that the gods govern everything in the universe. Don't neglect the gods. Beware of divine retribution.

---

101. Iamblichus, *On the Pythagorean Way of Life* (ch. 28, ¶¶137–8; pp. 156–7.

102. Peters, *Greek Philosophical Terms* (New York: New York University Press, 1967), s.v. *nomos.*

4. [1-1-4] Respect (thy) parents.

Grk.: Γονεῖς αἰδοῦ.

Lat.: Reverere parentes.

Respect: stand in awe of, fear, feel regard for, have compassion for, feel shame before, be reconciled with. *Parents*: ancestors, progenitors.

Respect those who have given you your existence and laid the foundations of your character (for better or worse). Respect parents and the ancestors in general. Show humility in the presence of your elders. Don't underestimate the power that parents have over their children. Be compassionate and reconciled with them.

The plain meaning, "respect your parents," is commonplace in ancient Greece, as in many cultures. However, I think we must interpret "parents" in a broad sense. In the ancient world it was common to adopt other people's children for political and social alliances; it was a kind of fostering. Moreover, spiritual teachers often adopted their students as spiritual children. They would address their students as "son" or "daughter," who would in turn address their teacher as "father" or "mother." Establishing this relationship constituted a spiritual rebirth.

5. [1-1-5] Yield to Justice.

Grk.: Ἥττω ὑπὸ δικαίου.

Lat.: Pro iusto etiam vinci sustine.

Yield to: be overcome by, give way to, be in thrall to, be defeated by. *Justice*: the right, the meet, the fitting, the lawful, the well-balanced, the moderate, the fair, the righteous, the genuine, the real, the true, the exact.

Do what is right or lawful. Be fair and just. Act with moderation. Yield to the truth. Resign yourself to reality. Ensure that each gets what they are due. Accept the judgment or punishment you deserve. Be appropriate in all your relationships and actions. Seek the common good. Yield to divine guidance and judgment.

Dikê (Justice) has to do with natural bounds in society and nature, which are enforced by Zeus, and with recompense for their transgression. They are the foundation of order among people and in the universe (*kosmos* refers to good order). The Pythagoreans teach that order in anything arises from a ruling first principle (*arkhê*), but for order to prevail, it is necessary for both the ruler and the ruled to be willing. Humans are complex beings, driven by hubris (see Oracle 41 [1-6-6] "Hate hubris") and other emotions, and therefore we should look to the gods to guide and aid our conduct. After them, we should look to the daimons, who are their assistants, and thereafter to ancient customs and to the divinely inspired sages who hand them down (see Oracle 2 [1-1-2] "Trust in Custom" on *nomos*, custom).[103]

Pythagoreans say that appropriateness in all relations is a principle of justice, for example, of learner to teacher and of the neophyte to one more experienced (and both parties must be willing). Of paramount importance is knowing the appropriate time to act (*kairos*, see Oracle 10 [1-2-3] "Know the right time" and B (Beta) in the Alphabet Oracle). In social relations, we should act as though all people share one body and one soul, and therefore strive for the common good. This common life extends as well to nonhuman animals, with whom we should be friendly. Treating people unjustly leads to civil strife. A Pythagorean *symbolon* (enigmatic, symbolic aphorism) is "Step not over the balance beam." Its interpretation is, "Yield to Justice." "Dikê" is also a Pythagorean name for 3 and 5.[104]

6. [1-1-6] Having learned, know.

Grk.: Γνῶθι μαθών.

Lat.: Cognosce, postquam didiceris.

Learned: noticed, perceived, understood, studied, practiced, formed a habit, been persuaded. *Know*: come to know, perceive, recognize, discern, determine, judge, think (about), make known, celebrate.

You have seen, learned, or studied something; now make it your own. Ponder it. Use it as a basis for judgment. Teach it and celebrate it. Insights are sterile unless cultivated so they bear fruit.

---

103. Iamblichus, *On the Pythagorean Way of Life* (ch. 30, ¶¶167–86; pp. 182–95).

104. See also Peters, *Greek Philosophical Terms*, s.v. *dikê*, on justice.

7. [1-1-7] Having heard, apprehend.

Grk.: Ακούσας νόει.

Lat.: Cum audieris, intellige.

Heard: heard of it, listened, heard and understood, been a pupil. *Apprehend*: perceive, observe, think, reflect, consider, devise, intend.

Think about what you have heard or learned (or what you will hear or learn). After reflecting on it, form a plan and act on it. Use your intuition to grasp and comprehend whatever you hear.

The verb translated "apprehend" (*noeô*) refers to the operation of the *nous*, which is the faculty of the mind capable of intuitively grasping connections. It is not the faculty of discursive reason (i.e., thinking things through).[105]

8. [1-2-1] Know thyself.

Grk.: Σαυτὸν ἴσθι.

Lat.: Nosce teipsum.

Know: be acquainted with.

Inquire into yourself. Cultivate self-awareness and self-knowledge. Investigate your motives. Look at yourself objectively. Be humble and don't boast. Don't overestimate your power or skill. Know your limitations. Seek to understand yourself first, before less relevant and less important matters. Understand your own character. Consider who you truly are. Accept yourself. Seek to understand human nature. Know that you are mortal, that you are body and soul in one. Know your true or higher self. Become acquainted with the gods and daimons in your soul. The truth is within.

Plato's *Charmides* addresses the meanings of "Know thyself," one of which is "Be moderate" (see Oracle 38 [1-6-3] "Nothing too much").[106] The verb in this sentence (ἴσθι) can mean either "know" (from οἶδα) or "be" (from εἰμί). Gessner reads it as "know," as is apparent from his Latin translation. On one hand, we expect "Know thyself" to be among

---

105. See also Peters, *Greek Philosophical Terms*, s.vv. *noêsis, noêton, nous.*

106. This most important Delphic maxim is discussed in a number of Platonic dialogues, including the *Alcibiades, Laws, Phaedrus, Philebus,* and *Protagoras.*

the Counsels of the Seven, but this is not the usual Greek expression of it (which is Γνῶθι σαυτόν). On the other hand, Oikonomides reads the verb as "be" and translates the maxim, "Be thyself" (an appropriate Latin translation is *Tu ipse esto*).[107] This way of reading the text is less likely than Gessner's, but if you prefer it, then the oracle may be interpreted:

> Be true to yourself. Don't pretend to be someone else. Manifest your true self. Act with authenticity. Live your destiny. Trust to your own nature.

9. [1-2-2] Intend to marry.
Grk.: Γαμεῖν μέλλε.
Lat.: Ducturus uxorem.

Intend: be destined, be about, delay. *Marry*: take a lover, betroth a child, give a child in marriage.

Be prepared or open to having a life partner. Expect to have a lover. It's your destiny; seek one, but don't jump into it. Plan for your child's marriage.

We have to understand this oracle in its cultural context. In the ancient world, it was a civic duty to marry and have children (for it helped ensure the continuity of the community), and sometimes you could be punished for not doing so. Things are different in the modern world, but I think most people are happier in a long-term relationship. It helps make us better people by shifting our focus of concern out of our egos. Nevertheless, the oracle has a sense of hesitancy and caution about it. It says "eventually, but maybe not now."

10. [1-2-3] Know the right time.
Grk.: Καιρὸν γνῶθι.
Lat.: Opportunitatem cognosce.

Know: come to know, perceive, recognize, discern, learn, determine, judge, think (about), make known, celebrate. *Right time*: opportunity, season, critical moment, vital part, advantage, fitness, due measure, *kairos*.

Consider carefully whether this is the right time for your action, and trust your intuition. Form the habit of discerning these right times, and teach others to do so.

---

107. Oikonomides, "Records of 'The Commandments of the Wise Men' in the 3rd c. B.C.": 67–76.

Timing is everything. Recognize an opportunity. Discern what is the due measure of something or its fitness to purpose. Perceive the heart of the matter. Discern what is right and appropriate; tell others about it.

On *Kairos* (opportunity, right time), see the Alphabet Oracle under B (Beta). "Kairos" is a Pythagorean name for the number seven.

11. [1-2-4] Think as a mortal.

Grk.: Φρόνει θνητά.

Lat.: Mortalia sapito.

Think: be minded, be wise, be prudent, have understanding, have thoughts, intend, consider, ponder, be sensible, be sane. *Mortal*: one who will die, human.

Use your human reason and be sensible. Do not be arrogant, acting like you have the wisdom or foresight of a god. Know your human limitations. Ponder your mortality. Remember that you will die someday and that you don't know how much time you have left; use it wisely. Now is a time to consider human matters, not to contemplate divine matters.

The word here translated as "think" (*phronêô*) is related to *phronêsis*, which is discussed under Oracle 17 [1-3-3] "Practice prudence."

12. [1-2-5] If thou'rt a guest-friend, know it.

Grk.: Ξένος ὢν ἴσθι.

Lat.: Hospes cum es, agnosce.

If thou'rt: being. *Guest-friend*: guest, stranger, outsider, alien, foreigner, wanderer, refugee, hireling. *Know*: recognize, acknowledge, admit, claim.

Be respectful when you are a visitor or guest. Accept hospitality, but don't make excessive demands. If you are wandering (literally or figuratively), don't act like you know your way; ask one who knows. Be grateful for offered friendship and aid, and reciprocate when possible. Claim your rights as a guest, foreigner, etc. Acknowledge that you are an outsider. If you are a hired contractor, consultant, etc., keep in mind that you are an outsider and don't know the local culture.

As in Oracle 8 [1-2-1] "Know thyself," the verb can mean either "be" or "know." Gessner understands it in the latter sense, and I think that is the simplest meaning. In any case, the interpretation is about the same.

Xenia (guest-friendship) was an important concept in ancient Greek culture from Homer onward. In fact, in the *Iliad* the Trojan War results from a violation of *xenia* (Paris's seduction of Helen, Menelaos's wife), and the *Odyssey* is framed by the suitors' violation of *xenia* by refusing to leave Odysseus's home. There are many other examples in both epics. *Xenia* was bound by rules of hospitality, binding on both host and guest, and their violation was punished by the gods, especially by Zeus Xenios, that is, Zeus in his role as protector of hospitality. For example, in the myth of Baucis and Philemon, Zeus and Hermes wander, disguised as beggars, and are turned away from the homes of rich people. But when they come to the modest home of Baucis and Philemon, an old couple who live happily despite their poverty, the gods are treated generously. In this myth, as in others, if the gods are treated well, they reward their hosts, otherwise the gods punish them severely. These sacred tales remind us to see the divinity in everyone, no matter how humble, and to be gracious hosts, but also, as guests, to be grateful for hospitality received.

13. [1-2-6] Honor the Hearth.

Grk.: Ἑστίαν τίμα.

Lat.: Focum honora.

Honor: revere, honor (as due a god), hold in honor, esteem, value. *Hearth*: Hestia, central fire, home-hearth, home, house, household, family, altar.

Respect the sanctity of the home (yours or someone else's). Value family life. Honor domesticity and value a well-ordered household. Make your prayers and offerings to Hestia (or to Vesta or whomever is your hearth god). Repair, cleanse, and consecrate your house. Respect the fire by which you cook. Clean your fireplace.

Traditionally, Hestia gets the first offering at a meal or sacrifice; as our Pagan ancestors often said, "Hestia comes first." She is an important goddess, the oldest Olympian, the virgin daughter of Kronos and Rhea. Before Zeus and the other Olympians were born, Hestia was there. The Vestal Virgins tended the sacred undying fire of Vesta, her Roman equivalent.

14. [1-2-7] Rule thyself.

Grk.: Ἄρχε σεαυτοῦ.

Lat.: Impera tibi ipsi.

Rule: control, govern, lead, begin with, begin from.

Exercise self-control. Determine your own direction. Guide yourself on the path. Begin by thinking about yourself and how you should act. The solution begins with you.

15. [1-3-1] Help thy friends.

Grk.: Φίλοις βοήθει.

Lat.: Succurre amicis.

Help: assist, aid, come to the aid of. *Friends*: dear ones, beloved ones, lovers, allies, kith and kin, one's own, things you love, pleasing things.

Help your friends and family. Help someone close to you. Assist an animal, plant, place, or organization dear to you.

See Oracle 20 [1-3-6] "Be fond of affection" for more on friendship.

16. [1-3-2] Control thy spirit.

Grk.: Θυμοῦ κράτει.

Lat.: Iram vince.

Control: master, conquer, take possession of, rule, command. *Spirit*: soul, breath, courage, strength, passion, heart, desire, appetite, mind, will, temper, anger.

Control your anger or temper. Don't get carried away. Control your breathing. Master your emotions. Conquer a desire or appetite. Master your thoughts so they don't master you. Learn to control your mental powers. Don't be willful. Conquer your spirit and make it your own. Guide your soul. Exercise your courage skillfully.

The spirit (*thymos*) is the part of soul that translates thought into action. Plato divided the soul (*psyche*) into three parts: the appetitive part (responsible for desires and aversions), the spirited part (responsible for will and the choice to act), and the rational part (responsible for judgment and knowledge). Above the soul is the *nous* (intuitive mind) (see chapter 2, "Theory of Divination").[108]

One of the Pythagorean *symbola* (enigmatic maxims) is "Turn away from thyself every sharp edge." Iamblichus interprets it to mean that we should use prudence and not succumb to anger, for like a sharp edge, it cuts every which way, destroying sound judgment.[109] See also Oracle 112 [3-2-7] "End hatreds."

17. [1-3-3] Practice prudence.

Grk.: Φρόνησιν ἄσκει.

Lat.: Prudentiam exerce.

Practice: exercise, form by art, honor. *Prudence*: practical wisdom, sense, judgment, purpose, intention.

Be prudent. Exercise good sense and judgment. Don't be foolhardy. Don't act aimlessly or haphazardly; consider your intention and purpose. Learn the arts of observation, judgment, and planning. "Practice makes perfect" applies to judgment and practical wisdom, as well as to other skills. Practice contemplation of the Platonic Ideas and the divine realm.

Phronêsis refers to prudence and practical wisdom, especially in ethical matters, but also to contemplation of the Platonic Ideas. For Plato it is sometimes synonymous with *nous* (see under Oracle 7 [1-1-7] "Having heard, apprehend"). "Phronêsis" is also a Pythagorean name for the number three.[110]

---

108. See also Peters, *Greek Philosophical Terms*, s.v. *psychê*.

109. Iamblichus, *Protrepticus* (Stuttgart: Teubner, 1996), ch. XXI, symbol 10; p. 113, θ'. See also Johnson, *The Collected Works of Thomas Moore Johnson* (King's Lynn: Prometheus Trust, 2015), 83.

110. Peters, *Greek Philosophical Terms*, s.v. *phronêsis*.

18. [1-3-4] Honor Forethought.

Grk.: Πρόνοιαν τίμα.

Lat.: Providentiam cole.

Honor: revere, honor (as due a god), hold in honor, esteem, value. *Forethought:* foresight, perceiving beforehand, foreknowledge, providence, Athena.

Think ahead. Respect foresight in yourself and others. Depend on your ability to foresee. Value the providence of the gods, who foresee all things. Pray to Athena for guidance. Honor the Providence of the gods.

Pronoia is literally fore-thought (*pro-noia*) and is related to the word *nous* for the intuitive mind (see discussion under Oracle 7 [1-1-7] "Having heard, apprehend"). It refers to the foresight that should govern individual behavior, but also to the divine Providence, proceeding from the Cosmic Nous, and governing the universe by means of the gods, Cosmic Soul, and other divine beings. "Pronoia" is therefore an epithet of Athena as goddess of foresight and is a Pythagorean name for the number five.[111]

19. [1-3-5] Do not use Oath.

Grk.: Ὅρκῳ μὴ χρῶ.

Lat.: Iureiurando abstine.

Use: suffer from, be subject to, indulge; make use of, use, consult; be intimate with. *Oath:* the object by which one swears, the witness of an oath, Horkos (the god of oaths, who enforces them).

Do not swear a solemn oath. Do not depend on oaths to establish your credibility. If you break your oath, you will suffer the consequences. Do not ask someone else to swear an oath. Do not invoke Horkos. Do not inquire of Horkos. Do not be friends with Horkos or subject yourself to him. I think this oracle is warning against casually swearing oaths by the gods. If you intend to swear such an oath, be sure you mean it!

In ancient Greece an oath (*horkos*) was more than a simple promise. The oath-swearer does indeed make a statement about the past or present, or a promise about the future,

---

111. See also Peters, *Greek Philosophical Terms*, s.v. *pronoia*.

but they also invoke one or more deities to punish them if they have sworn falsely or break the oath, and may even specify the punishment. The divine invocation can be emphasized by making an offering or by touching a sacred object, including the earth (a goddess). As a result, you have conditionally cursed yourself. Because of this invitation and expectation of divine retribution, the oath was fundamental to the stability and coherence of ancient Greek civilization. According to Hierocles of Alexandria (fifth century CE), the human oath is an image of the ineffable archetypal Oath by which Zeus maintains the order of the Cosmos, ensuring its stability and coherence.[112]

Respect for oaths is best preserved, Hierocles tells us, by using them sparingly—when absolutely necessary—or not at all. Swearing oaths rashly is impious and invites divine retribution. Those who have proved themselves to be trustworthy and reliable do not need to use oaths, for they have established their credibility through their actions.[113]

Horkos, the God of Oaths, is the son of Eris (goddess of strife). The Erinyes (Furies) attended his birth. He punishes perjurers and oath-breakers by sending the Erinyes to torment the criminal and destroy their home and family. Oaths support *Dikê* (Justice), the right functioning of society (see Oracle 5 [1-1-5] "Yield to Justice"), which is the special concern of Zeus. Therefore, Zeus Horkios, as Protector of Oaths, was depicted with a thunderbolt in each hand by which to punish intentional oath-breakers. See also the similar Oracle 69 [2-3-6] "Flee a pledge."

20. [1-3-6] Be fond of affection.

Grk.: Φιλίαν ἀγάπα.

Lat.: Amicitiam dilige.

Be fond of: love, desire, prize, welcome, tolerate. *Affection:* friendship, friendly love, affectionate regard, friendliness, amiability.

Value amiability over coldness and conflict. Welcome someone's friendship or friendliness, or at least tolerate it. Be friendly and amiable toward others. Treasure

---

112. Hierocles, *Commentary on the Pythagorean Golden Verses*, II.1–6 in Schibli, *Hierocles of Alexandria* (Oxford, Oxford University Press, 2002), 186–188. See also Sommerstein and Torrance, *Oaths and Swearing in Ancient Greece* (Berlin: De Gruyter, 2014) on oaths.

113. Hierocles, *Commentary on the Pythagorean Golden Verses*, II.6–11 in Schibli, *Hierocles of Alexandria*, 188–189.

your friends. Seek out a friend or friends. Be friendly toward people of every kind, toward animals, and toward the gods.

Philia (Affection, also translated as Love and Friendship) is a Pythagorean name for three. According to the Pythagorean sage and magician Empedocles, who first taught us the four elements, the two primary forces in the cosmos are Love (*Philia* or *Philotês*) and Strife (*Neikos*). Strife is the cause of separation, for it causes like to cling to like, and therefore separates things that are unlike each other. Love, in contrast, is the force of union, for it causes all things to cling together, whether alike or unalike. Love and Strife are ruled by Aphrodite and Ares, who are themselves inseparable. (This is symbolized by the net of Hephaistos, which binds them together. For when Hephaistos found them in bed together, joined in love, he ensnared them in his indestructible net—to the endless amusement of the other gods and goddesses, who came to see.)

Pythagoras was commonly called the discoverer and legislator of Friendship (*Philia*); in particular, he taught the *friendship of all for all*.[114] This included the friendship of people for one another, friendship among citizens by means of law, friendship for people of other races on the basis of correct science (which reveals that all humans have the same nature), friendship between husband and wife, between parents and children, and among kin. He extended this to friendship with animals on the basis of justice and our common nature. Friendship of all for all begins with the friendship between gods and mortals, which we express through piety and worship in accord with true knowledge (*epistêmê*) of the gods, according to Pythagoras. It extends to the friendship of philosophical and religious doctrines with one another. It applies to the friendship of body and soul, and to the friendship of the rational and irrational parts of the soul, which are reconciled through philosophy. It even includes the friendship that should permeate our mortal bodies, mediating and reconciling the opposed powers within it. This is accomplished through health and moderation, through a lifestyle patterned after the orderly mixture of elements in the cosmos.

Pythagoreans established a partnership concerning divine goods, unity of mind (*nous*), and divine soul, by encouraging one another, "Don't tear asunder the god in yourself." This is the Dionysos in each of us, which, in the absence of inner unity, the Titans will dismember. For according to the Orphic Mysteries, the Titans tore apart and ate Dionysos (the son of Zeus). Zeus blasted them, and made humans from the ash, thus combining

---

114. Iamblichus, *On the Pythagorean Way of Life,* ch. 16, ¶¶69–70, ch. 33, ¶¶229–30, 240; pp. 92–5, 226–7, 234–5.

in us Titanic (mortal) and Dionysian (divine) substance. By these concords Pythagoreans aimed at union with the Cosmic Soul, the Cosmic Mind, and The Inexpressible One; this is the supreme friendship. (See chapter 2 on these Neoplatonic concepts; see Oracle 107 [3-2-2] "Pursue unity of mind" on unity of mind.)

21. [1-3-7] Cling to education.

Grk.: Παιδείας ἀντέχου.

Lat.: Disciplinae incumbe.

Cling to: hold on by. *Education*: mental culture, learning, teaching, training, child-rearing, childhood, youth.

Depend on education (either giving or receiving). Don't forget what you have learned, or how you were brought up; depend on them. Commit yourself to another's education or rearing. Teach your children. Cultivate your mind. Focus on character development. Education is your mainstay. Seek training. Cling to your youthfulness; you are never too old to learn.

The ancient Greek concept of *paideia* (education) is a complex and rich topic (one scholar wrote a three-volume study!); I can only touch on it here. It was intended to produce the ideal citizen, noble in character, excellent in mind and body, beautiful and good (see Oracle 30 [1-5-2] "Practice nobility," Oracle 26 [1-4-5] "Praise Excellence," and Oracle 24 [1-4-3] "Speak well of the good"). Unlike strength and beauty, which cannot be given to others and diminish with age, learning does not decrease, and you can give it to others without losing it. Pythagoras called it "the sum total of natural excellence," which is passed on from each generation to the next; it separates humans from beasts, Hellenes from barbarians, and philosophers from other people. It separates free people, who govern their own lives, from slaves, who are governed by others (the original meaning of the *liberal* arts: the knowledge important for free people).[115]

---

115. See Iamblichus, *On the Pythagorean Way of Life*, ch. 8. The three-volume work is Jaeger's *Paideia* (Oxford: Oxford University Press, 1939).

22. [1-4-1] Chase opinion.

Grk.: Δόξαν δίωκε.

Lat.: Gloriam sectare.

Chase: pursue, seek after; chase away, banish; drive, urge, urge on. *Opinion*: expectation, (mere) opinion, judgment (good or bad), conjecture, fantasy; (good) reputation, honor, glory.

Strive for honor, glory, or a good reputation. Ask others' opinions, judgments, or expectations. Seek for a judgment or decision. Banish conjecture, mere opinion, and fantasy. Abandon expectations. Chase away other's baseless opinions and judgments.

This oracle has contradictory interpretations: pursue opinion, but in order to catch it or to chase it away? You will need to ponder this enigma, or do another divination to get guidance.

The distinction between opinion (*doxa*) and true knowledge (*epistêmê*) is fundamental to ancient Greek philosophy. *Doxa* includes the ordinary, often unreliable opinions and judgments of people, perception and judgment about the material world in its chaotic flux, and reasoning from uncertain premises and unjustified assumptions. *Epistêmê*, in contrast, is true knowledge, for it is grounded in contact with the eternal Platonic Ideas, which exist in the Cosmic Nous, and therefore have images in the nous of each person. (See Oracle 7 [1-1-7] "Having heard, apprehend" on *nous*, Oracle 118 [3-3-6] "Forsake not opinion" on opinion, and Peters, s.vv. *doxa, epistêmê*.)

The Pythagoreans said that it is foolish to worry about fame and the opinions of the multitude, because opinions are significant only if they are based on knowledge, which only a few people have. On the other hand, it is also foolish to despise all opinion, as ignorant and incorrigible people do. Those who don't know should learn from those who do, and especially from those who have lived well.[116]

---

116. Iamblichus, *On the Pythagorean Way of Life*, ch. 31, ¶¶200–1; pp. 204–5.

23. [1-4-2] Desire Wisdom.

Grk.: Σοφίαν ζῆλου.

Lat.: Aemulare Sapientiam.

Desire: admire, praise, strive after, affect. *Wisdom*: cleverness, skill, practical wisdom, speculative wisdom, craft, cunning, sound judgment, intelligence, learning.

Strive after wisdom. Appreciate and praise the wisdom of others. Study and learn. Think carefully and be shrewd and clever. Strive to learn your craft and become skillful. Be smart. Emulate cleverness. Worship the goddess Sophia. Be a true philosopher (*philo-sophia* = love of wisdom). Seek to know the truths of existence. Be a lifetime learner.

Sophia (wisdom) refers especially to the practical wisdom of the Seven Sages (*Hepta Sophoi*). It was an epithet of both Hephaistos, the craft god, and Athena, goddess of wisdom. Pythagoras, who coined the word *philosophia* (see Oracle 48 [1-7-6] "Become the philosopher"), says it is the desire and love of wisdom, and that wisdom is knowing the truth about what exists.[117] However, things in the material world "exist" only in a manner of speaking, for they come to be and pass away and are continually changing; so-called knowledge of them is unstable. *Epistêmê* (true knowledge) pertains only to what truly exists, that is, to that which is eternal and immaterial, the cause of material existence (see Oracles 22 [1-4-1] "Chase opinion" and 118 [3-3-6] "Forsake not opinion" on knowledge and opinion). Wisdom is founded on such knowledge. To this end, Pythagoreans taught the art of memory, which is essential in acquiring knowledge, experience, and prudence (see Oracle 17 [1-3-3] "Practice prudence" on prudence). Iamblichus says, "wisdom renders its possessors similar to divinity." [118] [119]

---

117. *Ibid.*, ch. 29, ¶¶159, 166; pp. 274–5, 178–9.

118. Iamblichus, "Epistle to Asphalios Concerning Wisdom" in Johnson, *The Collected Works*, 107.

119. See also Peters, *Greek Philosophical Terms*, s.v. *Sophia*.

24. [1-4-3] Speak well of the good.

Grk.: Καλὸν εὖ λέγε.

Lat.: Quod pulchrum est, pulchre dicito.

Speak of: tell of, say, wish to say, boast of, recite, recount; count, gather. *Well:* thoroughly, competently, kindly. *The good:* the beautiful, beauty, the noble, the honorable, honor, virtue.

Honor the good, noble, and beautiful in all things. Speak kindly about another's goodness or virtues. Recount the good deeds of others and boast of your own. Speak positively about virtue. Tell heroic tales. Collect instances of beauty and honor.

True beauty, as opposed to superficial beauty, resides in a noble and virtuous soul. In Neoplatonism, goodness and beauty are aspects of The Inexpressible One. The beauty of material things and processes is a reflection of their transcendent Forms, which descend from and look back toward the simplicity and unity of The One. Transcendent Beauty inspires Love (*Erôs*), which draws us upward to divine union.[120]

25. [1-4-4] Censure nobody.

Grk.: Ψέγε μηδένα.

Lat.: Neminem vitupera.

Censure: blame, find fault with. *Nobody:* not even one.

Don't judge. Don't concern yourself with others' failings. Focus on the virtues of others. Concern yourself with your own failings. Don't shift blame to others.

See Oracle 87 [2-6-3] "Censure the present" for a discussion of its apparently contradictory advice. Of course, different oracles apply in different situations.

---

120. See MacLennan, *The Wisdom of Hypatia*, chapter 10 for this spiritual practice.

26. [1-4-5] Praise Excellence.

Grk.: Ἐπαίνει ἀρετήν.

Lat.: *Lauda Virtutem.*

Praise: approve, applaud, commend, recommend. *Excellence*: goodness, manliness,[121] distinction, fame, good nature, kindness, prosperity; the glorious deed, the divine miracle.

Praise goodness in character. Recommend this trait to others. Approve of good nature and kindness in others. Appreciate glorious deeds, heroism, and fame. Encourage striving for distinction. Acknowledge the order and harmony in the best of anything. Reward excellence, especially moral excellence. If a divine miracle has occurred, praise it.

Interestingly, this oracle does not tell you to *be* excellent, it tells you to *praise* or *recommend* it. So it is directed more toward the improvement of others than of yourself. "Excellence" here translates the important Greek word *aretê*, often inadequately translated "virtue." *Aretê* is the excellence of anything (not just a person), its fitness to its purpose, its ability to fulfill its essential role. Iamblichus says that the excellence of anything resides in the inherent order and harmonious arrangement proper to the sort of thing it is. For a person, it is the character of being truly and authentically a human. Plato enumerated four *Cardinal Excellences*: prudence (Oracle 17 [1-3-3] "Practice prudence"), justice (Oracles 5 [1-1-5] "Yield to Justice" and 27 [1-4-6] "Do just things"), moderation (Oracle 38 [1-6-3] "Nothing too much"), and fortitude. Of course, there are many other excellences, some of which are advised in these oracles, and they are all aspects of a general excellence of character.[122] [123]

---

121. Originally, *aretê* referred to the manly virtues (like, indeed, Latin *virtus* < *vir*, man). However, it was generally applied to the excellence of anything, including women, and Aretê was personified as a goddess [see **P** (Rho) in the Alphabet Oracle].

122. Iamblichus, *Protrepticus*, ch. XIX; p. 88 and in Johnson, *The Collected Works*, 66; Plato, *The Dialogues of Plato* (New York: Scribners, 1899), vol. 2, *Republic* (Book IV, 427e).

123. See also Peters, *Greek Philosophical Terms*, s.v. *aretê*.

27. [1-4-6] Do just things.

Grk.: Πρᾶττε δίκαια.

Lat.: Fac quae iusta sunt.

Do: practice, do, accomplish, study, be busy with, experience, act. *Just*: right, meet, righteous, lawful, well-ordered, well-balanced, moderate, civilized, fair, genuine, real, true, exact.

Do what is right, fair, and lawful. Be orderly, balanced, moderate, and civilized. Be careful, accurate, and truthful. Study just acts and well-ordered things. Be honestly righteous. Concern yourself with fairness and the genuine. Treat animals, gods, and other people appropriately. The emphasis is on doing or being actively engaged with just things (as opposed to just talking about them).

See the discussion of *Dikê* (Justice) under Oracle 5 [1-1-5] "Yield to Justice." "Dikê" is also a Pythagorean name for three and five.

28. [1-4-7] Be well-inclined toward thy friends.

Grk.: Φίλοις εὐνόει.

Lat.: Amicis esto benevolus.

Be well-inclined toward: be favorable to, be at peace with, have kind thoughts for, be kindly disposed toward. *Friends*: dear ones, beloved ones, lovers, allies, kith and kin, one's own, things you love, pleasing things.

Think kindly of your friends and relatives. Be kind to them as well. Don't feud with friends and relatives; be reconciled with them. Be kind to those you love. Be grateful to your allies. Think fondly about the things you love.

See Oracle 20 [1-3-6] "Be fond of affection" for more on friendship.

29. [1-5-1] Ward off thine enemies.

Grk.: Ἐχθροὺς ἀμύνου.

Lat.: Inimicos ulciscere.

Ward off: keep off, defend against, beware; repay, punish, avenge thyself on. *Enemies*: hostile ones, hated ones, hateful ones.

Defend yourself against your enemies. Beware of them. Keep hateful people at bay. Don't allow yourself to be hurt by their hatred. Take practical measures for self-defense (physical, mental, financial, etc.). Use defensive magic and erect shields. Avenge yourself on those who have hurt you and repay the injury.

Personally, I don't think vengeance is usually advised. However, some people need to learn that bad behavior has its consequences. Tit for tat. The goal is not for you to feel better through their suffering, but to improve their behavior for their sake and everyone else's. Remember the Threefold Law.

30. [1-5-2] Practice nobility.

Grk.: Εὐγένειαν ἄσκει.

Lat.: Ingenuitatem exerce.

Practice: exercise, form by art, honor. *Nobility*: nobility of mind or birth, (bodily) excellence.

Make a practice of nobility. Honor noble ideals and strive to live by them. Behave nobly. Honor those who are noble by birth or who have made themselves noble by their character and behavior. Develop the excellence of your body. Practice premeditation of misfortunes, so you can be tranquil when they occur.

The literal (etymological) meaning of the Greek word is being "born well," but this oracle urges you to develop the traits associated with nobility. The Pythagoreans said that the surest foundation of nobility is the understanding that no human mishap should be unexpected, for those with intelligence will prepare themselves for anything that is out of their control.[124] In this way, the wise maintain their equanimity in the face of all circumstances.[125]

---

124. Iamblichus, *On the Pythagorean Way of Life*, ch. 31, ¶¶196, 224; pp. 200–1, 220–1.

125. Meditating on possible misfortunes is a Stoic spiritual exercise: see MacLennan, *The Wisdom of Hypatia*, chapter 6.

31. [1-5-3] Shun vice.

Grk.: Κακίας ἀπέχου.

Lat.: Abstine malitia.

Shun: abstain from, desist from, hold thyself away from, keep away from. *Vice*: badness, cowardice, evil, dishonor.

Don't do something bad, dishonorable, or evil. If you are engaged in anything of this kind, stop! Stay clear of any association with or appearance of vice. Don't be a coward or dishonor yourself. Stay away from the dark side.

In the Greek tradition, evil is rarely considered a force in the universe; usually it is a sort of absence. The closest to this may be the Indefinite Dyad, which in Platonism is the principle of multiplicity, indeterminateness, and disorder complementary to the Monad or One, which is the principle of unity, determinate existence, and order. The interaction of these two brings the cosmos into being (cf. Love and Strife, discussed under Oracle 20 [1-3-6] "Be fond of affection"). Similarly, another source of badness is the imperfection with which the divine Ideas are impressed on material reality. In general, the darkness of vice is simply the absence of the light of divine illumination. This oracle advises you to avoid the dark places.[126] See also the discussion of the goddesses Vice (*Kakia*) and Virtue (*Aretê*) under P (Rho) in the Alphabet Oracle.

32. [1-5-4] Become common.

Grk.: Κοινὸς γίνου.

Lat.: Esto communis.

Become: come into a new state of being, be born. *Common*: ordinary, general, kindred, public, colloquial, vulgar, affable, impartial, neutral.

You are like everyone else. Recognize that you are an ordinary person, and act like it. Be friendly to everyone. Don't put on airs or be a snob. Treat everyone equally. Become impartial.

---

126. See also Peters, *Greek Philosophical Terms*, s.v. *kakos*.

33. [1-5-5] Watch over personal things.

Grk.: Ἴδια φύλαττε.

Lat.: Propria custodi.

Watch over: watch, guard, ward, defend, preserve, maintain, cherish, hold fast to; beware of, avoid. *Personal:* one's own (property, interests, business); personal, private, peculiar, appropriate, proper, exceptional.

Take care of your property. Protect, maintain, and preserve it. Beware of theft. Manage your personal affairs carefully. Cherish what is yours. Protect your privacy. Preserve what is proper and appropriate. Defend the exceptional. Avoid the peculiar. Beware of privacy, personal matters, and property.

As is sometimes the case, this oracle can be interpreted in contradictory ways: beware of personal things—to protect them or to avoid being ensnared by them?

34. [1-5-6] Keep away from another's things.

Grk.: Ἀλλοτρίων ἀπέχου.

Lat.: Alienis abstine.

Keep away: desist, abstain. *Another's things:* what is another's, things belonging to another, things of another, things unlike thine own, foreign things, strange things, strangers.

Leave other people's things alone. Don't steal. Don't trespass. Stay out of someone else's business. Avoid strangers and strange things; keep to your own.

35. [1-5-7] Hear all.

Grk.: Ἄκουε πάντα.

Lat.: Audi omnia.

Hear: know by hearsay, listen to. *All*: all things, everything. Also, hearken in all points, in all ways, entirely.

Pay attention to what others are saying. Be aware of popular opinions. Don't ignore what you are hearing. Be willing to listen to what someone else has to say. Take in everything. Listen to nature.

36. [1-6-1] Be religiously silent.

Grk.: Εὔφημος ἴσθι.

Lat.: Verbis bene ominare.

Religiously silent: auspicious-speaking, fair-speaking, mild.

Say nothing inauspicious. Keep a holy silence. Speak no evil. Don't speak negatively. Speak words of praise. Think before you speak.

The etymological meaning of *euphêmos* is "well-speaking" and it is related to our word "euphemism." The sense is to speak only words of good omen, or to put it otherwise, the best way to avoid words of ill omen is to keep silent. This is because a chance utterance might become an omen, which then would come to pass. At the formal beginning of an ancient Greek sacrifice, the priest would command *Euphêmeite!* (Keep holy silence!). To speak inauspiciously might ruin the ritual.

As in Oracles 8 [1-2-1] "Know thyself" and 12 [1-2-5] "If thou'rt a guest-friend, know it," the verb (ἴσθι) can be read "be" or "know," but in this case, "be" is meant.

37. [1-6-2] Be favorable to a friend.

Grk.: Φίλῳ χαρίζου.

Lat.: Gratificare amico.

Be favorable to: do or say something agreeable to, do a favor for, be kind to, gratify, humor, grant (erotic) favors to. *Friend*: dear one, beloved one, lover, ally, kith and kin, one's own.

Help a friend. Make a friend feel good. Do them a favor. Humor a friend's desires or quirks. Do these things for your family, partners, and allies as well. Be kind to those close to you. Give them a good word. Gratify the sexual desires of your friend or lover.

38. [1-6-3] Nothing too much.

Grk.: Μηδὲν ἄγαν.

Lat.: Ne quid nimis.

Nothing: not at all, by no means. *Too much*: very much.

Nothing in excess. Everything in moderation (including moderation). Strive for balance and proportion, a well-ordered psyche. Avoid strong emotions (positive or negative). Moderate your feelings through meditation and contemplation. Seek happiness only in what is under your control. Prefer the mean (neither too much nor too little): the Goldilocks Principle.

This is one of the famous Delphic Maxims, the other being "Know thyself" (Oracle 8 [1-2-1]). Interestingly, Plato (*Charmides* 164e) says that the true meaning of "Know thyself" is "Have moderation" and therefore that the two Delphic Maxims have the same meaning. This oracle expresses one of the Cardinal Excellences of Greek philosophy: *sôphro-synê* ("self-control," also translated "moderation" or "temperance"). (See Oracle 26 [1-4-5] "Praise Excellence" on the Cardinal Excellences.) Its etymological meaning is moral sanity, and the Stoics say it refers to the ability to choose what is good and avoid what is bad. The Neoplatonist Olympiodorus (ca. 495–570 CE) says *sôphrosynê* inspires the desire to know the higher powers and give them priority in your life. In Pythagoreanism and Platonism it refers primarily to balance and harmony in the psyche. In terms of Plato's three-part model of the soul, there is harmony when the rational part governs the desiring and spirited parts (*thymos*, see Oracle 16 [1-3-2] "Control thy spirit"). Pythagoras said that one should "cut off with fire and sword" whatever is out of correct proportion. In life, we should seek the mean, neither too much nor too little. And so in our mental state, we should avoid the extremes of giddiness and grief, and of fear and anger, and strive for a state of calm joy. When Pythagoreans were troubled by strong emotions, they meditated in solitude to calm themselves. Iamblichus interpreted "nothing too much" to mean that it's best to depend on ourselves for happiness, without relying too much on circumstances or other people; doing so will make us moderate, valiant, just, and wise (the Cardinal Excellences) and therefore happy.[127] *Premeditation of misfortunes* was a spiritual practice that helped them prepare for inevitable setbacks and possible calamities.[128] [129]

39. [1-6-4] Use time sparingly.

Grk.: Χρόνου φείδου.

Lat.: Parce tempori.

Use sparingly: be thrifty in using, refrain from using. *Time*: the season, (your) lifetime, a delay.

Manage your time. Don't waste time. Make use of a delay. Don't use more time than necessary for something. Make hay while the sun shines. Time is flying, and you're not getting any younger. Don't waste your life.

40. [1-6-5] Look to the future.

Grk.: Ὅρα τὸ μέλλον.

Lat.: Prospice futurum.

Look to: see, have eyes for, look toward, take heed of, beware of, behold, look out for. *Future*: thing to come, event, issue; what is about, destined, likely or intended to happen.

Think ahead. Exercise your foresight. Consider what is coming. Anticipate and plan for the future. Beware of what is about to happen or likely to occur. Pay attention to the outcome. Perceive your destiny.

---

127. Iamblichus, *On the Pythagorean Way of Life*, ch. 31, ¶¶187, 196; pp. 196–7, 200–1; *Protrepticus*, ch. XIX; p. 88–93; and in Johnson, *The Collected Works*, 66–69.

128. MacLennan, *The Wisdom of Hypatia*, chapter 6.

129. See also Peters, *Greek Philosophical Terms*, s.v. *sôphrosynê*.

41. [1-6-6] Hate hubris.

Grk.: Ὕβριν μίσει.

Lat.: Iniuriam oderis.

Hubris: insolence, overweening pride, wanton violence, pride, or passion; rape or another outrage, lust.

Don't tolerate the wanton degradation of others. Hate overweening pride in yourself and others. Don't be insolent or tolerate it. Don't commit unjustified violence against others or tolerate it. Shun acting like a god.

Hubris is such an important concept that the Greek word has entered English. Fundamentally it refers to degrading another person for your own gratification or glorification. It has both sexual and violent overtones, somewhat like "rape" in both its literal and metaphorical uses. Such behavior is associated with wantonness and extreme egotism. It is often supposed that hubris is such an affront to the gods that they will punish it themselves (as in many Greek myths). Hubris is also the topic of Oracles 83 [2-5-6] "Ward off hubris" and 130 [3-5-4] "Don't begin to have hubris."

42. [1-6-7] Respect suppliants.

Grk.: Ἱκέτας αἰδοῦ.

Lat.: Famulos reverere.

Respect: stand in awe of, fear, feel regard for. *Suppliants*: those who seek aid or protection.

Suppliants are protected by the gods: respect them and try to help them. Feel compassion for those in need. Don't exploit those seeking aid or protection.

43. [1-7-1] Adapt thyself in all things.
Grk.: Πᾶσιν ἁρμόζου.
Lat.: Omnibus se apta.[130]

Adapt thyself: accommodate, suit, or adjust yourself; compose or "harmonize" yourself.

Be flexible. Learn and grow. Adapt and survive. Don't be rigid. Harmonize yourself within and with the world. Suit yourself to the world and the world to yourself.

44. [1-7-2] Educate thy sons.
Grk.: Υἱοὺς παίδευε.
Lat.: Filios erudito.

Educate: train, teach, bring up, rear, discipline, correct. *Sons:* children.

Educate your children. Teach the next generation. Correct the learners. Discipline them, if necessary. Bring children up to have good character. Inculcate excellence.

See Oracle 21 [1-3-7] "Cling to education" on *paideia* (education), which is related to the word here translated "educate." Compare this oracle to Oracle 127 [3-5-1] "Teach the younger."

45. [1-7-3] If you have, show kindness.
Grk.: Ἔχων χαρίζου.
Lat.: Si quid habes, aliis gratificare.

Have: hold (yourself), hold fast, possess, keep (yourself) safe, understand, are well off. *Show kindness:* show favor; give graciously or cheerfully; be gracious, agreeable or favorable; comply.

If you are well off, help others out; be generous. Do the same if you are safe and secure. Recognize your fortune and be cheerful and gracious. So long as your situation is secure, give in to others.

This oracle is similar to Oracle 55 [2-1-6] "Having got, give back."

---

130. This is my Latin translation, since Gessner doesn't provide one.

46. [1-7-4] Fear the trap.

Grk.: Δόλον φοβοῦ.

Lat.: Dolum metue.

The trap: any trick or stratagem; bait or a cunning device for deceiving or catching; cunning, treachery, craft.

Beware of being tricked or being caught by treachery or cunning. Avoid using trickery, treachery, or craft. Don't be too subtle or cunning. Avoid being lured into a trap. Watch out for deceit.

47. [1-7-5] Speak well of everyone.

Grk.: Εὐλόγει πάντας.

Lat.: Benedic omnibus.

Speak well of: praise, bless.

Praise everyone or some particular person. Make a habit of appreciating the best in each person. Don't criticize people. Spread blessings around. Pray for the best for everyone.

48. [1-7-6] Become a philosopher.

Grk.: Φιλόσοφος γίνου.

Lat.: Philosophus esto.

Become: come into a new state of being, be born. *Philosopher*: lover of wisdom.

Seek wisdom and live wisely. Desire wisdom and love it. Look at the situation philosophically, and let wisdom inform your attitude and guide your behavior. Undertake spiritual rebirth as a philosopher.

Ancient philosophy was not primarily an abstract study with little application to everyday life. Rather, it was a way of life rooted in the love of wisdom. As such, it involved living more thoughtfully, but especially living your day-to-day life in a better way, no matter what your circumstances. Pythagoras is supposed to have coined the word *philosophia*—for the love (*philo-*) of wisdom (*sophia*). (See Oracle 23 [1-4-2] "Desire Wisdom" on Wisdom, and

Peters, s.v. *philosophia*. MacLennan teaches ancient Greek philosophy as a way of living a more meaningful life today.[131])

49. [1-7-7] Choose holy things.

Grk.: Ὅσια κρῖνε.

Lat.: Quod bonum et aequum est, iudica.[132]

Choose: select, pick out; distinguish, separate. *Holy*: hallowed, sanctioned or allowed by divine or natural law (as opposed to human law), profane things not forbidden by divine law.

Distinguish what is holy from what is not. Keep away from what is forbidden by the gods. Prefer what is allowed by eternal law to what is allowed by temporal law. Do not mix the sacred and profane.

50. [2-1-1] If you know, act.

Grk.: Γνοὺς πρᾶττε.

Lat.: Ubi cognoveris rem, actioni incumbe.

Know: have come to know, perceive, observe, recognize, discern, learn, determine, think (about); have become aware; are one who knows or is prudent. *Act*: get busy, accomplish, achieve, experience things; manage things, negotiate; practice, study; exact payment, punishment or revenge.

Act on what you know. Study and practice what you have learned. Accomplish something with your knowledge. You've thought enough, now get busy. Manage the situation you have observed. Use your understanding to negotiate. If you are sure you know the facts, exact payment or punishment.

---

131. MacLennan, *The Wisdom of Hypatia*.

132. I think *Iudica sancta* is a better Latin translation than this, which is Gessner's.

51. [2-1-2] Shun slaughter.

Grk.: Φόνου ἀπέχου.

Lat.: Abstine caede.

Shun: keep away, desist, abstain from. *Slaughter*: murder, the death penalty; bloodshed, gore, a corpse; a murder weapon, any agent of slaughter.

Don't kill. Stop killing. Shun violence. Avoid the death penalty. Keep away from murder weapons. Don't touch lethal weapons. Avoid slaughter or a violent situation. Keep away from blood and gore. Avoid a corpse.

If a literal interpretation does not seem relevant, then this oracle can be taken metaphorically to mean that you should not take a person down psychologically, destroy their reputation (e.g., through gossip), or hurt them in other ways. Beware if you or others are using metaphors of violence or slaughter.

52. [2-1-3] Pray for the possible.

Grk.: Εὔχου δυνατά.

Lat.: Opta possibilia.

Pray for: long for, wish for; vow; boast (vainly) of, profess (loudly). *The possible*: possible or practicable things; strong, mighty, capable, powerful, influential or productive things.

Hope and pray only for the possible. Vow that you will do something practical, influential, or productive. Hope for what's possible. Don't wish for the impossible. Don't boast of what you cannot do. Pray for what is practicable or productive. Pray for what is strong, mighty, or influential.

53. [2-1-4] Consult with the wise.

Grk.: Σοφοῖς χρῶ.

Lat.: Utere sapientibus.

Consult with: suffer from, be subject to, indulge; make use of, use, consult; be intimate with. *The wise*: wise people, the prudent, the learned, the skilled, the clever, the ingenious, the subtle; wise or clever things.

Seek advice from wise people. Consult with those who are skilled, educated, smart, or clever. Follow their advice. Depend on those who know. Hang out with smart, educated folks. Make use of good ideas or clever methods. Follow the true philosophers.

The word here translated *sophos* (wise) is related to *Sophia* (Wisdom), on which, see Oracle 23 [1-4-2] "Desire Wisdom," and to the Seven Sages (Wise Ones): *Hepta Sophoi*. The philosophers, the lovers of wisdom (*philo-sophoi*), are those who devote their lives to pursuing wisdom.

54. [2-1-5] Test character.

Grk.: Ἦθος δοκίμαζε.

Lat.: Ingenium & mores explora.

Test: make trial of, assay; approve (as fit), sanction. *Character*: disposition; the accustomed place, custom, usage.

Test your own character; take a hard look at it. You don't know your own character until it has been tested. This is a test of your character. Test the character of others. Evaluate it and approve it as good or condemn it as bad. Don't assume that some person is good or bad. Don't trust a person's reputation or hearsay about them. Don't trust or condemn blindly; find evidence for the sort of person they are. Approve or recommend someone's character. Assess the customary and habitual, and decide if they are fit. Don't simply accept it.

I don't think this Oracle is usually recommending that we be vocal about our evaluations, but rather that you evaluate the character of yourself or another and act accordingly. Heraclitus (535–475 BCE) said that a person's *êthos* (character) is their *daimôn* (their inner divinity).

55. [2-1-6] Having got, give back.

Grk.: Λαβὼν ἀπόδος.

Lat.: Quod accepisti, restitue.

Got: taken, grasped, seized, caught, apprehended (by the senses or mind), taken in hand, undertaken; received, gained, won, profited. *Give back*: give up, give freely, deliver, restore, return, make payment.

When you are successful, be generous. Make a gift from your gains. Reward those who have helped you succeed. Pay for what you have received. Pay the price. If you have taken something, give it back or make restitution. Return what you have borrowed. Release what you have caught. Tell what you have observed or understood. Deliver freely the fruits of your undertaking.

This oracle is similar to Oracle 45 [1-7-3] "If you have, show kindness." One of the Pythagorean *symbola*, the enigmatic sayings through which they teach their wisdom, is "Rear nothing that has crooked nails." Iamblichus explains its hidden meaning as follows. The animals with crooked nails, that is talons, snatch things quickly and do not let them go. The gods, however, have granted humans straight nails on hands that are capable of giving as well as taking. Therefore, we should not grasp at things insatiably without ever giving back. Hence, we should act with justice, as taught in philosophy, repay what we have received, and equalize inequality through reciprocal gifts.[133] See Oracle 5 [1-1-5] "Yield to Justice" on Justice.

56. [2-1-7] Suspect no one.

Grk.: Ὑφορῶ μηδένα.

Lat.: De nemine suspicare.

Suspect: view with suspicion or jealousy, eye stealthily; look from below at. *No one*: not even one.

Don't be suspicious or jealous; be trusting. Don't spy. Don't be a voyeur.

---

133. Iamblichus, *Protrepticus*, ch. XXI, symbol 20; pp. 117–118, ιθ'; in Johnson, *The Collected Works*, 86–87.

57. [2-2-1] Use craft.

Grk.: Τέχνῃ χρῶ.

Lat.: Utitor arte.

Use: suffer from, be subject to, indulge; make use of, consult; be intimate with. *Craft*: (professional) skill, art, cunning; a system or method, rules of art, manner or means of doing something.[134]

Use your skill, your craft. Use the techniques you have learned. Follow the rules of your art; subject yourself to them. Learn your craft. Study it. Apply the methods you know. Use your professional expertise. Know your art and let it flourish. Be clever.

58. [2-2-2] Give what you intend.

Grk.: Ὃ μέλλεις, δός.

Lat.: Daturus non differes.

Give: be ready to give, offer (to the gods); forgive. *Intend*: are destined or are about to; put off, are always going to (but never do).

Give what you intend to give. Make your intended offering to the gods. Do what you intend to do. Do not put it off. Forgive as you have intended. Do these things if you have been putting them off, or never got around to them. It is your destiny or fate.

59. [2-2-3] Honor good deeds.

Grk.: Εὐεργεσίας τίμα.

Lat.: Beneficia honorato.

Honor: revere, honor (as due a god), hold in honor, esteem, value. *Good deeds*: kindnesses, public services.

Esteem good deeds, kind acts, and public service; value them. Have reverence for good deeds; the gods love them.

---

134. See also Peters, *Greek Philosophical Terms*, s.v. *technê*.

60. [2-2-4] Envy no one.

Grk.: Φθόνει μηδενί.

Lat.: Invideto nulli.

Envy: be envious of, be jealous of, resent, be indignant at; feel ill-will or malice toward; begrudge, refuse due to envy or ill-will. *No one*: not even one; nothing.

Don't be envious or jealous. Don't resent others or be indignant at their actions. Don't harbor bad feelings against anyone. Don't deny someone out of spite. Don't be hateful.

Pythagoreans teach their wisdom through *symbola*, enigmatic sayings that have to be interpreted symbolically. One of these is "Eat not the heart." On one level, this could be interpreted as a dietary restriction, but Iamblichus reveals its deeper meaning: don't be envious. For envy dissolves the unity and cohesion of the world, and so philosophy teaches us not to envy the goods of others or to rejoice in their misfortunes. The *symbolon* "exhorts us to sympathy and mutual love" for all people are alike by nature and subject to a common fortune.[135]

61. [2-2-5] Pay attention to protection.

Grk.: Φυλακῇ πρόσεχε.

Lat.: Custodiam ne contempseris.

Pay attention to: turn (thy mind) toward, be intent upon, devote thyself to, don't neglect. *Protection*: a watch(ing), a guard(ing), a keeping or preserving; a ward, a watch post, a night watch; a safeguard, a precaution.

Be on guard, watch out, etc. Pay attention to security. Take precautions. Dedicate yourself to protection. Look to your wards. Shield yourself. Take care for yourself. Set up surveillance. Post a guard. Pay attention to cybersecurity and use malware protection on your digital devices.

---

135. Iamblichus, *Protrepticus*, Ch. XXI, Symbol 30; p. 123, λ'; Johnson, *The Collected Works*, 90–91.

62. [2-2-6] Praise hope.

Grk.: Ἐλπίδα αἴνει.

Lat.: Spem approbato.

Praise: speak (well) of, recommend, be content with, vow. *Hope*: a hope, the thing hoped for, expectation; fear, apprehension.

Be optimistic. Give others reason to hope. For now, be satisfied with the hope of a better future. Advocate for your hopes. Make a vow that your hopes will be fulfilled. Acquiesce in your fear or apprehension.

An expectation can be a hope or a fear, and I believe this oracle is recommending that you acknowledge it, either way. I think optimism is the better attitude. "We should all be optimistic," Seneca said, "but ready at the same time to meet trouble and difficulties whenever they arise." Hope for the best, but prepare for the worst.

63. [2-2-7] Hate slander.

Grk.: Διαβολὴν μίσει.

Lat.: Calumniam oderis.

Slander: false accusation, ill-repute, quarrel, enmity, prejudice.

Don't slander or tolerate others slandering. Don't accuse falsely. Don't listen to gossip or spread it. Avoid quarrels. Stamp out prejudice. Be aware of your own prejudices and strive to eliminate them.

64. [2-3-1] Acquire justly.

Grk.: Δικαίως κτῶ.

Lat.: Posside iure.

Acquire: get, gain, procure for oneself or another, bring upon yourself, win. *Justly*: lawfully, rightly, fairly, decently, in due form, exactly, with reason, really and truly.

Don't cheat or steal. Obey the law in business and commerce. Win by the rules. Be fair and decent in your business dealings. Be scrupulous in them. Be a rational and careful consumer. Get for yourself what really matters. Do the same for others.

See Oracle 5 [1-1-5] "Yield to Justice" for more on justice. This oracle is similar to Oracle 117 [3-3-5] "Be rich justly."

65. [2-3-2] Honor good people.

Grk.: Ἀγαθοὺς τίμα.

Lat.: *Honora bonos.*

Honor: revere, honor (as due a god), hold in honor, esteem, value. *Good*: noble, gentle, brave, capable.

Respect good people. Be thankful for those who are noble, brave, competent, and gentle. Honor and praise them. Have reverence for the best of humanity.

66. [2-3-3] Know the judge.

Grk.: Κριτὴν γνῶθι.

Lat.: *Iudicem nosce.*

Know: come to know, perceive, recognize, discern, learn, determine, judge, think (about), make known, celebrate. *Judge*: decider, umpire.

Determine who will be making the decision and understand them. Think about them. Praise them as judges. Discern whose judgments really matter. If you are facing any decision or judgment, then you should determine who is really making the decision (who might not be the apparent decision maker) and understand them thoroughly.

67. [2-3-4] Control weddings.

Grk.: Γάμους κράτει.

Lat.: *Nuptias admitte.*

Control: master, conquer, take possession of, rule, command, control, seize, hold fast. *Weddings*: wedding feasts, nuptials, marriages.

Control weddings and don't let them get out of hand (e.g., too expensive or a cause for arguments). Control the wedding celebrations socially or psychologically.

What if no one is getting married? Then I think you need to interpret this oracle meta-phorically. A wedding is a sort of alliance between two families, a connection manifest in the wedded couple. Therefore, this oracle may be advising you to take control of some alliance (personal, business, political) that is in progress or will arise soon. Don't let it go; manage it.

68. [2-3-5] Acknowledge Fortune.

Grk.: Τύχην νόμιζε.

Lat.: Fortunam ne neges.

Acknowledge: consider, believe in, esteem, use customarily. *Fortune*: good luck, suc-cess, the good obtained by a god's favor, the goddess Tychê or Fortuna, providence, destiny, chance, a chance event; bad luck, an accident, misfortune; station in life; physical necessity.

Don't ignore the role of chance, luck, and accidents in your life; make use of them. Know that some things happen due to simple physical necessity. Be thankful when your luck is good and be prepared for inevitable misfortune. Watch for a change of fortune. Trust in your ultimate success. Know that the gods can help you, so pray to them for aid. Believe in the Providence of the gods, which guides the Cosmos. Know that you have an individual destiny, granted by the gods, so strive to fulfill it. True philosophy teaches you how to fulfill your destiny in accord with divine Provi-dence. Acknowledge your station in life.

Tychê (Roman Fortuna) was generally considered a rather fickle goddess, and therefore she was often depicted standing on a sphere to symbolize the instability of both good and bad fortune. In an instant you can tumble from good luck to bad, and just quickly regain your good fortune. Therefore, philosophers advised placing your trust in a more depend-able goddess, *Sophia* (Wisdom) (see Oracle 23 [1-4-2] "Desire Wisdom" on Wisdom and Oracle 48 [1-7-6] "Become a philosopher" on philosophy). Nevertheless, it is foolish (the opposite of wisdom) to neglect a goddess, and I think this oracle is advising you to recog-nize the enormous power of Fortune in our lives. Moreover, Iamblichus says it is a mistake to think that Tychê is a source of disorder in the cosmos. In fact, she acts both as a goddess who brings higher, spiritual causes into manifestation (vertical causation), and as a daimon who governs natural causation in the material realm (horizontal causation).[136] "Tychê" is also a Pythagorean name for the number seven. [137]

69. [2-3-6] Flee a pledge.

Grk.: Ἐγγύην φεῦγε.

Lat.: Sponsionem fuge.

Flee: avoid, escape, flee consequence of. *Pledge*: pledge given or received, surety, security, betrothal.

Avoid making a pledge or requiring someone else to make one to you. The oracle implies that you will come to regret doing so. Don't give security for an agreement. If you have made a pledge, try to get released from it. Cancel the engagement.

See the similar Oracle 19 [1-3-5] "Do not use Oath."

70. [2-3-7] Discuss simply.

Grk.: Ἁπλῶς διαλέγου.

Lat.: Colloquere simpliciter.[138]

Discuss: converse, discourse, lecture, argue, reason, practice dialectic, write prose; have sex. *Simply*: plainly, openly, frankly, in good faith, in one way, absolutely, generally; loosely, superficially, foolishly.

Talk plainly. Eschew obfuscation. Discuss matters and argue in good faith. Converse openly and frankly. Lecture so people can understand. Write simply and clearly. Prefer simple reasons and arguments. Have intercourse (sex) honestly and in good faith. Keep it simple (missionary position?).

The plain meaning is to talk simply, frankly, and honestly, but this is also a euphemism for open, honest, and simple intercourse in a sexual sense. Granted, the Seven Sages are unlikely to have intended this meaning, but we have to include it for divinatory purposes.

---

136. Iamblichus, "Epistle to Macedonios Concerning Fate" in Johnson, *The Complete Works*, 104.

137. See also Peters, *Greek Philosophical Terms*, s.v., *tychê*.

138. My Latin translation, since Gessner has a different Greek text here, and therefore a different translation.

71. [2-4-1] Associate with peers.

Grk.: Ὁμοίοις χρῶ.

Lat.: Utere similibus.

Associate with: consult; be intimate with, indulge, make use of, use, suffer from, be subject to. *Peers*: equals, those who are similar, matches, or equal rank or station.

Stick with your own kind. Don't put on airs, but also avoid slumming, pretending to be like those less advantaged. Have your friends among your equals. Indulge them, but also depend on them. Do as they do. The oracle is telling you to avoid being someone who you are not, and that you should be a participating member of your community.

72. [2-4-2] Govern luxuries.

Grk.: Δαπανῶν ἄρχου.

Lat.: Sumptus facere ne differ.

Govern: command, rule; begin with. *Luxuries*: expensive, lavish, or consuming things.

Keep your luxury expenses in check; begin with them. Buy what you need and what you can afford. Don't try to "keep up with the Joneses." The oracle does not prohibit luxuries, it simply advises that they be kept in bounds.

Pythagoras warned that the first evil to slip unseen into houses, or whole cities, is luxury. The second evil to appear is hubris (see Oracles 41 [1-6-6] "Hate hubris" and 83 [2-5-6] "Ward off hubris"). The third is ruin. Therefore, keeping luxury in check is the first line of defense.[139]

---

139. Iamblichus, *On the Pythagorean Way of Life*, ch. 30, ¶171; pp. 184–5.

73. [2-4-3] Having got, be glad.

Grk.: Κτώμενος ἥδου.

Lat.: Acquisitis gaude.

Got: acquired, gained, procured for oneself or another, brought upon yourself, won. *Be glad:* enjoy, be delighted.

Be happy with what you have obtained or won. Enjoy your possessions and accomplishments. Delight in what you have obtained for someone else. Take time out to be satisfied. Don't be disappointed or dissatisfied with what you have got. Avoid buyer's remorse.

74. [2-4-4] Honor shame.

Grk.: Αἰσχύνην σέβου.

Lat.: Verecundiam cole.

Honor: revere, worship, respect. *Shame:* sense of shame, (dis)honor, modesty.

Respect your feeling of shame, which will guide you. Avoid doing something that will make you feel ashamed or dishonorable. Inculcate an appropriate sense of shame in someone else. Honor the sense of what is right and honorable in yourself or someone else. Cultivate modesty.

Shame is not a popular idea nowadays, but to be shameless means to have no sense of right or wrong, or of what is proper or improper. Therefore, I think shame should be understood as this sense, the feeling that you have done less than expected (by yourself or others). Shame (*Aiskhunê*) is occasionally treated as a goddess, and so this oracle can be interpreted literally to mean that you should worship this goddess; give her the respect she is due.

75. [2-4-5] Achieve grace.

Grk.: Χάριν ἐκτέλει.

Lat.: Gratias refer.

Achieve: accomplish, bring to an end. *Grace*: charm, graciousness; kindness, goodwill, a favor, a kindness, loving-kindness, homage, gratitude.

Be gracious. Be friendly and helpful. Be kind to someone and do them a favor. Practice loving-kindness. Be pleasant and helpful. Embody the grace of the gods (which benefits even imperfect mortals). Be grateful; thank someone for a kindness. Thank the gods.

Grace (Grk., *kharis*, also transcribed *charis*; Lat., *gratia*) is a complicated concept. Fundamentally, it is something that gives delight, joy, or pleasure. Therefore, a favor or kindness, a kind word or action, verbal pleasantries. Something that is graceful (exhibiting grace in form or movement). It is the favor, goodwill, or kindness of someone, which is delightful to the recipient. In particular, *kharis* is the kindness of the gods and, especially in a Christian context, the Grace of God.

The Graces (Charites) are the goddesses who embody the various aspects of grace in the above senses. The Three Graces are depicted often in art and are commonly named Euphrosynê (Merriment), Aglaia (Splendor), and Thalia (Blooming). (Many others are also listed.) "Charis" is also the name of a goddess, the wife of Hephaistos, and in a sense his complement, for she is as graceful as he is awkward (due to his lameness). Since Aphrodite (Venus) is also named as the wife of Hephaistos, "Charis" may be another name for her. Sometimes the Charites are the attendants of Aphrodite, so they are closely connected.

76. [2-4-6] Pray for good luck.

Grk.: Εὐτυχίαν εὔχου.

Lat.: Bonam fortunam optes.

Pray for: make a vow for, repay your vow for, wish for; boast of, profess. *Good luck*: prosperity, success.

Pray for good luck, success, or prosperity. For these benefits, make a vow to an appropriate god. If you have made such a vow, you must fulfill it. Be optimistic. If you have been fortunate, then publicly thank the gods.

77. [2-4-7] Love Fortune.

Grk.: Τύχην στέργε.

Lat.: Fortunam dilige.

Love: be fond of, like; be content with, bear with, submit to. *Fortune:* good luck, success, the good obtained by a god's favor, the goddess Tychê or Fortuna, providence, destiny, chance, a chance event; bad luck, an accident, misfortune; station in life; physical necessity.

Be happy with the lot granted you by Fortune. If you can't be happy, then submit to it and bear with it, knowing it is either meaningless happenstance, your destiny, or the will of the gods. Put up with misfortune; roll with the punches. Appreciate happy accidents. Devote and submit yourself to divine Providence. Be happy with your station in life.

See Oracle 68 [2-3-5] "Acknowledge Fortune" on Fortune (*Tychê*), which is similar to this Oracle. This one goes further: not only should you acknowledge Lady Luck and her fickle ways, you should love her for them. Be amazed and amused at the curve balls she can throw! Compare Oracle 142 [3-7-2] "Trust not Fortune." "*Tychê*" is also a Pythagorean name for the number seven.

78. [2-5-1] Having heard, see.

Grk.: Ἀκούων ὅρα.

Lat.: Audiens vide.

Heard: listened, understood, been called, obeyed. *See:* look, have sight, take heed, beware, behold, look out, observe, perceive, discern, have visions.

Use your own eyes to check what you have heard. See for yourself; don't trust to hearsay. Inspect carefully that which you've heard about. If you have been called, watch out. Take heed for what you have understood. You obeyed, now beware. If you have been called by the gods, seek visions of them.

79. [2-5-2] Work for things worth getting.

Grk.: Ἐργάζου κτητά.

Lat.: Labora pro rebus quae acquiri possunt.

Work for: make, earn, practice, work at. *Things worth getting*: acquisitions, desirable things, what may be gotten.

Discern what is truly worthwhile, and go for it. Work for something you desire. Earn your acquisitions. Practice for what you want to accomplish. Work for the obtainable.

80. [2-5-3] Hate Strife.

Grk.: Ἔριν μίσει.

Lat.: Contentionem oderis.

Strife: discord, quarrel, rivalry, dispute, debate; the goddess Eris.

Avoid a quarrel. Seek agreement rather than an argument. Avoid pointless competition and rivalry. Don't enter into a debate. Seek concord and consensus. Don't invoke Eris (though you must acknowledge her divinity).

81. [2-5-4] Detest blame.

Grk.: Ὄνειδος ἔχθαιρε.

Lat.: Opprobrium detestare.

Blame: censure, reproach; a matter of reproach, a disgrace.

Don't blame someone or try to disgrace them; it is better to teach them respectfully. Don't play the blame game. Don't seek out a reason to reproach someone; regret that the matter has occurred. Avoid being censured or blamed by striving to do things right. Don't be disgraceful.

82. [2-5-5] Hold thy tongue.

Grk.: Γλῶτταν ἴσχε.

Lat.: Linguam cohibe.

Hold: restrain; have (possession).

The plain meaning is to hold your tongue, to keep quiet or keep to yourself your opinions or ideas. However, the verb can also mean to have something in the sense of possession, so perhaps the oracle is advising that you have a tongue and should use it wisely; consider what you say.

This oracle is similar to Oracle 36 [1-6-1] "Be religiously silent," but more general. Interestingly, when the Romans called for religious silence, they said, *Favete linguis!* (Hold your tongues!), so perhaps the meanings are not very different.

One of the Pythagorean *symbola*, or enigmatic maxims, is "Above all things, govern your tongue when you follow the gods." The hidden meaning, revealed by Iamblichus, is that the job of wisdom is to convert discursive reason from external expression of thoughts (jabbering) to inward contemplation of the Ideas. In this way, we can perfect the intellect (*nous*) and follow the gods (Oracle 1 [1-1-1] "Follow the god"). This is also the turn from theology ("god-talk") to theurgy ("god-work").[140]

83. [2-5-6] Ward off hubris.

Grk.: Ὕβριν ἀμύνου.

Lat.: Iniuriam repelle.

Ward off: keep off, defend against; avenge. *Hubris*: insolence, overweening pride, wanton violence, pride, or passion; rape or another outrage, lust.

Guard yourself against having overweening pride. Don't be insolent. Resist violence and passion (in yourself or someone else). Don't degrade someone else to gratify your ego. Avenge the wanton violence or outrage committed by another person.

---

140. Iamblichus, *Protrepticus*, ch. XXI, symbol 7; p. 112, ϛ'; in Johnson, *The Complete Works*, 82.

Don't act like a god, or the gods will punish you. Don't be overcome by your own lust or by the lust of someone else. Drive off a rapist or other aggressor; protect yourself.

See Oracle 41 [1-6-6] "Hate hubris" on hubris. Compare Oracle 130 [3-5-4] "Don't begin to have hubris."

84. [2-5-7] Choose just things.

Grk.: Κρῖνε δίκαια.

Lat.: Iudica iuste.

Choose: select, pick out; distinguish, separate. *Just*: right, meet, righteous, lawful, well-ordered, well-balanced, moderate, civilized, fair, genuine, real, true, exact.

Distinguish what is right and lawful from what is not, and prefer the former. Choose those things that are well-ordered and balanced, that are genuine and real. Prefer moderation, civilization, and fairness. Opt for the truth. Choose appropriate relationships over inappropriate. The focus here is on opting for what is just.

See Oracle 5 [1-1-5] "Yield to Justice" for more on justice, especially as understood by Pythagoreans. [141]

85. [2-6-1] Use what you have.

Grk.: Χρῶ χρήμασιν.

Lat.: Ute re pecuniis.

Use: suffer from, be subject to, indulge; make use of, consult; be intimate with. *What you have*: your gear, goods, property, money; what is needed; the thing, event, affair, matter.

Use your own resources; be constrained by them. Don't depend on someone else's money, supplies, or equipment. Make use of what is at hand. Use what is needed. Be aware of your resources. Make use of circumstances. Submit to the event or the matter at hand. Indulge the affair. Put up with the situation. Immerse yourself in it.

---

141. Peters, *Greek Philosophical Terms*, s.v. *dikê*, on justice.

86. [2-6-2] Judge incorruptibly.

Grk.: Ἀδωροδόκητος δίκαζε.

Lat.: Muneribus incorruptus res examina.

Judge: give judgment, decide. *Incorruptibly*: without bribery.

Pass judgment fairly. Make your decision or judgment without thought of advantage or disadvantage to you. Beware of attempts to sway your judgment unfairly.

The literal meaning of *adôrodokêtos* (incorruptible) is to have an opinion (*-dokêtos*) without gifts (*a-dôro-*). The plain meaning, of course, is not to accept bribes if you are in a position of passing judgment. I think it can be interpreted more broadly to remind us to be fair in our decisions and not be biased by previous kindness (or lack thereof) from those concerned. Are you making decisions about someone or some thing? Do it fairly, without consideration of past or future advantage to you.

87. [2-6-3] Censure the present.

Grk.: Αἰτιῶ παρόντα.

Lat.: Incusa praesentia.

Censure: accuse, charge, blame; allege as cause. *The present*: things at hand, present times; one who is present.

Accuse or blame someone to their face (not behind their back). Don't make a scapegoat of someone not present or blame a foreigner. Don't excuse present company who are guilty. Be willing to acknowledge that the cause of a problem is close to home. Blame present circumstances or the time we live in. Criticize our current culture or society.

This oracle apparently contradicts Oracle 25 [1-4-4] "Censure nobody." On the one hand, this is not a problem in divination, for different queries call for different answers, but we might wonder why the Counsels of the Seven contain contradictory advice. Remember, however, that wisdom pays attention to context, and it is foolish to follow these rules blindly. Often, the opposite of good advice is also good advice. ("Look before you leap." "He who hesitates is lost.") Different advice applies in different situations. Moreover, this oracle can be understood as saying, "if you must censure someone, do it to their face," which is similar to Oracle 125 [3-4-6] "Fight not those absent." Alternately, like Gessner, we can interpret the oracle to mean that we should censure *things* that are present, what is near at hand in time and place, present circumstances.

88. [2-6-4] Knowing, speak.

Grk.: Λέγε εἰδώς.

Lat.: Dic sciens.

Speak: tell, say, explain, boast, recite, recount, count, gather.

You know, so speak. If you know, then say what you know. Recite, recount, or explain what you know. You should display your knowledge, don't hide it. Use your knowledge to organize things.

89. [2-6-5] Do not hold force.

Grk.: Βίας μὴ ἔχου.

Lat.: Vim non facias.

Hold: have, possess, use habitually, depend on, cling to, be close to, hold fast; bear up against, hold out; hold back, keep away from, refrain from. *Force*: bodily strength, might, power; acts of violence or force; mental strength or power.

Don't use force, don't depend on it. Keep away from violence. Don't cling to strength of mind or body. Yield to violence or force (don't fight it). Don't hold back your strength or power. You have power; use it wisely.

A simple statement pregnant with ambiguity! The form *bias* (force) can be accusative plural or genitive singular, and how we read it modulates the meaning of the verb. Moreover, the verb (*ekhou*) is very versatile, and so the oracle has a range of interpretations, some contradictory. The meanings center around holding and physical force, but whether we are being advised not to cling to it or not to withhold it, is unclear. Perhaps the conclusion is that we should consider carefully the use of physical force or strength, neither using it out of habit nor refraining from using it when appropriate. The oracle can also be interpreted to refer metaphorically to mental strength of power, which may apply in some cases. Your challenge is to solve this enigma.

90. [2-6-6] Live painlessly.

Grk.: Ἀλύπως βίου.

Lat.: Vive iucunde.

Live: pass your life. *Painlessly*: without pain or sorrow; without causing pain or sorrow; pleasantly.

Don't cause yourself unnecessary grief. Don't cling to what you cannot control, and you will live with tranquility. Don't bring pain and suffering on yourself through your attitudes and actions. Avoid causing another person to suffer.

Living without pain and sorrow might seem impossible, but they can be minimized by adopting the ancient spiritual practices of the Stoics. If you understand where your freedom resides, that is, what is in your control and what is not, then you can learn to derive your happiness only from what you can control and not to suffer from what you cannot.[142]

91. [2-6-7] Engage mildly.

Grk.: Ὁμίλει πράως.

Lat.: Conversare mansuete.

Engage: consort, join in company, be friends, be married, busy oneself; join battle. *Mildly*: gently, softly, meekly.

Be gentle with your friends and family. Treat your spouse with gentleness. Deal mildly with those around you. Don't be harsh or aggressive with them. Be meek among those others. Be a gentleman or woman in conflicts. Be gentle and soft in your relationships and interactions.

---

142. See MacLennan, *The Wisdom of Hypatia*, on Stoic spiritual practices.

92. [2-7-1] Fearlessly accomplish the end.

Grk.: Πέρας ἐπιτέλει μὴ ἀποδειλιῶν.

Lat.: Finem coeptis intrepidus impone.

Fearlessly: without fear, cowardice, or flinching from danger or effort. *Accomplish*: complete, finish; fulfill (especially a promise, vow, religious service, oracle, or vision). *End*: finish, completion, object, limit, perfection, boundary; final decision.

Go forward boldly to the destination. Keep up your effort and you will reach your goal. Be brave and you will reach the finish line. With effort you will accomplish your object. Drive onward to the final decision. Practice tirelessly and you will attain perfection. With courage you will fulfill your spiritual destiny.

"End" translates *peras*, which means limit or bound. *Limit* and the *Unlimited*, or *Bound* and the *Boundless*, are the principal Pythagorean opposites. Although, like Yang and Yin, both are necessary, Limit is the more positive, for it confers definiteness and determination. The oracle commands you to strive bravely toward the state of completeness and perfection.[143]

93. [2-7-2] Be kind to everyone.

Grk.: Φιλοφρόνει πᾶσιν.

Lat.: Omnibus esto benignus.

Be kind: show favor.

Be kind to everyone. Help them out. Think kindly and generously about others. Don't be unpleasant or uncooperative. Don't be selfish.

The oracle literally commands you to be kind-minded (*philo-phrôn*).

---

143. Peters, *Greek Philosophical Terms*, s.vv. *apeiron, peras*.

94. [2-7-3] Curse not thy sons.

Grk.: Υἱοῖς μὴ καταρῶ.

Lat.: Filios non exsecrare.[144]

Curse: lay curses upon, damn, denounce, abominate.

Don't condemn your children. Don't hate them. Don't denounce your students or followers. Don't denounce young people. Don't pronounce a formal curse on such people.

Literally, this oracle refers to your sons, but I think we must interpret it metaphorically to refer to any children, and to others in a similar relationship to you, such as your students or those you are mentoring. In the ancient world, students often referred to their spiritual teacher as "Father" or "Mother," and the teacher might call the student "Son" or "Daughter."

95. [2-7-4] Lead the woman.

Grk.: Γυναικὸς ἄρχε.

Lat.: Impera mulieri.

Lead: command, rule, govern; begin with, begin from. *Woman*: lady, wife, spouse.

Guide the woman involved in this matter. Guide your spouse. Provide guidance to a woman. Be a leader. Dissuade her from acting unwisely. Begin by considering, dealing with, or thinking of the woman or your spouse.

We have to remember that this maxim was most likely a man's opinion intended for other men in a society that was much more patriarchal in its customs than ours. No doubt, such opinions led to the oppression of women in ancient Greece, who for the most part had less opportunity for an education. (Typically, women were married when they were about fifteen years old to men twice their age.) For our time, a more progressive interpretation is that you should try to provide guidance for your spouse (male or female) or for a woman who is involved in the matter of inquiry.

Interestingly, Gessner read the Greek manuscripts differently, and for this oracle he has "Rule the tongue" (Grk., Γλώττης ἄρχε; Lat., *Impera linguae*), which is similar to Oracle 82 [2-5-5] "Hold thy tongue." If you don't like the patriarchal oracle above, you can substitute Gessner's reading. Interpret it like Oracle 82 [2-5-5] "Hold thy tongue."

---

144. My Latin translation, since Gessner has a different Greek text here, and therefore a different translation.

96. [2-7-5] Do thyself well.

Grk.: Σεαυτὸν εὖ ποίει.

Lat.: Benefac tibi ipsi.

Do well: benefit, treat well, make well off, make happy; create well, compose well, make well, produce well.

Be kind to yourself. Take care for your own happiness. Enjoy yourself! Charity begins at home. Earn some money. Take care of your health. Get your personal life sorted out. Take time for your personal development.

97. [2-7-6] Become affable.

Grk.: Εὐπροσήγορος γίνου.

Lat.: Affabilis esto.

Become: come into a new state of being, be born. *Affable*: courteous, easy to address.

Become polite and approachable. Don't be rude, arrogant, or aloof. It's time to begin your new life as a nice person. In particular, be friendly with a person involved in the matter.

98. [2-7-7] Answer at the right time.

Grk.: Ἀποκρίνου ἐν καιρῷ.

Lat.: Responde in tempore.

Answer: reply; answer charges, defend yourself. *Right time*: critical moment, opportune time, in season.

In making a reply or defending yourself, timing is everything! Think carefully about the right time, but also trust your intuition. If you make your answer too soon or too late, it will not have the result you want. There is a time and place for your reply.

On *Kairos* (opportunity, right time), see Oracle 10 [1-2-3] "Know the right time" and also the Alphabet Oracle under B (Beta). "Kairos" is a Pythagorean name for the number seven. This oracle is similar to Oracle 103 [3-1-5] "Counsel in time."

99. [3-1-1] Labor with glory.

Grk.: Πόνει μετ᾽εὐκλείας.

Lat.: Labora cum iustitia.

Labor: toil, suffer toil; be hard pressed, suffer. *With*: along with, by means of, according to. *Glory*: good repute; Eukleia.

Work hard and you will have a good reputation. Bear your suffering nobly and honorably. Don't labor or suffer shamefully. Use your good reputation to aid your work. Your burden will be your glory. You have the goddess Artemis Eukleia by your side in your travails.

"Eukleia" (Glory) is an epithet of Artemis.

100. [3-1-2] Act unrepentantly.

Grk.: Πρᾶττε ἀμετανοήτως.

Lat.: Ea fac, quorum te non paeniteat.

Act: get busy, accomplish, achieve, experience things; manage things, negotiate; practice, study; exact payment, punishment, or revenge. *Unrepentantly*: in a way not to be repented or regretted.

Act in a manner you will not regret. Manage things so you will not repent later. Achieve your goals without regret. Practice and study, or you will regret it. If you are going to do something, do it without repentance. Live life without regrets. If you seek revenge or to punish someone, do so in a manner you will not regret. Negotiate wisely, so you will not regret the consequences.

See also the remarks on "repentance" in Oracle 101 [3-1-3] "Failing, repent," which follows.

101. [3-1-3] Failing, repent.

Grk.: Ἁμαρτάνων μετανόει.

Lat.: Peccans paenitudi ne afficiaris.

Failing: missing the mark, failing your purpose, going or doing wrong, erring, sinning. *Repent*: change your mind or purpose, awake spiritually; perceive with hindsight.

If you have failed in some way, change your thinking. Reconsider your goals and desires. You didn't achieve your aims, which gives you an opportunity to change your means and ends. Are you barking up the wrong tree? If you have behaved badly, reform your thinking. If you've sinned, repent! Take responsibility for your failings. Look back on your mistakes and learn from them. You are not living a fulfilling life; wake up and live by a new philosophy!

In summary, acknowledge your mistake, but then free yourself by a change in your thinking. The word translated "repent" is related to *metanoia*, often translated "repentance," but literally a change of mind (*meta* + *noia*). It's also used for a spiritual awakening, conversion, or change of heart. Books have been written about this word! See also Oracle 100 [3-1-2] "Act unrepentantly."

102. [3-1-4] Control the eye.

Grk.: Ὀφθαλμοῦ κράτει.

Lat.: Oculo moderare.

Control: master, conquer, take possession of, rule, command, control, seize, hold fast. *Eye*: eye of a master, ruler, or god; dearest, best.

Keep your wandering eyes in check. Manage your attention. Observe the situation carefully. Control envy (yours or someone else's). Manage how you are seen by those in charge. Take control of your image. Attract and hold the attention of the gods. Keep control of that which is most important to you. Hold fast to it.

Metaphorically, the eye can stand for what is dearest or most important.

103. [3-1-5] Counsel in time.

Grk.: Βουλεύου χρόνῳ.

Lat.: Consule utilia.

Counsel: take counsel, deliberate; counsel another. *In time*: in season, at last.

Think the matter through at the right time. Consult with someone at the appropriate time. Give timely advice (neither too soon nor too late). Finally, you should give or receive advice.

This oracle is similar to Oracle 98 [2-7-7] "Answer at the right time."

104. [3-1-6] Act quickly.

Grk.: Πρᾶττε συντόμως.

Lat.: Absolve cito.

Act: get busy, accomplish, achieve, experience things; manage things, negotiate; practice, study; exact payment, punishment, or revenge. *Quickly*: shortly, briefly, concisely, immediately.

Act quickly, get busy now. Finish your task soon. Sprint to the finish line. Don't dilly dally or drag things out. Negotiate the agreement quickly. Don't put off getting your payment—or revenge; make it quick and to the point. Study or practice quickly; don't do more than necessary. Be efficient.

105. [3-1-7] Watch over affection.

Grk.: Φιλίαν φύλαττε.

Lat.: Amicitiam custodi.

Watch over: watch, guard, ward, defend, preserve, maintain, cherish, hold fast to; beware of, avoid. *Affection*: friendship, friendly love, affectionate regard, friendliness, amiability.

Cultivate your friendships; don't let them wither. Watch over your friendships and don't let others damage them. Cherish friendliness and affectionate feelings toward others. Try to be friendly and amiable; hold fast to these feelings. Beware of people using your friendship against you. Watch out for unhealthy or dangerous entanglements.

You are advised to watch over affection, but does that mean to care for it or to guard yourself from it? That is the riddle. See Oracle 20 [1-3-6] "Be fond of affection" on affection.

106. [3-2-1] Become sensible.

Grk.: Εὐγνώμων γίνου.

Lat.: Sis gratus.

Become: come into a new state of being, be born. *Sensible*: of good mind or feeling, prudent, reasonable; considerate, kind.

Exercise prudence and good judgment. Be reasonable. Don't be foolish. Commit to being kind and considerate.

The sense of the oracle is that you should be of good mind or judgment, kind, and considerate toward others.

107. [3-2-2] Pursue unity of mind.

Grk.: Ὁμόνοιαν δίωκε.

Lat.: Concordiam sequere.

Pursue: chase, seek after; drive, urge; chase away, banish. *Unity of mind*: unity of thought, concord, unity.

Seek concord and unity. Strive for consensus. Get everyone on the same page. Work toward psychological integration. Strive for a unified mindset and attitude. Don't be of two minds. On the other hand: Banish group-think (a lack of diversity in ideas). Encourage constructive disagreement.

Unity of mind is the property of being *homonous* or "of one mind" (*homo* + *nous*). Pythagoras began his speech to the Thousand in Croton by extolling unity of mind (*homonoia*), and told them to ensure concord in the city by building a temple to the Muses, for the Muses are called by one name and always sing and dance in unity and harmony.[145] In a letter,

---

145. Iamblichus, *On the Pythagorean Way of Life,* ch. 9, ¶45; pp. 68–9.

Iamblichus describes *homonoia* as "a communion and unity that brings together kindred minds," which spreads out to encompass homes and the community.[146] But, he says, it also applies to individuals, for you have unity of mind if you are "governed by a single mindset and attitude," that is, if you are not of two minds. "Homonoia" is a Pythagorean name for the numbers three and nine, and Homonoia is sometimes viewed as a goddess (Roman Concordia). (See Oracle 20 [1-3-6] "Be fond of affection" on Pythagorean friendship.)

The opposing meaning—to chase concord away or to banish unity of thought—is less obvious, but might be appropriate in a divinatory context. In both cases we are told to pursue it, but we must decide whether to catch it or chase it away.

108. [3-2-3] Conceal the unspeakable.

Grk.: Ἄρρητον κρύπτε.

Lat.: Arcanum non profer.

Conceal: hide, keep secret; cover, cloak, bury. *Unspeakable*: inexpressible, unsayable, unutterable; not to be spoken, not to be divulged, sacred mystery, arcana; unspoken, unsaid; horrible, shameful to be spoken; (mathematical) irrational.

Don't divulge a secret. Don't try to say that which cannot be said. It is best not to speak of some things. Respect your vows of secrecy; do not reveal the Sacred Mysteries or the inner teachings of your craft. Hide those things that should be kept secret. Don't talk about things that are shameful or horrible. Some things are better left unsaid.

In a religious or spiritual context, "the unspeakable" (*to arrhêton*) is that which cannot be spoken, either because it is so ineffable that it cannot be expressed in words, or because it is a sacred mystery that is unlawful to divulge to the uninitiated. "The unspeakables" (*ta arrhêta*) refers to the sacred secrets of the Mysteries (such as the Eleusinian Mysteries), and in Neoplatonic philosophy, The Unspeakable One (*To Arrhêton Hen*) is the highest principle, which confers unity on everything in heaven and on earth (discussed in chapter 2).

---

146. Iamblichus, "Letter 9, To Macedonius, On Concord," *Iamblichus of Chalcis* (Atlanta: Society of Biblical Literature, 2009), 28–9.

109. [3-2-4] Fear being mighty.

Grk.: Τὸ κρατοῦν φοβοῦ.

Lat.: Potentius time.

Being mighty: being powerful, holding sway, ruling, commanding, controlling; prevailing, defeating.

If you are in control of something, watch out. Being in command or the one holding power is not enviable; think twice before stepping into these shoes. The strong have many problems. You have much to fear and worry about; you have many responsibilities. Beware of defeating someone or of always being the winner. Your strength can be your weakness.

110. [3-2-5] Seek utility.

Grk.: Τὸ συμφέρον θηρῶ.

Lat.: Venare utile.

Seek: hunt for, pursue eagerly, chase after. *Utility*: use, advantage, expediency, profit, the useful, the fitting, assistance.

Pursue the useful, profitable, or expedient, that which gives an advantage. Seek it out. Figure out what you really need and go after it. Get help.

111. [3-2-6] Accept opportunity.

Grk.: Καιρὸν προσδέχου.

Lat.: Occasionem expecta.

Accept: receive favorably, admit, undertake; await, expect. *Opportunity*: right time, season, critical moment, vital part, advantage, fitness, due measure.

An opportunity is coming; watch for it and welcome it. Wait for the right time and seize it. Watch for the appropriate season for the matter. Look for an advantage and take it; don't pass it by. Accept what is in due measure, fit, or appropriate. The sense of the oracle seems to be that the opportunity is not to be sought, but watched for and awaited.

On *Kairos* (opportunity, right time), see Oracle 10 [1-2-3] "Know the right time" and also the Alphabet Oracle under B (Beta). "Kairos" is a Pythagorean name for the number seven.

112. [3-2-7] End hatreds.

Grk.: Ἔχθρας διάλυε.

Lat.: Inimicitias dissolve.

End: do away with, reconcile; dissolve, break up, put asunder. *Hatreds*: enmities.

Become reconciled with your enemies. Stop hating. Let anger and hatred dissolve. Build bridges, not walls.

Hatred is rarely a worthwhile emotion. As someone said, it's like drinking poison and expecting it to hurt the other person. One of the Pythagorean *symbola* (enigmatic maxims) is "Cut not fire with sword." Iamblichus reveals the hidden meaning: It's unwise to direct sharp words at an angry person. He quotes Heraclitus: "It is difficult to fight with anger," for it cannot be stopped. "But by governing the tongue," Iamblichus says, "and being quiet, friendship is produced from strife, the fire of anger being extinguished; and you yourself will not appear to be destitute of reason."[147] See also Oracle 16 [1-3-2] "Control thy spirit."

113. [3-3-1] Accept old age.

Grk.: Γῆρας προσδέχου.

Lat.: Senectutem expecta.

Accept: receive favorably, admit, undertake; await, expect.

Accept becoming old, whether you are old already or it's far in the future. Welcome it, for in spite of its challenges, it brings rewards, experience, and, if you are fortunate, wisdom. Reject the cult of youth and embrace your seniority (present or future). Prepare for your old age (both practically and spiritually). Welcome an old person into your life. Expect to encounter a mentor.

---

147. Iamblichus, *Protrepticus*, ch. XXI, symbol 9; pp. 112–113, η'; Johnson, p. 83.

114. [3-3-2] Boast not because of strength.

Grk.: Ἐπὶ ῥώμῃ μὴ καυχῶ.

Lat.: De viribus ne glorieris.

Boast: vaunt yourself, speak loud. *Because of*: as a result of, from a position of, for the purpose of, depending on, in addition to, against. *Strength*: bodily strength, might, force.

If you are in a position of strength, don't brag about it or be arrogant. Don't use your position of power to promote yourself. Don't boast to increase your power or influence, or to resist or diminish another's power.

115. [3-3-3] Practice auspicious speech.

Grk.: Εὐφημίαν ἄσκει.

Lat.: Benedicentiam usurpa.

Practice: exercise, form by art, honor. *Auspicious speech*: speech of good omen, abstinence from inauspicious speech, religious silence; prayer, praise, or worship offered to gods, praise or honor for people.

Think about what you say, and make a habit of saying auspicious, positive things. If you cannot speak in this way, it is better to keep silent. Don't make a negative prediction, which may become self-fulfilling. It is better to interpret omens positively, or to keep silent. Praise the gods, and praise godlike honorable people. Worship and pray to the gods regularly; make it a practice.

See Oracle 36 [1-6-1] "Be religiously silent" on auspicious speech and religious silence.

116. [3-3-4] Flee hatred.

Grk.: Ἀπέχθειαν φεῦγε.

Lat.: Simultatem fuge.

Flee: avoid, escape, flee consequence of. *Hatred*: toward others or toward yourself.

Avoid hating other people or yourself, for it's a destructive, unproductive emotion. Flee these feelings like a plague! Beware the consequences of another's hatred of you; don't let them hurt you.

The best way to escape hatred is to cultivate feelings of compassion, both for others and for yourself. See also Oracle 112 [3-2-7] "End hatreds" on hatred.

117. [3-3-5] Be rich justly.

Grk.: Πλούτει δικαίως.

Lat.: Divitias possideto iure.

Be rich: be wealthy. *Justly*: rightly, in due form, decently, fittingly, lawfully, moderately, reasonably, fairly, righteously, genuinely, really, truly, exactly.

Acquire wealth in just, lawful, fair, and righteous way. If you are wealthy, behave decently and moderately; don't be ostentatious or act as though privileged. Be genuine. Be rich in the things that really matter (not money).

This oracle is similar to Oracle 64 [2-3-1] "Acquire justly."

118. [3-3-6] Forsake not opinion.

Grk.: Δόξαν μὴ λεῖπε.

Lat.: Gloriam non defere.

Forsake: abandon, desert, leave behind. *Opinion*: expectation, (mere) opinion, judgment (good or bad), conjecture, fantasy; (good) reputation, honor, glory.

Judge, even if you cannot be absolutely certain. Pay attention to what others say and to their opinions. Pay attention to the reputations of others. Take heed for your own honorable reputation; don't forsake it. Be willing to speculate, to conjecture, and to imagine. Don't be hamstrung by certainty.

In ancient Greek philosophy, true knowledge (*epistêmê*) is contrasted with mere opinion (*doxa*). We prefer true knowledge (certainty) when we can have it, but in this material world of flux and uncertainty, which we try to understand with our limited cognitive capacities and experience, opinion (uncertain knowledge) is often the best we can have. See also Oracle 22 [1-4-1] "Chase opinion" and Peters, *Greek Philosophical Terms*, s.v. *doxa*.

119. [3-3-7] Hate vice.

Grk.: Κακίαν μίσει.

Lat.: Malitiam habeas odio.

Vice: badness, cowardice, evil, dishonor.

Don't behave badly, dishonorably, or cowardly. Detest the bad, dishonorable, or cowardly behavior of someone else. Eliminate vice from your life. Be good; strive for excellence, nobility, honor, and bravery.[148]

120. [3-4-1] Be daring prudently.

Grk.: Κινδύνευε φρονίμως.

Lat.: Periclitare prudenter.

Be daring: take a risk or risks, make a venture or ventures; be in danger. *Prudently*: wisely, sensibly, discreetly.

Now is the time to take risks, but be smart, not rash, about it. Start a new enterprise, but think it through. Be daring, but be wise. Be bold, but don't make a show of it.

121. [3-4-2] Tire not of learning.

Grk.: Μανθάνων μὴ κάμνε.

Lat.: Discendo non defatigeris.

Tire: be weary, work; suffer, be distressed; be sick, suffer illness. *Learning*: learning from study, practice, or experience; being a learner; perceiving, noticing; understanding.

---

148. Peters, *Greek Philosophical Terms*, s.v. *kakos*.

Continue to study, practice, and learn. Work hard at them and don't be weary. Don't be bored or upset by new experiences. Strive to pay attention, observe, learn, and understand. They are worth your effort.

122. [3-4-3] Forsake not sparing.

Grk.: Φειδόμενος μὴ λεῖπε.
Lat.: Parcitatem ne defere.[149]

Forsake: abandon, desert, leave behind. *Sparing*: being merciful; using sparingly, being thrifty.

Do not become unforgiving or unmerciful. Don't become cruel. Spare those you have bested and show them mercy. Don't become wasteful; be frugal and thrifty.

123. [3-4-4] Marvel at oracles.

Grk.: Χρησμοὺς θαύμαζε.
Lat.: Oracula admirare.

Marvel at: wonder at, be astonished by; admire, honor, worship. *Oracles*: oracular responses.

Honor oracles, for they are revelations from the gods. Treat oracles with respect and worship the gods who deliver them. Honor the oracular responses you have received. Don't consult oracles frivolously.

The word here translated "oracle" (*khrêsmos*) refers etymologically to a proclamation from the gods, and therefore to any divine revelation.

---

149. Gessner reads "Forsake not enjoying yourself" (Grk., Ἡδόμενος μὴ λίπε; Lat., *Ea quibus gaudes ne defere*), so I have provided a Latin translation.

124. [3-4-5] Be fond of those you have reared.

Grk.: Οὓς τρέφεις, ἀγάπα.

Lat.: Dilige eos quos alis.

Be fond of: love, desire, prize, welcome, tolerate. *Reared:* brought up, caused to grow or increase, let grow, bred; fostered, supported, nurtured, maintained; cherished.

Love your children and grandchildren; be tolerant of their failings. Cherish your students, look kindly on them, and forgive their failures. Take care of those who depend on you. Be welcoming to all whom you have supported and helped to grow. Be proud of them, for you have helped them to become who they are.

125. [3-4-6] Fight not those absent.

Grk.: Ἀπόντι μὴ μάχου.

Lat.: Absentem ne impugnes.

Fight: quarrel with, dispute with, oppose, gain say. *Those:* things. *Absent:* away.

Don't denounce or sabotage someone behind their back or in their absence. If you must oppose them, do it to their face. Don't libel or spread vicious rumors. Don't fight distant battles; concern yourself with what is close to home.

This oracle is similar to Oracle 87 [2-6-3] "Censure the present."

126. [3-4-7] Respect the older.

Grk.: Πρεσβύτερον αἰδοῦ.

Lat.: Maiorem te natu reverere.

Respect: stand in awe of, fear, feel regard for. *Older:* elder; more important, greater; presbyter.

Respect your elders. Treat them kindly. Recognize people who are superior to you in some way and acknowledge their superiority. In some cases you should fear them. Respect priests, religious elders, and spiritual teachers.

127. [3-5-1] Teach the younger.

Grk.: Νεώτερον δίδασκε.

Lat.: Iuniorem doce.

Teach: instruct, teach about. *Younger*: young, more youthful; newer, more recent, later, fresher; less expected, strange, worse, rebellion.

Instruct the younger generation or the newcomers. Or teach *about* them. Teach about surprising things, the new and strange, revolutions. Advise about changes to the worse.

Compare Oracle 44 [1-7-2] "Educate thy sons."

128. [3-5-2] Distrust wealth.

Grk.: Πλούτῳ ἀπίστει.

Lat.: Divitiis non confide.

Distrust: disbelieve, disobey. *Wealth*: riches; Ploutos (god of riches).

Distrust the wealthy. Distrust those who have a financial stake in the matter. Don't let wealth be your unquestioned guide. What the God of Riches gives, he also takes back (when you die).

129. [3-5-3] Respect thyself.

Grk.: Σεαυτὸν αἰδοῦ.

Lat.: Verere teipsum.

Respect: stand in awe of, fear, feel regard for.

Respect yourself. Treat yourself kindly; be compassionate to yourself. You are awesome! But watch out for yourself.

130. [3-5-4] Don't begin to have hubris.

Grk.: Μὴ ἄρχε ὑβρίζειν.

Lat.: Iniurius esse ne coeperis.

Hubris: insolence, overweening pride, wanton violence, pride, or passion; rape or another outrage, lust.

Don't even *think* of having hubris! Don't let overweening pride or insolence get a foothold in your attitude or behavior. Don't pump up your ego by debasing or humiliating someone else. Don't even contemplate violence against another. Control your lust.

See also Oracle 41 [1-6-6] "Hate hubris" on hubris. The gist of this oracle is to nip hubris in the bud. Compare Oracle 83 [2-5-6] "Ward off hubris."

131. [3-5-5] Crown the ancestors.

Grk.: Προγόνους στεφάνου.

Lat.: Maiores tuos corona.

Crown: wreathe (as a victor), honor. *Ancestors*: forefathers; progenitor gods; stepchildren.

Honor those who have come before you, your ancestors, the founders of your country, culture, or tradition. Thank them for their gifts and their benefits, which have come down to your time. Lay a wreath for them. Worship the ancestral gods of your people. Respect stepchildren.

The literal meaning of *progonos* is "one who was born before" (*pro* + *gonos*), and hence an ancestor or forefather, but that phrase can also refer to a child by a previous marriage, and hence a stepchild.

Iamblichus says that for anyone with self-respect, it is unacceptable to be honored only for your ancestors and not for your own sake. For the honor of your ancestors is like an inherited treasure which you should increase, or at least not squander. Therefore, everyone should conduct their lives so as to acquire their own honor, to win their own glory, which can be passed on to their successors.[150]

---

150. Iamblichus, *Protrepticus*, ch. XIX; p. 91; in Johnson, *The Complete Works*, 68.

132. [3-5-6] Die for the fatherland.

Grk.: Θνῆσκε ὑπὲρ πατρίδος.

Lat.: Pro patria mortem oppetas.

Die for: perish for, be slain by. *Fatherland:* country, native land or town; something derived from your fathers, something hereditary.

Defend to the death your country or your native land. Devote your life to your homeland or to your community. Devote your life to your cultural heritage. Serve your country. Defend things such as these with all that you have got.

This oracle has a straightforward literal meaning, but it can also be understood metaphorically.

133. [3-5-7] Be not burdened by thy life.

Grk.: Τῷ βίῳ μὴ ἄχθου.

Lat.: Non pugna adversus vitam.

Burdened: oppressed, vexed, grieved; loaded. *Life:* course of life, biography; manner or means of living, livelihood; lifetime.

Don't let life drag you down. Don't be oppressed by your job; live a balanced life. Don't be depressed by your past. Don't be angry at your life circumstances. Always look on the bright side of life (thank you, Monty Python!).

In some circumstances, this oracle might seem impossible to obey, but Stoic spiritual practices can help you to center your happiness in what is truly under your control and to face with equanimity what is not.

134. [3-6-1] Laugh not at the dead.

Grk.: Ἐπὶ νεκρῷ μὴ γέλα.

Lat.: De mortuo non riseris.

The dead: a corpse.

Don't mock the dead; respect them. Don't abuse a corpse.

Compare Oracle 140 [3-6-7] "Wrong not the dead." When the Stoic philosopher Zeno of Citium (ca. 334–ca. 262 BCE) asked an oracle how to live his life, he was told to converse with the dead. He understood this to mean that he should study the writings of the ancients. Likewise, this oracle can warn you not to ridicule or disparage ancient ideas.

135. [3-6-2] Suffer with the unfortunate.

Grk.: Ἀτυχοῦντι συνάχθου.

Lat.: Cum infelice condoleto.

Unfortunate: unlucky, unsuccessful.

Have sympathy for the unfortunate. Feel compassion for them. Feel sympathy for those whose lives have not turned out well. Share their sadness.

136. [3-6-3] Show kindness without harm.

Grk.: Χαρίζου ἀβλαβῶς.

Lat.: Gratificare citra iacturam.

Show kindness: show favor; give graciously or cheerfully; be gracious, agreeable or favorable; comply. *Without harm*: harmlessly, innocently; without suffering harm, securely.

Be kind and helpful, but do so honestly and without a hidden agenda. Be genuinely cooperative. Comply honestly, not in appearance only. Be generous, but not too your own detriment. Don't take undue risks when you give aid.

137. [3-6-4] Grieve not for anyone.

Grk.: Μὴ ἐπὶ παντὶ λυποῦ.

Lat.: Non quavis de causa tristeris.

Grieve: be distressed; vex, annoy, give pain. *Anyone*: anything.

Don't grieve for someone else. Don't grieve the dead. In fact, don't be distressed at anything. Don't annoy other people or cause them pain.

I think that this oracle is telling you to put aside any grief or distress you might feel, for you shouldn't suffer from things outside your control. See Oracles 90 [2-6-6] "Live painlessly" and 133 [3-5-7] "Be not burdened by thy life" for the remarks on Stoic spiritual practices.

138. [3-6-5] Beget from the well-born.

Grk.: Ἐξ εὐγενῶν γέννα.

Lat.: Ex ingenuis prolem suscipe.

Beget: bring forth, produce, create. *Well-born*: highbred, noble, noble-minded, generous.

Create from what is already noble or of high quality, be that a spouse, or an animal to be bred. Use the best materials in your creations. Engage generous and noble-minded people in your creative endeavors.

139. [3-6-6] Promise to nobody.

Grk.: Ἐπαγγέλλου μηδενί.

Lat.: Nemini promitte.

Promise: offer, profess, tell, proclaim, give orders.

Don't make a promise. Don't make an offer or proclamation. Don't speak out or lecture someone; keep quiet. Don't order others around or take a commanding position.

140. [3-6-7] Wrong not the dead.

Grk.: Φθιμένους μὴ ἀδίκει.

Lat.: Ne fueris iniquus in defunctos.

Wrong: treat unjustly, be unrighteous to, injure, harm. *Dead*: slain; perished, wasted away.

Treat the dead with justice. Don't libel the dead, rob their estates, or rob or vandalize their tombs. Don't abuse a corpse. Don't take advantage of those who have perished.

See Oracle 5 [1-1-5] "Yield to Justice" on justice (*dikê*), for the root meaning here is not to treat the dead without *dikê*. Compare Oracle 134 [3-6-1] "Laugh not at the dead." Metaphorically, treat the ancients and their ideas justly.

141. [3-7-1] Be well off, as thou'rt mortal.

Grk.: Εὖ πάσχε ὡς θνητός.

Lat.: Suscipe beneficia, tanquam mortalis.

Be well off: receive benefits, be well disposed; suffer well. *As*: since, because. *Mortal*: one who will die, human.

Accept the human condition and be tranquil, for soon enough each of us will die. Be willing to be helped. Be grateful that you will not live forever. Accept with equanimity what is out of your control, and anchor your happiness in what is in your control.

As mentioned in Oracles 90 [2-6-6] "Live painlessly," 133 [3-5-7] "Be not burdened by thy life," and 137 [3-6-4] "Grieve not for anyone," Stoic spiritual practices can help you to be tranquil in spite of life's inevitable disappointments and misfortunes.

142. [3-7-2] Trust not Fortune.

Grk.: Τύχῃ μὴ πίστευε.

Lat.: Fortunae ne credas.

Trust: put faith in, trust to, rely on, believe in, comply with. *Fortune*: good luck, success, the good obtained by a god's favor, the goddess Tychê or Fortuna, providence, destiny, chance, a chance event, bad luck, an accident, misfortune, station in life; physical necessity.

Fortune is fickle; don't trust her! Don't rely on good luck or chance events. Don't assume you will be successful or that your current success will continue. Don't assume the gods will help you. Don't assume the outcome is destined and inevitable. Don't allow yourself to be tossed about by fortune, whether good or bad. Don't be constrained by your station in life, whether high or low.

I think that the import of this oracle is that you should not simply hope for success or a good outcome, but should take some action to get the result you desire. The gods help those who help themselves. Also, Neoplatonic spiritual practices are directed toward escaping Fortune and living joyously in conformity with divine Providence (see for example MacLennan, 2013). See Oracle 68 [2-3-5] "Acknowledge Fortune" for more on Tychê (Fortune); see also Peters, *Greek Philosophical Terms*, s.v., *tychê*. Compare Oracle 77 [2-4-7] "Love Fortune." "Tychê" is a Pythagorean name for the number seven.

143. [3-7-3] As a child, be well-behaved.

Grk.: Παῖς ὢν κόσμιος ἴσθι.

Lat.: Modestus esto in pueritia.

Child: servant, slave. *Well-behaved*: orderly, regular, discreet, quiet, moderate.

You are a young person, so be well-behaved. You are metaphorically a child (beginner, learner, subordinate), so be humble, discreet, and quiet (so you can learn and grow). You will learn more by listening than by talking. Be orderly in your studies.

Oracles 143–147 form an obvious series, from childhood to the end of life, and they are generally treated as a connected statement. However, there is no punctuation in the original inscription, and each of the five lines is an independent clause in this context. Therefore, each of these lines is understandable as an independent oracle. Moreover, I think these oracles can be applied to any phase of life that begins, matures, and inevitably ends, such as a career or a relationship.

144. [3-7-4] As a youth, be strong.

Grk.: ἡβῶν ἐγκρατής.

Lat.: adolescens quidem sis temperans.

As a youth: as an adolescent, as one past puberty, being in the prime of youth; being fresh or vigorous. *Be strong*: be stout, hold fast, have power.

You are in your prime, so be strong and use your power. Don't be lazy or weak, wasting your youthful vigor. You are at the height of your strength, so stand firm. You have established yourself in your career, so be bold. Go for it!

This oracle is part of a series, Oracles 143–147; see the discussion under Oracle 143 [3-7-3] "As a child, be well-behaved." The plain meaning refers to youth, but as an oracle it can refer to any vigorous person or someone who has come into their strength.

145. [3-7-5] In the middle, be just.

Grk.: μέσος δίκαιος.

Lat.: vigente aetate iustus.

In the middle: between youth and elder; being moderate, of middle rank. *Just*: right, meet, righteous, lawful, well-ordered, well-balanced, moderate, civilized, fair, genuine, real, true, exact.

You are an adult, so act like one. Be civilized, honest, fair, and just. Be careful and do what is right. Be impeccable in the midpoint of your career or in your middle-management position. Obey the law and do what is right. Midway through your life or career, stay balanced and live with moderation. If you are stuck in the middle, keep your balance and do what is right and fair.

In the context of Oracles 143–147 (see discussion under Oracle 143 [3-7-3] "As a child, be well-behaved"), the plain meaning relates to someone between youth and elder in age (and, in this sense, "middle-aged"). As an independent oracle, we may take it as applying to anyone in the middle of some role, relationship, or process. See Oracle 5 [1-1-5] "Yield to Justice" on justice.[151]

146. [3-7-6] As an elder, be sensible.

Grk.: πρεσβύτης εὔλογος.

Lat.: senex autem prudens.

Elder: old man; chief, president, ambassador. *Sensible*: reasonable, fair.

If you are an elder or have attained an exalted position, stay sensible, reasonable, and fair. Don't let your status go to your head; be dignified yet humble. Use your experience to act sensibly. Use your authority to ensure fairness.

In the context of Oracles 143–147 (see discussion under Oracle 143 [3-7-3] "As a child, be well-behaved"), the plain meaning relates to old age. As an independent oracle, we may take it as applying to any dignified person.

147. [3-7-7] Coming to the end, be without pain.

Grk.: τελευτῶν ἄλυπος.

Lat.: moriaris absque tristitia.

Coming to the end: ending life, dying; finishing, at the end, at last; accomplishing, completing, bringing to pass; fulfilling (especially an oath, promise, etc.). *Be without pain*: be without bodily pain; be without mental pain, distress, or grief; cause no pain.

If you are approaching the end of your life, do so without regret or fear. When the part that the gods have written for you in the drama of life requires your final exit, be thankful for your time on stage and don't complain that you should have been given a bigger part or more lines to speak. Be tranquil in the face of pain, sickness, infirmity, and the other inevitabilities of old age. Don't grieve for what might have been (it's too late for that). Don't inflict your pain on others. At the end of your career, be thankful for your experiences; celebrate your freedom and make way for

---

151. Peters, *Greek Philosophical Terms*, s.v. *dikê*.

those who will come after. Having reached your goal or fulfilled your promise, accept the end and prepare for what is to follow.

In the context of Oracles 143–147 (see discussion under Oracle 143 [3-7-3] "As a child, be well-behaved"), the plain meaning relates to end of life. As an independent oracle, we may take it as applying to any sort of end, completion, or accomplishment. As discussed under Oracle 90 [2-6-6] "Live painlessly," Stoic spiritual practices can help you to be tranquil and not suffer as things come to their inevitable conclusion.

Conclusion

You have now learned two systems of divination based on inspired wisdom engraved on ancient stone tablets. The Alphabet Oracle, which we know from tablets more than 1,800 years old, is under the patronage of Apollo and Hermes, and the Oracle of the Seven Sages, which was inscribed on tablets in Apollo's temple at Delphi, is at least 2,400 years old (and perhaps 2,600: the era of the Seven Sages). These two Oracles of Apollo are complementary. The Alphabet Oracle is most suited to answering practical questions about your plans and how best to pursue them (or, sometimes, to abandon them). Whatever your journey, it is your guide along the way. The Oracle of the Seven Sages gives a different kind of advice, for it offers broad philosophical and moral principles to guide you through your life.

You have learned also that oracles are enigmas, for Apollo and Hermes are riddlers, whose words are obscure and ambiguous. In this way they challenge you to exercise and improve your intelligence so that you can understand their wisdom and act wisely in any situation. You must look through the most obvious or desirable meanings of an oracle to see what its meaning is for you now. Accept it and do what is best.

In order to use these oracles more effectively, you have learned rituals for consecration and divination, and magical operations to manifest your destiny better. These are supported by symbolic actions, signs, and correspondences that connect you with divinity. Practice will improve your skill in using them.

Finally, you have learned how our Pagan ancestors used divination to improve their lives. Although our world is very different from theirs, the gods are the same, and you can use these ancient sacred tools to live better today. Through this ancient sacred art you may, as Iamblichus taught, share in the divine life of the gods, partaking of their wisdom and providence.[152] That has been my goal in writing *The Oracles of Apollo*.

---

152. Iamblichus, *Iamblichus on the Mysteries*, X.4 (¶289; p. 346).

Appendix A

Glossary

Many Hellenist and Roman Neopagans like to know the Greek and Latin words used in their practice, and so I have collected them here, with a guide to their approximate pronunciation in Ancient (Attic) Greek and Classical Latin. Of course, you do not need to know any Greek or Latin to use these divination systems. In each case, I list the word in its singular form, followed in parentheses by its pronunciation, its plural form, the plural's pronunciation, and an indication of the language (Grk., Lat., or Eng.). (Note that G's are always hard in Ancient Greek and Latin.) Then follows the meaning *in the context of divination* (most of these words have non-divinatory meanings as well). I have also included a few relevant English words, such as "astragalomancy."

Abacus (AH-bah-kuss; *abaci,* AH-bah-key; Lat.): dice tray or game board.

Ainigma (AI-nig-mah; *ainigmata,* ai-NIG-mah-tah; Grk.): enigma, riddle.

Alveus (AHL-weh-us; *alvei,* AHL-weh-ee; Lat.): dice tray.

Astragalomancy (ah-STRA-gah-low-Mahn-see; Eng.): Divination by means of huckle-bones or dice; a kind of cleromancy. In Greek, *astragalomanteía* (ah-stra-gah-law-mahn-TAY-ah).

Astragalos (ah-STRAH-gah-loss; *astragaloi,* ah-STRAH-gah-loy; Grk.): hucklebone.

Bolos (BAW-loss; *boloi,* BAW-loy; Grk.): a throw or cast of the lots.

Chrêsmologikê (khrase-maw-law-gih-KAY; *chrêsmologikai,* khrase-maw-law-gih-KAI; Grk.): (art of) divination, especially from collected oracles.

Chrêsmologos (khrase-maw-LAW-goss; *chrêsmologoi,* khrase-maw-LAW-goy; Grk.): diviner, especially a collector and interpreter of oracles.

Chrêsmos (khrase-MOSS; *chrêsmoi*, krase-MOY; Grk.): oracle.

Cleromancy (KLEH-row-Man-see; Eng.): divination by lots (things chosen by chance), or sortilege; *see Klêros*. (The Greek word for it would be *klêromanteía*, but I don't know of any ancient evidence for it.)

Cubomancy (KYOO-bow-Man-see; Eng.): a rare word for dice divination (see *kubos*).

Daimôn (DIE-moan; *daimones*, DIE-maw-ness; Grk.): daimon (Lat. *daemon*, pl. *daemones*, pronounced the same as Greek), an intermediate spirit between gods and mortals.

Divinatio (dee-wee-NAH-tih-oh; *divinationes*, dee-wee-nah-tih-OH-nase; Lat.): divination.

Fritillus (frih-TILL-us; *fritilli*, frih-TILL-ee; Lat.): dice cup or box.

Gramma (GRAH-mah; *grammata*, GRAH-mah-tah; Grk.): written letter of the alphabet or other character.

Grammatomancy (gram-MAT-o-man-see): divination by means of letters of the alphabet. (The Greek word for it would be *grammatomanteía*, but I don't know of any ancient evidence for it.)

Iactus (YAHK-tuss; *iacti*, YAHK-tee; Lat.): a throw or cast of the lots.

Isopsêphos (ih-SAW-psay-foss; *isopsêphoi*, is-SAW-psay-foy; Grk.): numerically equal words (equal in terms of *psêphoi*, pebbles; see *psêphos*).

Klêros (KLAY-ross; *klêroi*, KLAY-roy; Grk.): lot, something chosen by chance.

Kubos (KOO-boss; *kuboi*, KOO-boy; Grk.): die (pl. dice).

Lamella (lah-MEL-lah; *lamellae*, lah-MEL-lie; Lat.): thin metal sheet or leaf.

Manteia (mahn-TAY-ah; *manteiai*, mahn-TAY-eye; Grk.): power of divination, oracle.

Mantikê (mahn-tih-KAY; *mantikai*, mahn-tih-KAI; Grk.): (art of) divination.

Mantis (MAHN-tiss; *manteis*, MAHN-tase; Grk.): diviner, seer.

Onoma barbaron (AW-naw-mah BAR-bah-rawn; *onomata barbara*, aw-NAW-mah-tah BAR-bah-rah; Grk.): barbarian name (i.e., a magical name).

Oraculum (aw-RAH-kuh-lum; *oracula*, aw-RAH-kuh-lah; Lat.): oracle.

Phimos (fih-MOSS; *phimoi*, fih-MOY; Grk.): dice cup or box.

Pinax (PIH-nahks; *pinakes*, PIH-nah-kess; Grk.): tablet, dice tray or table.

Psêphos (PSAY-foss; *psêphoi*, PSAY-foy; Grk.): pebble or small stone, especially as used in divination, magic, counting, calculating, voting, etc.

Purgos (PURR-goss; *purgoi*, PURR-goy; Grk.): dice tower.

Signum (SIG-num; *signa*, SIG-nuh; Lat.): sign, token, symbol.

Sors (SOURCE; *sortes*, SOAR-tayss; Lat.): lot, something chosen by chance.

Sortilegus (soar-TIH-leh-guss; *sortilegi*, soar-TIH-leh-gee; Lat.): diviner, lot caster.

Sumbolon (SÜM-baw-lawn; *symbola*, SÜM-baw-lah; Grk.): symbol, sign, token, secret sign or token, allegory, enigmatic saying, oracle.

Tabula (TAH-buh-lah; *tabulae*, TAH-buh-lie; Lat.): tablet, dice tray or table.

Talus (TAH-luss; *tali*, TAH-lee; Lat.): hucklebone.

Tessera (TEH-seh-rah; *tesserae*, TEH-seh-rai; Lat.): die (pl. dice).

Theourgia (theh-oor-GIH-ah; *theourgiai*, theh-oor-GIH-ai; Grk.): theurgy, the art of ritual communication with and ascent to gods.

Thriai (three-AI; Grk.): pebbles used in divination; the Thriai nymphs; oracles from the preceding. (The singular does not occur.)

Turricula (tur-RIH-kuh-lah; *turriculae*, tur-RIH-kuh-lie; Lat.): dice tower.

Vox magica (WOX MAH-gih-kah; *voces magicae*; WOE-case MAH-gih-kai; Lat.): magic word or phrase.

Appendix B

Probabilities

If you know a little about probability theory, you might have realized that with some methods of casting the Alphabet Oracle the letters are not equally likely to occur. For example, with alphabet stones or leaves and with the coin and Three-Out-of-Four Methods, each letter has the same probability, but with the ancient astragalos and dice methods, some of the sums can occur in several different ways, and so the corresponding letters are more likely to occur by chance. Furthermore, due to the irregular shape of astragaloi, their four sides are not equally likely to occur (0.1 each for 1 and 6, 0.4 each for 3 and 4),[153] and many ancient dice were not perfectly "fair" (all six sides equally likely). This concerns some practitioners of the ancient divinatory arts, since it seems to imply that certain oracular responses are more likely than others. In this appendix, I will explain why there is no reason to be concerned.

I'll discuss the issues by using a simple example. The laws of probability tell you what you can expect to happen if you repeat a "trial" (test) a large number of times. For example, if you toss a fair coin a large number of times (and if you toss it fairly!), you can expect about the same number of heads and tails. Probability theory says *nothing* about what will happen in an individual trial. If it is a fair trial, then (by definition) a head will be just as likely as a tail. Even if you have just tossed four heads in a row, on the next toss a head is just as likely as a tail. Many people find this surprising, but it is true. In fact, runs are more common than most people suspect, and when people try to act randomly (e.g., in playing games like Rock-Paper-Scissors), they tend to have too few runs. For example, you could expect to have one run of five heads out of every thirty-two tests of five tosses. Indeed, even a run of one hundred heads in a row does not violate the laws of probability,

---

153. David, *Games, Gods, and Gambling*, 7.

although it is very unlikely (and might lead you to suspect you have an unfair coin!). To state it plainly, no sequence of tosses violates the laws of probability, although sequences with approximately the same number of heads and tails are more likely (their probability fits a bell-shaped curve called the binomial distribution).

Now let's bring this discussion back to cleromancy (divination by lots), and in particular to casting the Alphabet Oracle. You can see that the laws of probability do not limit in any way its ability to deliver a particular oracle to you. Even if the oracle has answered Ω on your last four questions, there is nothing preventing it from answering Ω again on your next question. If you kept track of the oracular responses over a lifetime of divination (perhaps tens of thousands of readings), I expect that each letter would turn up *about* the number of times you would expect by chance (e.g., 1/24 for drawing alphabet stones). All this means is that all twenty-four oracles are approximately equally useful; it does not in any way contradict the appropriateness of each individual oracular response.

This raises an obvious question: "Suppose I ask the same question a large number of times? Shouldn't I get the same answer each time?" The answer is that we are talking about divination (contact with a divinity), not a game of chance or the repetition of a scientific experiment. In his collaborations with the Nobel Laureate quantum physicist Wolfgang Pauli, Carl Jung distinguished statistical laws from synchronistic laws.[154] Statistics deals with causation in the material world, which is repeatable and therefore subject to statistics. Synchronicity (meaningful coincidence) connects material and mental phenomena by means of their shared meaning. Individual synchronistic events are unrepeatable and therefore statistics does not apply to them. Synchronistic laws do indeed describe regularities in experience, but different from the regularities described by statistical and physical laws. Divination uses the laws of synchronicity to set up a synchronistic event, which coordinates the physical and psychical realms and allows the psychical to manifest in the physical.

From a spiritual perspective, divination is the art of contacting a god or other spirit in order to gain knowledge or advice in a matter of some importance. How do you think a human sage would react if we came to them to ask a question, and having received their answer, came back ten minutes later and asked the same question, and then came back again, and again and again, until we had enough "samples" for statistical analysis? I expect that they would reward our arrogance and mistrust by not answering (i.e., "letting the

---

154. Atmanspacher, "Dual-Aspect Monism à la Pauli and Jung," *Journal of Consciousness Studies* 19, 9-10 (2012): 96–120.

chips fall where they may"), or perhaps teach us a lesson in humility in some other way. There is a long tradition in many cultures that the gods withdraw our prophetic powers if they are misused. Without the guiding hand of the god, you will get exactly what would be expected by chance: random readings.

"The master speaks but once." This was Carl Jung's comment about repeating a divination, which he wrote in his Forward to the *I Ching*,[155] which is well worth reading. Does this mean that you should never ask the same question more than once? Not necessarily. There is nothing wrong with repeating a question to obtain clarification, although in this case you should be explicit about what is unclear, which means it's really a different question. It is also appropriate to repeat a question if circumstances have changed since the first time you asked it. Again, that really makes it a different question, since its context has changed. If you just keep in mind that you are addressing a divinity to whom you owe respect, and that you are not playing a game (or running a scientific experiment), then you will not go wrong.

To come back to the original question, it does not matter that different ways of casting the oracle give different probabilities to the letters. Use whichever methods work best for you.

---

155. *The I Ching or Book of Changes: The Richard Wilhelm Translation rendered into English by Cary F. Baynes, Forward by C. G. Jung*, 3rd ed. (Princeton: Princeton University Press, 1967), xxix.

Bibliography

Addey, Crystal. *Divination and Theurgy in Neoplatonism: Oracles of the Gods*. Surrey: Ashgate, 2014.

Agrippa, H. C. *Three Books of Occult Philosophy*. Translated by J. Freake, edited and annotated by D. Tyson. St. Paul, MN: Llewellyn, 1999.

Allen, W. S. *Vox Graeca: A Guide to the Pronunciation of Classical Greek*. Cambridge: Cambridge University Press, 1968.

Apollodorus. *The Library*. 2 vols. Translated by James G. Frazer. Loeb Classical Library. Cambridge: Harvard University Press, 1921.

Atmanspacher, Harald. "Dual-Aspect Monism à la Pauli and Jung." *Journal of Consciousness Studies* 19, 9–10 (2012): 96–120.

Bernardus Silvestris. *Commentary on the First Six Books of Virgil's* Aeneid. Translated by Earl G. Schreiber and Thomas E. Maresca. Lincoln, NE: University of Nebraska Press, 1979.

Betz, Hans Dieter, ed. *The Greek Magical Papyri in Translation, Including the Demotic Spells*, 2nd ed. Chicago, IL: University of Chicago Press, 1992.

Browning, Elizabeth Barrett. *Prometheus Bound and Other Poems*. New York: C. S. Francis, 1851.

Budge, E. A. Wallis. *An Egyptian Hieroglyphic Dictionary*, Vol. I. New York: Dover, 1978.

Burkert, Walter. *Greek Religion*. Translated by John Raffan. Cambridge, MA: Harvard University Press, 1985.

Butterworth, E. A. S. *Some Traces of the Pre-Olympian World in Greek Literature and Myth.* Berlin: Walter de Gruyter, 1966.

Cicero. M. *Tulli Ciceronis De Divinatione Liber Primus.* A. S. Pease, ed. *University of Illinois Studies in Language and Literature*, Vol. VI, No. 2 (May 1920).

———. *On Divination Book I.* Translation, introduction, and commentary by D. Wardle. Oxford: Clarendon, 2006.

Cook, Arthur Bernard. "The Bee in Greek Mythology." *Journal of Hellenic Studies* 15 (1895): 1–24.

———. *Zeus: A Study in Ancient Religion.* 3 vols. New York: Biblo and Tannen, 1965.

David, Florence Nightingale. *Games, Gods, and Gambling: The Origins and History of Probability and Statistical Ideas from the Earliest Times to the Newtonian Era.* New York: Hafner, 1962.

Davis, Gil. "*Axones* and *Kurbeis*: A New Answer to an Old Problem." *Historia* 60, 1 (2011): 1–35.

Decker, Ronald, Thierry Depaulis, and Michael Dummett. *A Wicked Pack of Cards: The Origins of the Occult Tarot.* New York: St. Martins, 1996.

Diogenes Laertius. *Lives of the Eminent Philosophers.* 2 vols. Translated by R. D. Hicks. Loeb Classical Library. Cambridge, MA: Harvard University Press, 1925.

Fowler, Robert L. *Early Greek Mythography II: Commentary.* Oxford: Oxford University Press, 2013.

Franklin, Stephen E. *Origins of the Tarot Deck: A Study of the Astronomical Substructure of Game and Divining Boards.* Jefferson, NC: McFarland and Company, 1988.

Gantz, Timothy. *Early Greek Myth: A Guide to Literary and Artistic Sources.* Baltimore, MD: Johns Hopkins University Press, 1993.

Gardner, Alan. *Egyptian Grammar: Being an Introduction to the Study of Hieroglyphs*, 3rd ed. Cambridge: Oxford University Press, 1957.

Godwin, Joscelyn. *The Mystery of the Seven Vowels: In Theory and Practice.* Grand Rapids, MI: Phanes, 1991.

Goodwin, W. W. *A Greek Grammar.* Revised and Enlarged Edition. Boston, MA: Ginn & Co, 1892.

Gordon, Cyrus H. "The Accidental Invention of the Phonemic Alphabet." *Journal of Near Eastern Studies* 29 (1970): 193–197.

Guthrie, Kenneth Sylvan. *The Pythagorean Sourcebook and Library: An Anthology of Ancient Writings Which Relate to Pythagoras and Pythagoreanism.* Edited by David Fideler. Grand Rapids, MI: Phanes, 1987.

Halliday, W. R. *Greek Divination: A Study of Its Methods and Principles.* London: Macmillan, 1913.

Hansen, William. *Anthology of Ancient Greek Popular Literature.* Bloomington, IN: Indiana University Press, 1998.

Heinevetter, Franz. *Würfel- und Buchstabenorakel in Griechenland und Kleinasien.* Breslau: Universität Breslau, 1912.

Hesiod. *Hesiod, the Homeric Hymns, and Homerica.* Translated by Hugh G. Evelyn-White. Loeb Classical Library. Cambridge: Harvard University Press, 1936.

Hornblower, S., and A. Spawforth. *The Oxford Classical Dictionary*, 3rd ed. Oxford: Oxford University Press, 1996.

Hyginus. *Hygini Fabulae*, 2nd ed. Edited by Herbert Jennings Rose. Leiden, Holland: A. W. Sijthoff, 1963.

Iamblichus. *Iamblichus of Chalcis: The Letters.* Translation and commentary by John M. Dillon and Wolfgang Polleichtner. Atlanta, GA: Society of Biblical Literature, 2009.

———. *Iamblichus on the Mysteries.* Translation and introduction by Emma C. Clarke, John M. Dillon, and Jackson P. Hershbell. Atlanta, GA: Society of Biblical Literature, 2003.

———. *On the Pythagorean Way of Life: Text, Translation, and Notes.* Translated by John Dillon and Jackson Hershbell. Atlanta, GA: Scholars Press, 1991.

———. *Protrepticus: Ad Fidem Codicis Florentini.* Edited by Hermenegildus Pistelli. Stuttgart, Germany: Teubner, 1996.

———. *The Theology of Arithmetic: On the Mystical, Mathematical and Cosmological Symbolism of the First Ten Numbers Attributed to Iamblichus.* Translated by Robin Waterfield. Grand Rapids, MI: Phanes, 1988.

———. *Theoulogumena Arithmeticae.* Edited by V. De Falco. Stuttgart, Germany: Teubner, 1975.

The I Ching or Book of Changes: The Richard Wilhelm Translation rendered into English by Cary F. Baynes, Forward by C. G. Jung, 3rd ed. Princeton: Princeton University Press, 1967.

Jaeger, Werner. *Paideia: The Ideals of Greek Culture*. 3 vols. Translated by G. Highet. Oxford: Oxford University Press, 1939.

Johnson, Thomas Moore. *The Collected Works of Thomas Moore Johnson: The Great American Platonist*. King's Lynn, England: Prometheus Trust, 2015.

Johnston, Sarah Iles. *Ancient Greek Divination*. Chichester, England: Blackwell, 2008.

Johnston, Sarah Iles, and Peter T. Struck, eds. *Mantikê: Studies in Ancient Divination*. Leiden, Holland: Brill, 2005.

Keightley, Thomas. *The Mythology of Ancient Greece and Italy*, 4th ed. Edited by Leonhard Schmitz. London: George Bell & Sons, 1896.

Kelley, David H. "Calendar Animals and Deities." *Southwestern Journal of Anthropology* 16 (1960): 317–337.

Kerényi, Karl. *Apollo: The Wind, the Spirit, and the God. Four Studies*. Translated by Jon Solomon. Dallas, TX: Spring, 1983.

————. *The Gods of the Greeks*. Translated by Norman Cameron. London: Thames & Hudson, 1979.

————. *Hermes: Guide of Souls*, revised edition. Translated by Murray Stein. Dallas, TX: Spring, 1995.

Kingsley, Peter. *A Story Waiting to Pierce You: Mongolia, Tibet and the Destiny of the Western World*. Point Reyes, CA: Golden Sufi, 2010.

Larson, Jennifer. *Greek Nymphs: Myth, Cult, Lore*. Oxford: Oxford University Press, 2001.

Liddell, Henry George, Robert Scott, and Henry Stuart Jones. *A Greek-English Lexicon, with Supplement*. Oxford: Clarendon Press, 1968.

Lindsay, A. D. *Socratic Discourses by Plato and Xenophon*. London: J. M. Dent, 1910.

Livrea, Enrico. "From Pittacus to Byzantium: The History of a Callimachean Epigram." *The Classical Quarterly* 45, 2 (1995): 474–480.

Luck, Georg. *Arcana Mundi: Magic and the Occult in the Greek and Roman Worlds*. Baltimore, MD: Johns Hopkins University Press, 1985.

MacLennan, Bruce J. *The Wisdom of Hypatia: Ancient Spiritual Practices for a More Meaningful Life*. Woodbury, MN: Llewellyn, 2013.

Moran, Hugh A., and David H. Kelley. *The Alphabet and the Ancient Calendar Signs*, 2nd ed. Palo Alto, CA: Bell's, 1969.

Nollé, Johannes. *Kleinasiatische Losorakel: Astragal- und Alphabetchresmologien der hochkaiserzeitlichen Orakelrenaissance*. München, Germany: C.H. Beck, 2007.

Oikonomides, A. N. "Records of 'The Commandments of the Wise Men' in the 3rd c. B.C. The Revered 'Greek Reading-book' of the Hellenistic World." *Classical Bulletin 63* (1987): 67–76.

Opsopaus, John. "Apollo's Dagger." *Circle Magazine*, issue 108 (Spring 2011): 10–12. Published online as "Apollo's Demon Dagger" at http://omphalos.org/BA/ADD.html. Revised version in Lawrence, Jennifer, ed., *With Lyre and Bow: A Devotional in Honor of Apollo*. Bibliotheca Alexandrina, 2016: 76–91.

———. "A Greek Alphabet Oracle." *Circle Network News*, issue 57 (Fall 1995): 12–13. Reprinted in *Mythos* (Spring 1996); in *Manteia: A Magazine for the Mantic Arts*, No. 16 (Spring 1996): 54–56; and as "Un Oracolo dell' Alfabeto Greco" in *Mercurio: Pubblicazione Interna della Federazione Pagana*, num. 4 (Beltane 1996): 5–8.

———. "Greek Esoteric Music Theory." 1999. Found at http://omphalos.org/BA/GEM.

———. "Greater Tool Consecration." 1996. Found at http://omphalos.org/BA/Cmaj .html.

———. *The Guide to the Pythagorean Tarot: An Interpretation Based on Pythagorean and Alchemical Principles*. St. Paul, MN: Llewellyn, 2001.

Otto, Walter F. *The Homeric Gods: The Spiritual Significance of Greek Religion*. Translated by Moses Hadas. New York: Pantheon, 1954.

Papalexandrou, Nassos. *Warriors, Youths, and Tripods in Early Greece*. Lanham, MD: Lexington Books, 2005.

Pausanias. *Description of Greece*. 2 vols. Translated by W. H. S. Jones. Loeb Classical Library. Cambridge, MA: Harvard University Press, 1918.

———. *Pausanias Guide to Greece, vol. I: Central Greece*. Translated by Peter Levi. London: Penguin Books, 1979.

Peck, Harry Thurston, ed. *Harper's Dictionary of Classical Literature and Antiquities*. New York: Harper & Bros., 1898.

Peters, F. E. *Greek Philosophical Terms: A Historical Lexicon.* New York: New York University Press, 1967.

Plato. *The Dialogues of Plato.* 4 vols. Translated by Benjamin Jowett. New York: Scribners, 1899.

Plutarch. *Plutarch's Complete Works.* 6 vols. New York: Wheeler, 1909.

Salt, Alun, and Efrosyni Boutsikas. "Knowing when to consult the oracle at Delphi." *Antiquity* 79 (2005): 564–572.

Scheinberg, Susan. "The Bee Maidens of the Homeric Hymn to Hermes." *Harvard Studies in Classical Philology* 83 (1979): 1–28.

Schibli, Hermann S. *Hierocles of Alexandria.* Oxford: Oxford University Press, 2002.

Schimmel, A. *The Mystery of Numbers.* Oxford: Oxford University Press, 1993.

Sommerstein, Alan H., and Isabelle C. Torrance. *Oaths and Swearing in Ancient Greece.* Berlin, Germany: De Gruyter, 2014.

Stanford, W. B. *The Sound of Greek: Studies in the Greek Theory and Practice of Euphony.* Berkeley, CA: University of California Press, 1967.

Stanley, Thomas. *The History of Philosophy Containing the Lives, Opinions, Actions and Discourses of the Philosophers of Every Sect,* 4th ed. London: A. Millar, 1743.

Sterrett, J. R. Sitlington. *Leaflets from the Notebook of an Archæological Traveler in Asia Minor.* Austin, TX: University of Texas, 1889.

———. *The Wolfe Expedition to Asia Minor. Papers of the American Classical School at Athens,* Vol. III (1884–1885). Boston, MA: Damrell & Upham, 1888.

Stobaeus, Johannes. *Sententiae ex Thesauris Graecorum,* 3rd ed. Edited and translated by Conrad Gessner. Tiguri (Zurich): Christophorum Frosch, 1559.

Tytler, Henry William. *The Works of Callimachus, Translated into English Verse.* London: Davison, 1793.

Virgil. *The Æneid of Virgil Translated into English by E. Fairfax Taylor.* London: Dent & Sons, 1907.

De Vogel, C. J. *Pythagoras and Early Pythagoreanism: An Interpretation of Neglected Evidence on the Philosopher Pythagoras.* Assen, Netherlands: van Gorcum, 1966.

Watkins, Calvert, ed. *The American Heritage® Dictionary of Indo-European Roots,* 2nd ed. Boston, MA: Houghton Mifflin, 2000.

Weinstock, Stefan. "Lunar Mansions and Early Calendars." *The Journal of Hellenic Studies* 69 (1949): 48–69.

Woodard, Roger D. *Greek Writing from Knossos to Homer: A Linguistic Interpretation of the Origin of the Greek Alphabet and the Continuity of Ancient Greek Literacy.* Oxford: Oxford University Press, 1997.

Index

To Write to the Author

If you wish to contact the author or would like more information about this book, please write to the author in care of Llewellyn Worldwide Ltd. and we will forward your request. Both the author and publisher appreciate hearing from you and learning of your enjoyment of this book and how it has helped you. Llewellyn Worldwide Ltd. cannot guarantee that every letter written to the author can be answered, but all will be forwarded. Please write to:

John Opsopaus, PhD
℅ Llewellyn Worldwide
2143 Wooddale Drive
Woodbury, MN 55125-2989

Please enclose a self-addressed stamped envelope for reply,
or $1.00 to cover costs. If outside the U.S.A., enclose
an international postal reply coupon.

Many of Llewellyn's authors have websites
with additional information and resources.
For more information, please visit our website at
http://www.llewellyn.com

THE WISDOM OF

HYPATIA

ANCIENT SPIRITUAL PRACTICES FOR A MORE MEANINGFUL LIFE

BRUCE J. MACLENNAN, PHD

The Wisdom of Hypatia
Ancient Spiritual Practices for a More Meaningful Life
BRUCE J. MacLENNAN, PhD

Hypatia was the most famous female spiritual teacher of ancient Alexandria. The mix of classical philosophies she taught to Pagans, Jews, and Christians in the fourth century forms the very foundation of Western magic and mysticism as we know it today.

The Wisdom of Hypatia offers a progressive, nine-month program based on the teachings of this inspiring Pagan Neoplatonic philosopher. Discover how to bring purpose, tranquility, and spiritual depth to your life through exercises and techniques divided into three stages of wisdom: Epicureanism, Stoicism, and Neoplatonism. This virtual course in philosophy, well-being, and divine union is an essential and practical introduction to the ancient wisdom of the West.

978-0-7387-3599-3, 384 pp., 7 ½ x 9 ⅛   **$21.99**

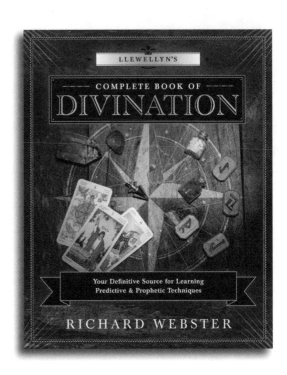

COMPLETE BOOK OF
DIVINATION

Your Definitive Source for Learning
Predictive & Prophetic Techniques

RICHARD WEBSTER

Llewellyn's Complete Book of Divination
Your Definitive Source for Learning Predictive & Prophetic Techniques
RICHARD WEBSTER

Richard Webster, one of the world's bestselling new age authors, explores the incredible wide variety of divination techniques from around the world. Discover explanations and in-depth techniques for thirty divination practices, including common methods such as tarot, astrology, palmistry, numerology, pendulums, runes, and the I Ching, as well as less well-known forms such as automatic writing, candle reading, coin divination, flower reading, sand divination, and many more.

978-0-7387-5175-7, 8 x 10 $29.99

December 2017 release
